DICTIONARY
of
MODERN
BIOGRAPHY

DICTIONARY
of
MODERN
BIOGRAPHY

EDWIN MOORE

GEDDES&
GROSSET

First published 1992
© 1992 Geddes & Grosset Ltd,
New Lanark, Scotland.

Cover design by Cameron Graphics Ltd,
Glasgow, Scotland.

ISBN 1 85534 074 7

Printed and bound in Great Britain.

A

Achebe, Chinua (1930-) Nigerian novelist and poet. Regarded as one of Africa's greatest writers in English, Achebe's work focuses on Ibo society and the legacy of colonialism. His works include the novels *Things Fall Apart* (1958), *Arrow of God* (1964) and the poetry collections *Beware Soul Brother* (1972) and *Christmas in Biafra* (1973).

Acheson, Dean [Gooderham] (1893-1971) American lawyer and statesman. As secretary of state under President TRUMAN, he was responsible for formulating and developing several important strands of American foreign policy, notably the MARSHALL Plan for reconstructing war-stricken Europe and the establishment of NATO.

Adams, Ansel [Easton] (1902-84) American photographer, notable for his detailed, deep-focus studies of the American landscape, e.g. his collection *This is the American West* (1960).

Adams, Richard [George] (1920-) English novelist. His best-known work is *Watership Down* (1972), an occasionally grim little fantasy about a colony of rabbits, which has become a modern classic of children's literature. Other novels include *The Plague Dogs* (1977) and *The Girl in a Swing* (1980).

Adenauer, Konrad (1876-1967) German statesman. A member of the Centre Party during the 1930s, he was imprisoned twice by the Nazi regime (1934 and 1944). He became mayor of Cologne in 1945 and a co-founder of the Christian Democratic Union. In his role as chancellor of West Germany (1949-63) he played a major part in world politics.

Adler, Alfred (1870-1937) Austrian psychiatrist. He was an associate of FREUD, whose emphasis on sexuality he rejected, founding a school of psychoanalysis based upon the individual's quest to overcome feelings of inadequacy (the "inferiority complex," as it came to be known). His works include *The Practice and Theory of Individual Psychology* (1923).

Adorno, Theodor [Wiessengrund] (1903-69) German philosopher, sociologist and music critic. His theorizing on the oppressive nature of all philosophical inquiry, e.g. in *Dialectic of the Enlightenment* (1947), is regarded as a significant influence on the 1960s radical movement. Adorno was associated with MARCUSE in the left-wing Frankfurt School of critics.

Aga Khan III [Sultan Sir Mohammed Shah] (1877-1957) spiritual leader of the Ismaili Muslim sect and statesman. He was president of the All-India Muslim League (1906-9) and became president of the League of Nations in 1937. He was succeeded by his son **Karim** (b. 1936), who, like his father, is a renowned breeder of racehorses.

Agnew, Spiro T[heodore] (1918-) American Republican politician, vice-president (1969-73) in NIXON's administration. A noted critic of the morality of his "effete" liberal opponents, he resigned office following revelations of political corruption and was sentenced to three years' probation.

Albee, Edward [Franklin] (1928-) American dramatist. His plays, which are predominantly satires on middle-class life, include *The Zoo Story* (1959), *Who's Afraid of Virginia Woolf* (1962) and *A Delicate Balance* (1966).

Aldrin, Edwin "Buzz" *see* **Armstrong, Neil**.

Alexandra, Feodorovna *see* **Nicholas II**.

Ali, Muhammad [Cassius Clay] (1942-) American boxer and world heavyweight champion (1964-9, 1974-78, 1978-79). His licence to box was withdrawn in 1967, after his refusal to be conscripted into the armed forces to serve in Vietnam, service he saw as incompatible with his conversion to Islam (at which he rejected his given "slave" name of Clay). Widely regarded as one of the greatest boxers of all time, he was also much loved for his wit and concern for the plight of the black poor.

Allen, Woody [Allen Stewart Konigsberg] (1935-) American film director, actor and writer, noted for his satirical, often autobiographical films about the (primarily sexual) neuroses of New York intellectuals, e.g. *Annie Hall* (1977) and *Manhattan* (1979).

Allende [Gossens], Salvador (1908-73) Chilean Marxist politician. He was elected president of his country in 1970 (at the fourth attempt), thus becoming the first freely elected Marxist president in Latin America. He was overthrown and killed in the coup that brought PINOCHET to power.

Amin [Dada], Idi (1925-) Ugandan dictator. He wrested power from OBOTE in 1971, and ruled Uganda until 1979 (appointing himself president for life in 1976). He fled Uganda following the Tanzanian army's invasion in 1979, and lived in Saudi Arabia from 1980. He was chairman of the Organization of African Unity (1975-6).

Amis, Sir Kingsley (1922-) English novelist and poet. His first novel, *Lucky Jim* (1954), a satire on academic life, is widely regarded as a comic masterpiece. His later novels also have streaks of anarchic humour, but are much darker in tone, dealing as they do with such issues as the problem of suffering and the nature of God (*The Anti-Death League*, 1966), and modern sexuality (*Stanley and the Women*, 1984). He is the father of **Martin Amis** (1949-) who is also a novelist.

Amundsen, Roald (1872-1928) Norwegian explorer and navigator, leader of the first expedition to reach the South Pole in 1911, which journey is described in his book *The South Pole* (1913).

Anderson, Carl David *see* **Hess, Victor Francis**.

Anderson, Sherwood (1876-1941) American novelist and short-story writer. His best-known work is *Winesburg, Ohio* (1919), a collection of naturalistic and gloomy short stories about small-town American life.

Andrew, Prince *see* **Elizabeth II**.

Andropov, Yuri [Vladimirovich] (1914-84) Soviet statesman, president of the USSR (1983-4). Andropov, a former head of the KGB, was rumoured to be a potential reformer when he succeeded to the Soviet presidency following BREZHNEV'S death.

Anne, Princess *see* **Elizabeth II**.

Anouilh, Jean (1910-87) French dramatist. The best known of his plays is his reworking of Sophocles' tragedy *Antigone* (1944), which was produced as a subversive interpretation of Nazi rule in occupied France. Other notable plays are the *The Waltz of the Toreadors* (1952) and *Beckett* (1959).

Antonioni, Michelangelo (1912-) Italian film director. His films include *L'Avventura* (1959) and *Blow-Up* (1967), the latter being commonly regarded as a landmark of the "Swinging Sixties" English cultural landscape.

Apollinaire, Guillaume *see* **Delaunay, Robert**.

Aquino, [Maria] Corazon (1933-) Filipino politician. Following the assassination of her husband Benigno Aquino, the most prominent opponent of MARCOS, she became the leader of the popular movement against Marcos's rule, and was elected President of the Philippines in 1986.

Arafat, Yasser (1929-) Palestinian leader, who helped found the anti-Israeli guerrilla force *Al Fatah*, and became chairman of the Palestine Liberation Organization in 1968. Arafat survived numerous attempts on his life from 1968, primarily from factions within the Palestinian movement, and came to be regarded by many Westerners as a "moderate" spokesman for the Palestinian cause. His leadership of the PLO entered its most crucial phase when he backed Saddam HUSSEIN's 1990 invasion of Kuwait.

Aragon, Louis (1897-1982) French poet, essayist and novelist. One of the founders of both Dadaism and Surrealism, his works include the Surrealist novel *Nightwalker* (1926) and several collections of verse. He became a member of the French Communist Party in the late 1920s, for which cause he became a prolific propagandist.

Arden, John (1930-) English dramatist, regarded as one of the leading left-wing playwrights of his generation. His best-known works are the satire *Live Like Pigs* (1958) and the passionately pacifist *Serjeant Musgrave's Dance* (1959).

Arendt, Hannah (1906-75) German-born American philosopher. Her best-known work is *The Origins of Totalitarianism* (1951), which argued that the similarities between HITLER's Germany and STALIN's Russia could be traced back to a common 19th-century ancestry. Her other works include *Eichmann in*

Jerusalem (1961), *On Revolution* (1963) and *On Violence* (1963).

Armstrong, [Daniel] Louis "Satchmo" (1900-71) American jazz trumpeter, singer and leader of many very popular jazz bands, notably the All-Stars. A highly gifted musician and singer with a genius for improvization, Armstrong became one of the best-loved entertainers of the century.

Armstrong, Neil [Alden] (1930-) American astronaut. He commanded the Apollo 11 moon landing mission, in which he became the first man to walk on the moon, followed by the lunar module pilot **Edwin "Buzz" Aldrin** (1930-). The other member of the mission was the orbiting module pilot **Michael Collins** (1930-).

Arp, Jean *or* **Hans** (1887-1966) German-born French sculptor and painter. One of the founders of Dadaism, Arp's work is characterized by the use of organic forms to create abstract shapes in disparate media.

Artaud, Antonin (1896-1948) French stage director, actor and dramatist. He was the creator of the "Theatre of Cruelty," a form of drama that attempts to restore humans to their spiritual roots by a process of communication involving symbolism and ritualistic gestures rather than language. Artaud's works include *Manifesto of the Theatre of Cruelty* (1932) and *The Theatre and its Double* (1938).

Ashcroft, Dame Peggy (1907-91) English actress. One of the most popular stage and film actresses of her generation, she is perhaps best known for her part in the television series *The Jewel in the Crown* (1983). She won an Oscar for best supporting actress in *A Passage to India* (1984).

Ashdown, Paddy [Jeremy John Dunham Ashdown] (1941-)

English Liberal politician. After service with the Marines and Special Boat Squadron, he joined the diplomatic service in 1971 (he was by then a fluent Mandarin speaker). He was elected leader of the Liberal and Social Democratic Party in 1988.

Ashkenazy, Vladimir [Davidovich] (1937-) Russian-born Icelandic pianist and conductor, best-known for his recordings of works by Mozart and Russian composers such as SCRIABIN and RACHMANINOV.

Ashton, Sir Frederick [William Mallandaine] (1906-88) Ecuadorian-born British choreographer and co-founder of the Royal Ballet. Ashton's ballets include *Facade* (1931, and *A Month in the Country* (1976).

Asquith, Herbert Henry [1st Earl of Oxford and Asquith] (1852-1928) British statesman. He was leader of the Liberal Party (1908-26) and prime minister (1908-16). Regarded as the leader of the conservative wing of the Liberals, he refused to serve under his successor LLOYD GEORGE (who had engineered Asquith's downfall).

Astaire, Fred [Frederick Austerlitz] (1899-1987) American dancer, singer and actor. His partnership with **Ginger Rogers** [Virginia McMath] (1911-) resulted in a series of classic song-and-dance films, e.g. *Flying Down to Rio* (1933) and *Top Hat* (1935).

Astor, Nancy Witcher [Langhorne] [Viscountess Astor] (1879-1964) American-born British politician. She was elected to parliament as a Conservative MP, becoming the first woman to take her seat in Parliament. She was an active campaigner for the temperance movement, and for women's and children's welfare.

Atatürk, Kemal [Mustafa Kemal Atatürk] (1881-1938) Turkish general and statesman, first president of Turkey (1923-38). He introduced wide-ranging reforms to westernize and secularize Turkish society, and is regarded as the creator of the modern Turkish state.

Atget, [Jean] Eugène (1856-1927) French photographer. He began selling his documentary photographs of Paris to museums in his late 1940s, and became recognized by artists such as BRAQUE as a master at recording the atmosphere of the city.

Attenborough, Sir David [Frederick] (1926-) English naturalist and broadcaster, best known for his highly popular TV series, e.g. *Life on Earth* (1978, on evolution), *The Living Planet* (1983, on the adaptation of life to the environment) and *The Trials of Life* (1989, on animal behaviour). He is Richard ATTENBOROUGH's brother.

Attenborough, Sir Richard [Samuel] (1923-) English film director, producer and actor. Films he has starred in include *Brighton Rock* (1947), *The Angry Silence* (1959) and *Seance on a Wet Afternoon* (1963). Films he has directed include *Oh! What a Lovely War* (1968), *A Bridge Too Far* (1976) and *Gandhi* (1982), the last winning eight Oscars. He is David ATTENBOROUGH's brother.

Attlee, Clement [Richard] [1st Earl Attlee] (1883-1967) British statesman. He was leader of the Labour Party (1939-55) and prime minister (1945-51). Attlee's 1945 administration introduced widespread nationalization and a programme of social security reforms (based on the BEVERIDGE Report).

Auden, W[ystan] H[ugh] (1907-73) English poet (US citizen from 1946). With such volumes as *Look, Stranger* (1936), he became the leading left-wing poet of his generation (the "Auden generation") but later drifted away from Marxism towards a Christian and socially conservative position. His works include *Collected Shorter Poems* (1966).

Austin, John Langshaw (1911-60) English philosopher. He stressed the need for simplicity and use of ordinary language in philosophical speculation, as seen in his posthumously published lectures *Sense and Sensibilia* and *How to do Things with Words* (both 1962).

Ayckbourn, Alan (1939-) English dramatist, noted for such satirical comedies as *Absurd Person Singular* (1973) and *The Norman Conquests* (1974).

Ayer, Sir A[lfred] J[ules] (1910-89) English philosopher, whose work is based on "logical positivism" and the rejection of metaphysics. His early short work *Language, Truth and Logic* (1936) has been highly influential on British "commonsense" philosophy. His later work, e.g. *The Problem of Knowledge* (1956), qualifies and in part rejects the more strident assumptions of his earlier writing.

Ayub Khan, Mohammed (1907-74) Pakistani field marshal and statesman, president of Pakistan (1958-69). He was the first commander-in-chief of his country's army (1951-58), and introduced some reforms during his presidency. His suspension of civil liberties and increasingly dictatorial style of leadership eroded his power base and led to his fall in 1969.

Azikiwe, [Benjamin] Nnamdi (1904-) Nigerian statesman, first president of Nigeria (1963-66). During the Nigerian civil war he joined the (Ibo) Biafran secessionist government, but accepted the reunification process once the war was over, when he (unsuccessfully) stood once more for president. He has been described as the "father of modern Nigeria."

13

B

Baader, Andreas *see* **Meinhoff, Ulrike**.

Babbitt, Milton [Bryon] (1916-) American composer. Babbitt became America's foremost exponent of serial twelve-tone music with his advocacy of "total serialization" in all aspects of composition. His works include *Composition for Orchestra* (1941) and *Philomel* (1964).

Babel, Isaac Emmanuilovich (1894-1941) Russian short-story writer and dramatist. He joined the Bolshevik forces in the Russian civil war in 1917, serving with the Cossack cavalry. His experiences with the Cossacks form the basis for the stories in his best-known work, *Red Cavalry* (1926). Another notable work is the (also autobiographical) collection of stories on Jewish life in Odessa, *Stories from Odessa* (1924). He died in a Soviet labour camp.

Bacall, Lauren *see* **Bogart, Humphrey**.

Bacon, Francis (1909-92) Anglo-Irish painter. Bacon's work is characterized by vivid colours and brutally distorted figures of humans, animals and cadavers. One of his best-known works is his macabre version of Velazquez's portrait of Pope Innocent X.

Baekeland, Leo Hendrik (1863-1944) Belgian-born American chemist. He made his fortune in the 1890s by selling a photographic process to EASTMAN for $1 million (Baekeland would have settled for $25,000), and subsequently invented the thermosetting resin Bakelite.

Baez, Joan (1941-) American folksinger, renowned for her "protest songs" on civil rights and the Vietnam war in the 1960s. She was closely associated with Bob DYLAN in the peace movement in the mid-60s. Baez and Dylan made a film together, *Renaldo and Clara* (1978).

Bailey, David (1938-) English photographer, whose work, particularly his fashion photographs of models such as Jean Shrimpton and "personalities" such as Mick JAGGER, were seen as epitomizing the "Swinging 60s" pop culture era in London.

Baird, John Logie (1888-1946) Scottish engineer, who invented a mechanically scanned system of television in the mid-1920s. Baird's system was used to transmit pictures (of poor quality) across the Atlantic, and he also produced colour and stereoscopic pictures. Baird's system became redundant in the late 1930s, when it was superseded by an electronic form of scanning.

Baker, Dame Janet [Abbott] (1933-) English mezzosoprano. Baker became one of Britain's most popular opera singers in the 1960s, and had parts created for her by composers such as BRITTEN. She published her memoirs, *Full Circle*, in 1982.

Balanchine, George (1904-83) Russian-born American choreographer and dancer. The best known of his productions are to music by Russian composers, particularly STRAVINSKY, e.g. *Apollo* (1928). He founded the New York City ballet in 1928.

Balcon, Sir Michael (1896-1977) English film producer. One of the most influential of all British producers, Balcon produced such films in the 1930s as the documentary *Man of Aran* (1933) and the thriller *The Thirty-Nine Steps* (1935), but is particularly associated with the great Ealing comedies of the 1940s and 50s, e.g. *Whisky Galore* (1949) and *The Lavender Hill Mob* (1952).

Baldwin, James [Arthur] (1924-87) American novelist, dramatist and essayist. Baldwin's main concern was with the role of blacks in American society, and, to a lesser extent, that of homosexuals. His novels include *Go Tell it on the Mountain* (1953) and *Giovanni's Room* (1956). His polemical work, *The Fire Next Time* (1963), on the oppression of blacks, was much discussed in the 1960s.

Baldwin, Stanley [1st Earl Baldwin of Bewdley] (1867-1947) British statesman and Conservative prime minister (1923-4, 1924-29, 1935-37). Notable aspects of his premierships include the passing of a state of emergency during the 1926 General Strike, his refusal to accept Wallis Simpson as Edward VIII's wife (see WINDSOR), which resulted in the latter's abdication, and his failure to deal with unemployment and the rise of European totalitarianism.

Bancroft, Anne *see* **Brooks, Mel.**

Banda, Hastings [Kamuzu] (1905-) Malawi statesman, first president of Nyasaland from 1963 and president of Malawi (formerly Nyasaland) from 1966. Banda, one of the longest-ruling leaders in the world, was appointed president for life in 1971. His rule has been autocratic by Western standards, and he was the only black leader to recognize and (officially) trade with South Africa.

Bandaranaike, Mrs Sirimavo Ratwatte Dias (1916-) Sri Lankan stateswoman, prime minister of Ceylon (later Sri Lanka) (1960-65, 1970-77). She succeeded her husband **S[olomon] W[est] R[idgeway] D[ias] Bandaranaike** (1899-1959) to the premiership following his assassination. A socialist and a nationalist, she fostered nationalization, the use of Sinhalese rather than Tamil as the official language, and Buddhism. She was expelled from parliament in 1980, following "abuse of power" charges.

Bankhead, Tallulah [Brockman] (1903-68) American actress, noted for her sharp wit, beauty and distinctive low-timbred voice. Her best-known stage role was that of Regina in *The Little Foxes* (1939). She published her memoirs, *Tallulah*, in 1952.

Bannister, Sir Roger [Gilbert] (1929-) British athlete and doctor, who became the first man to run a mile in four minutes in 1954, the circumstances of which are described in his memoir, *First Four Minutes* (1955). He has also published several papers on neurology.

Banting, Sir Frederick [Grant] (1891-1941) Canadian physician. His research into diabetes with the American physiologist **Charles Herbert Best** (1899-1978), initially under the supervision of the Scottish physiologist John MacLeod, resulted in the isolation of the pancreatic hormone insulin, in a form suitable for treating diabetes.

Barber, Samuel (1910-81) American composer. Barber is regarded as a "traditional" modern composer working with recognizably 19th-century harmonies and forms. His works include the popular *Adagio for Strings*, an adaptation of a movement from his string quartet (1936).

Barbirolli, Sir John (1899-1970) English conductor, cellist and founder of the Hallé Orchestra (1943-68). Barbirolli was particularly associated with the music of modern British composers, particularly DELIUS, ELGAR and VAUGHAN WILLIAMS. Vaughan Williams dedicated his 8th symphony to him.

Barbusse, Henri (1873-1935) French novelist and poet. His works are naturalistic, often grim accounts of war and the lives of the poor and the demimonde. His best-known work is the novel *Under Fire* (1916), a strongly pacifist account of trench warfare in World War I.

Bardeen, John (1908-91) American physicist and electrical engineer. He won two Nobel prizes, the first in 1956 for research that led to the invention of the transistor, the second in 1972 for research into the theory of superconductivity.

Bardot, Brigitte (1934-) French actress. Starring in such films as *And God Created Woman* (1956), she became the leading "sex symbol" of the 1950s. Few of her films are now seen as of any worth. Since the 1970s, she has lived in virtual seclusion in France, where she devotes herself to animal rights and welfare.

Barenboim, Daniel (1942-) Argentinian-born Israeli concert pianist and conductor. Among his many recordings are complete sets of the Mozart piano concertos and Beethoven's piano sonatas and concertos. He married the cellist Jacqueline DU PRÉ in 1967, and was appointed music director of the Orchestre de Paris in 1975.

Barnard, Christian [Neethling] (1923-) South African surgeon, who performed the first heart transplant in 1967. The patient, Louis Washansky, died not long after the operation.

Barrie, Sir J[ames] M[atthew] (1860-1937) Scottish dramatist and novelist, remembered principally for his remarkable fantasy play for children, *Peter Pan* (1904).

Barrymore, Lionel (1878-1954) American actor. One of a family of distinguished theatricals, notably his sister **Ethel Barrymore** (1879-1959) and brother **John Barrymore**

(1882-1942), Barrymore achieved great popularity as a character actor with his roles in such films as *You Can't Take It With You* (1938) and in the first Dr Kildare series of films. His memoir, *We Barrymores*, was published in 1951.

Barth, Karl (1886-1968) Swiss Protestant theologian. Barth's theology was based on an orthodox "theocentric" conception of divine grace and is seen as a reaction against the simplifications of 19th-century liberal theology. Barth was a committed and courageous opponent of Nazism. His theology is summarized in *Church Dogmatics* (1932-62).

Barthes, Roland (1915-80) French literary and cultural critic, whose semiological studies on subjects as diverse as washing powder and national monuments, influenced by McLUHAN and SAUSSURE, were regarded as necessary reading in the 1960s and 70s. His works include *Writing Degree Zero* (1953) and *Elements of Sociology* (1964).

Bartók, Béla (1881-1945) Hungarian composer and pianist. Bartók's compositions, based on Hungarian folk motifs and modern atonal techniques, have been very influential on modern music. His works include the opera *Bluebeard's Castle* (1918) and *Concerto for Orchestra* (1943).

Basie, Count [William] (1904-84) American jazz composer and bandleader. He was a jazz pianist of great ability, and his band, featuring singers such as ELLINGTON and SINATRA, became one of the best-loved big bands of their day.

Bates, H[erbert] E[rnest] (1905-74) English novelist and short-story writer. His works include two very popular novels, *Fair Stood the Wind for France* (1944), which centres on an RAF bombing crew, and a comic novel featuring the unruly farming family the Larkins, *The Darling Buds of May* (1958).

Bateson, William (1861-1926) British geneticist. Although highly unorthodox in some of his viewpoints, e.g. in opposing his "vibratory" theory of inheritance against the now accepted principle of chromosomal carriage of genes, Bateson's work in confirming Mendel's principles of heredity was of great importance in the study of genetics.

Batista [y Zaldivar], Fulgencio (1901-73) Cuban military leader, president of Cuba (1940-4, 1952-59). Initially a reformer who took power during a general strike, his rule became increasingly corrupt and he fled Cuba after the success of the insurrection led by CASTRO in 1959.

Bax, Sir Arnold [Edward Trevor] (1883-1953) English composer, noted for his traditional style of composition and interest in Celtic myth and legend, e.g. his tone poem *Tintagel* (1917). He was Master of the King's Music from 1941.

Beadle, George Wells *see* **Tatum, Edward Lawrie.**

Beaton, Sir Cecil [Walter Hardy] (1904-80) English society and fashion photographer, stage and costume designer, and writer. Beaton's design credits include *My Fair Lady* (1956), with its famous black-and-white racecourse scene. His society portraits, e.g. of the royal family and GARBO, have a strong period flavour.

Beatty, Warren (1938-) American film actor, producer and director. Films in which he has starred include *Bonnie and Clyde* (1967), *Heaven Can Wait* (1978) and *Reds* (1981).

Beauvoir, Simone de (1908-86) French novelist and essayist whose works explore the female predicament from the standpoint of existential feminism, e.g. her essay *The Second Sex* (1949). Her work was much affected by her lifelong relationship with SARTRE.

Beaverbrook, Max [William Maxwell Aitken, 1st Baron Beaverbrook] (1879-1964) Canadian-born British newspaper proprietor and Conservative politician. His newspapers, notably *The Daily Express*, were used as vehicles for Beaverbrook's usually imperialist and often eccentric enthusiasms. In World War I he served as minister of information (1918) and in World War II as minister of aircraft production (1940-41).

Bechet, Sidney (1897-1959) American jazz saxophonist and clarinettist. Bechet never learned to read music, but became recognized as one of the greatest soprano saxophone virtuosos of the century. He settled in France in 1951.

Beckett, Samuel (1906-89) Irish dramatist and novelist. He settled in Paris in the 1930s (where he befriended James JOYCE and wrote down *Finnegans Wake* at Joyce's dictation), and wrote in both French and English. His works, generally bleak and existentialist in philosophy, include the play *Waiting for Godot* (1952) and the short novel *Malone Dies* (1951).

Becquerel, Antoine Henri *see* **Curie, Marie**.

Beecham, Sir Thomas (1879-1961) English conductor, noted for his promotion and dashing interpretation of the works of DELIUS, STRAUSS and SIBELIUS, and for his sharply witty ripostes.

Beerbohm, Sir [Henry] Max[imilian] (1872-1956) English parodist, caricaturist and essayist. The parodies of authors such as Henry JAMES and KIPLING in such collections as *A Christmas Garland* (1912) established him as one of the greatest of all parodists, and his caricatures of his contemporaries are also much admired. His only novel, *Zuleika Dobson* (1911), is a surreal and satirical portrait of Oxford undergraduate life.

Begin, Menachem (1913-92) Polish-born Israeli statesman. He was commander of the Irgun militant Zionist group (1943-48)

Behan

and prime minister of Israel (1977-84). He and SADAT were awarded the Nobel Peace Prize in 1978, after Egypt and Israel signed a peace treaty.

Behan, Brendan (1923-64) Irish dramatist and poet. He was an Irish Republican Army supporter from an early age, and two of his works are directly based on his imprisonment for IRA activity, the play *The Quare Fellow* (1954) and the memoir *Borstal Boy* (1958).

Behrens, Peter (1868-1940) German architect. A self-taught architect, his industrial buildings, e.g. the AEG turbine factory (1909) in Berlin, were among the first 20th-century industrial structures to have artistic merit claimed for them. He was a major influence on GROPIUS and LE CORBUSIER.

Beiderbecke, [Leon] Bix (1903-31) American jazz cornetist, pianist and composer, who is regarded as one of the few white jazz musicians to have had any significant influence on the development of jazz. He died at 28 of alcoholism.

Belloc, [Joseph] Hilaire [Pierre] (1870-1953) French-born English poet, essayist, historian and Liberal MP. Noted in his own day for his prolific output of all kinds of books, and for his robust Roman Catholicism, anti-imperialism and bucolic nationalism, Belloc is now chiefly remembered as a writer of children's verse, e.g. *The Bad Child's Book of Beasts* (1896).

Bellow, Saul (1915-   ) Canadian-born American novelist, widely regarded as one of the greatest living writers for his humane yet ironic portrayal of the individual's struggle for identity in the modern world. His novels include *Dangling Man* (1944) and *More Die of Heartbreak* (1987). He was awarded the Nobel prize for literature in 1976.

Ben Bella, [Mohammed] Ahmed (1916-   ) Algerian statesman. One of the leading figures of his country's independence movement in the late 1940s and 50s, he was imprisoned twice by the French and became prime minister of Algeria in 1962 shortly after independence. He was deposed in 1965 after a military coup, and was imprisoned until 1980.

Benes, Eduard (1884-1948) Czech statesman. One of the founders of Czechoslovakia, with MASARYK, he was minister of foreign affairs (1919-35), prime minister (1921-22) and president (1935-38, 1945-48). He lived in London during the Nazi occupation of his country. A liberal, he resigned from office when the communists took power in Czechoslovakia in 1948.

Benét, Stephen Vincent (1898-1943) American poet and short-story writer. His work focuses on people and incidents central to American history and folklore, e.g. his long narrative poem on the Civil War, *John Brown's Body* (1928)

Ben-Gurion, David [David Gruen] (1886-1973) Polish-born Israeli statesman. He settled in Palestine in 1906, where he became active in the socialist wing of the Zionist movement. He was the first prime minister of Israel (1948-53, 1955-63).

Benn, Tony [Anthony Neil Wedgwood Benn, formerly Viscount Stansgate] (1925-) British politician. Since the late 1970s he has been regarded as one of the leading figures of the radical left in the Labour Party and in British politics generally. He has held several government posts in the past, e.g. minister of technology (1966-70).

Bennett, [Enoch] Arnold (1867-1931) English novelist, dramatist and essayist. His novels, which are centred on industrial life in the Staffordshire Potteries, include *The Old Wives' Tale* (1908) and the Clayhanger trilogy, *Clayhanger* (1910), *Hilda Lessways* (1911) and *These Twain* (1916).

Bennett, Richard Rodney (1936-) English composer and pianist. His works include symphonies, concertos and the opera, *All the King's Men* (1969). He has also written music for films, e.g. *Murder on the Orient Express* (1974).

Bentine, Michael *see* **Milligan, Spike.**

Bentley, Edmund Clerihew (1875-1956) English journalist, noted for his invention of the "clerihew," a short comic form of verse consisting of two irregular lines, and for his classic detective novel, *Trent's Last Case* (1913).

Berberian, Cathy *see* **Berio, Luciano.**

Berdyaev, Nikolai Alexandrovich (1874-1948) Russian philosopher. He was exiled from the USSR in the early 1920s, and spent the rest of his life developing a religious philosophy based on man's free will to choose between good and evil. His books include *The Meaning of History* (1936) and *The Destiny of Man* (1937).

Berenson, Bernard (1865-1959) Lithuanian-born American art critic. Berenson became an arbiter of taste for rich collectors in the course of his long career, particularly on Renaissance art. His best-known work is *Italian Painters of the Renaissance* (1952), but many of his judgments are now regarded as having been seriously compromised by his financial interests.

Berg, Alban (1885-1935) Austrian composer. He studied under SCHOENBERG, and adopted his teacher's atonal twelve-tone technique. His works include songs, chamber works and the operas *Wozzeck* (1921) and *Lulu* (1935).

Bergman, Ingmar (1918-) Swedish film and stage director. His films are claustrophobic psychological studies focusing on themes such as man's relations with God and the Devil and highly charged family tensions. The films, which include *The Seventh Seal* (1956), *Wild Strawberries* (1957) and *Cries and Whispers* (1972), have been very influential on many other directors.

Bergman, Ingrid (1915-82) Swedish actress. She was regarded as one of the most talented and beautiful actresses of her generation. Her films include several classics, e.g. *Casablanca* (1942) and *Gaslight* (1944).

Bergson, Henri Louis (1859-1941) French philosopher. His writings expound his theory of a "vital spirit" moving in the world, bridging the apparent chasm between metaphysics and hard science. His works include *Time and Free Will* (1889) and *Creative Evolution* (1907). He was awarded the Nobel prize for literature in 1927.

Beria, Lavrenti Pavlovich (1899-1953) Georgian-born Soviet politician. He rose to power in the 1930s under STALIN, and became head of the secret police (1938-53). He was one of the most feared men in the USSR by the time of his death, which was arranged by his rivals for the succession after Stalin's death, who had him tried for treason and executed.

Berio, Luciano (1925-) Italian composer. His works, which are based on a system of serialism and often feature electronic components, include *Homage to Joyce* (1958, a tribute to James JOYCE) and *Circles* (1960). From 1950-66 he was married to the American soprano **Cathy Berberian** (1928-83), for whom many of his works were written.

Berkeley, Busby [William Busby Enos] (1895-1976) American film director, noted especially for his elaborate, often surreal, dance choreography in such musicals as *42nd Street* (1933) and *The Gang's All Here* (1942).

Berkeley, Sir Lennox [Randal Francis] (1903-89) English composer. His early compositions are tonal in construction, but he drifted towards serialism in the 1960s. His works include operas, symphonies, film scores and song cycles, such as *Songs of the Half-Light* (1964).

Berlin, Irving [Israel Baline] (1888-1989) Russian-born American songwriter. He began his career as a street singer, and eventually wrote around a thousand songs, many of which achieved worldwide popularity, e.g. "Alexander's Ragtime Band," "God Bless America," and "White Christmas." His songs featured in many highly successful shows, e.g *Annie Get Your Gun* (1946) and in several film musicals, e.g.*Top Hat* (1935) and *Easter Parade* (1948).

Berlin, Sir Isaiah (1909-) Latvian-born British philosopher and historian. His works focus on the history of ideas, with particular reference to historical determinism, which he regards as discredited. His works include *Karl Marx* (1939), *The Hedgehog and the Fox* (1953, a study of TOLSTOY's determinism) and *Vico and Herder* (1976).

Bernal, J[ohn] D[esmond] (1901-71) British physicist. Bernal's most important work was in the field of the structure of complex molecules, in which he used X-ray crystallography. He was a member of the Communist Party from 1923, and one of MOUNTBATTEN's personal advisers during World War II.

Bernstein, Leonard (1918-90) American composer and conductor. He was musical director of the New York Philharmonic (1958-70), and a tireless popularizer of classical music. His works include *Kaddish Symphony* (1963), chamber and choral music, and several very popular musicals, e.g. *West Side Story* (1957).

Berryman, John (1914-72) American poet and critic. His works include the verse monologue *Homage to Mistress Bradstreet* (1956), *Berryman's Sonnets* (1967), and *Delusions, etc.* (1972). He was depressive and an alcoholic, and killed himself by drowning.

Bertolucci, Bernardo (1940-) Italian film director. His films include the sexually explicit *Last Tango in Paris* (1972, starring BRANDO and butter), *1900* (1976), a historical epic on the rise and death of Italian fascism, and *Tragedy of a Ridiculous Man* (1982).

Best, Charles Herbert *see* **Banting Sir Frederick**.

Best, George (1946-) Northern Irish soccer player. He signed for Matt BUSBY's Manchester United team while still at school, and soon came to be regarded as one of the world's finest and most entertaining wingers. His playing career slowly folded in a haze of alcohol abuse and general dissipation.

Bethe, Hans Albrecht (1906-) German-born American physicist. Persecuted in Germany for being a Jew, Bethe settled in the US in the mid-1930s, where he became established as a leading theorist in physics. During World War II, he helped develop the atom bomb as director of the theoretical physics division at Los Alamos. He was awarded the 1967 Nobel prize for physics for his work on solar and stellar energy.

Betjeman, Sir John (1906-84) English poet and essayist. His deceptively simple poems, which feature a dislike for the cruder excesses of modern commercialism and nostalgia for a quieter, nobler England, were very popular with critics and public alike. His *Collected Poems* were first published in 1958. He also wrote widely on architecture, e.g. *Ghastly Good Taste* (1933), and raised public consciousness about the worth of Victorian architecture. He was appointed poet laureate in 1972.

Bevan, Aneurin (1897-1960) Welsh statesman. He was Labour MP for Ebbw Vale for 30 years (1929-60), and was regarded as one of the main spokesmen for the radical socialist opposition during World War II. As minister of health (1945-51) during the postwar ATTLEE administration, he oversaw the formation of the welfare state (*see* BEVERIDGE). He resigned from the government in 1951 in protest at the reinstatement of charges for medical treatment.

Beveridge, William Henry [1st Baron Beveridge] (1879-1963) Indian-born English economist. His "Beveridge Report," the *Report on Social Insurance and Allied Services* (1942), became the basis for the welfare state introduced by ATTLEE's postwar administration.

Bevin, Ernest (1881-1951) English trade unionist and statesman. He helped found the Transport and General Workers Union (1922) and was minister of labour (1940-45) in the coalition war government and Labour's foreign secretary (1945-51).

Bhutto, Zulfikar Ali (1928-79) Pakistani statesman. He was the first civilian president of Pakistan (1971-73), then prime minister (1973-77). He was deposed in a coup and executed, despite worldwide appeals for clemency. His daughter **Benazir Bhutto** (1953-) became prime minister of Pakistan in 1988, but was defeated in elections in 1990. She was the first prime minister to give birth to a child while in office.

Biko, Steve [Stevan] (1946-77) South African black radical leader. Biko helped found the Black People's Convention in order to build confidence ("black consciousness") in South

African blacks that they could defeat apartheid. His death in police custody while awaiting trial was universally regarded as murder, and was widely condemned throughout the world.

Birtwhistle, Sir Harrison (1934-) English composer. Birtwhistle is regarded, with Maxwell DAVIES and others, as a leading postwar avant-garde composer. His works include the operas *Punch and Judy* (1967) and *Gawain and the Green Knight* (1991).

Blackett, Patrick Maynard Stuart, Baron (1897-1974) English physicist. He was awarded the 1948 Nobel prize for physics for his work on cosmic rays and rock magnetism. He discovered the positron in 1933.

Blériot, Louis (1872-1936) French aviator and aeronautical engineer. A pioneer in aircraft design, he made the first flight across the English Channel in one of his monoplanes in 1909.

Bliss, Sir Arthur [Edward Drummond] (1891-1975) English composer. His works include the choral symphony *Morning Heroes* (1930), music for ballets, e.g. *Miracle in the Gorbals* (1944), and the film score for KORDA's *Things to Come* (1934). He was Master of the Queen's Music (1953-75).

Bloch, Ernest (1880-1959) Swiss-born American composer. Bloch was strongly influenced by the Jewish musical tradition in both liturgies and folk music. His works include the symphonies *Israel* (1916) and *America* (1926).

Blok, Aleksandr Aleksandrovich (1880-1921) Russian poet. By the time of the Bolshevik Revolution in 1917, which he welcomed, Blok was widely recognized within Russia as one of the country's leading Symbolist poets with a passionate vision of Russia as a great creative force ready to shock the world. "The Twelve" (1918), in which Christ marches at the head of a band of Red Guards, is his best-known poem.

Blum, Léon (1872-1950) French statesman. Blum was the first socialist and Jewish prime minister of France (1936-37, 1938, 1946-47). His socialist and humanist beliefs are summarized in his *À l'échelle humaine* (1945), which was written during his imprisonment by the Nazis (1943-45).

Blunt, Anthony [Frederick] (1907-83) English art historian. He was one of the most influential art historians of his day, knighted in 1956, and was appointed Surveyor of the Queen's Pictures in 1945, a post he held until 1972. He was stripped of his knighthood in 1979, following the public revelation that he had been a Soviet spy.

Blyton, Enid [Mary] (1897-1968) English children's writer. The most famous character in her more than 400 books for young children is Noddy, whose escapades in Toyland with Big Ears, etc., have delighted millions of children. She also wrote adventure stories for older children, featuring heroes such as the "Famous Five." Her work has been much criticized by educationalists as irredeemably politically incorrect and middle-class.

Boas, Franz (1858-1942) German-born American anthropologist. His emphasis on linguistic structure and scientific methodology, and respect for individual societies and cultures, e.g. in his much admired studies of North American Indian societies, has been very influential on anthropology. His works include *Race, Language and Culture* (1940).

Boccioni, Umberto (1882-1916) Italian painter and sculptor. He became the leading futurist artist of the early 20th century, and one of the movement's principal theorists. Only four of his sculptures survive.

Bogarde, Sir Dirk [Derek Jules Gaspard Ulric Niven van den Bogaerde] (1920-) English actor and author. Films he has starred in include LOSEY'S *The Servant* (1963) and VISCONTI'S *The Damned* (1969) and *Death in Venice* (1970). He has also written three highly acclaimed volumes of autobiography, *A Postilion Struck by Lightning* (1977), *Snakes and Ladders* (1978) and *An Orderly Man* (1983), and two best-selling novels, *A Gentle Occupation* (1980) and *Voices in the Garden* (1981).

Bogart, Humphrey [De Forest] (1899-1957) American actor. Bogart's screen persona (not unlike his true personality) was that of the cynical tough guy with a heart of gold. His films include *Casablanca* (1942) and HAWKS' *To Have and to Have Not* (1945) and *The Big Sleep* (1946), the latter two also starring his (fourth) wife **Lauren Bacall** [Betty Joan Perske] (1924-).

Bohr, Niels [Henrik David] (1885-1962) Danish physicist. His greatest achievement was to apply quantum theory to explain the stability of the nuclear model of the atom. He was awarded the 1922 Nobel prize for physics.

Bokassa, Jean Bedel (1921-) president of the Central African Republic (1972-76), who changed his country's name to the Central African Empire and became its self-proclaimed emperor, Bokassa I (1976-79). After his deposition in 1979, his country reverted to its former name.

Böll, Heinrich Theodor (1917-) German novelist and short-story writer. His works, which are usually critical of the endemic militarism of postwar German society, include the novels *Group Portrait with Lady* (1971) and *The Lost Honour of Katharina Blum* (1974), the latter work being a brave and harrowing account of the excesses of the German gutter press.

Bolt, Robert [Oxton] (1924-) English dramatist and screen-writer. His best-known play is *A Man for All Seasons* (1960, filmed 1967), based on the martyrdom of Sir Thomas More, which won Bolt an Oscar. His screenplays include LEAN'S *Lawrence of Arabia* (1962) and *Dr Zhivago* (1965).

Bond, Edward (1934-) English dramatist and screenwriter. His plays include notoriously violent scenes, e.g. the stoning of a baby in its pram in *Saved* (1965), his justification for the violence being that it is needed for an accurate portrayal of capitalist society. (The furore over *Saved* resulted in the aboli-tion of stage censorship in the UK.) He has also written librettos for opera, e.g. HENZE'S *We Come to the River* (1976) and screenplays, e.g. ANTONIONI'S *Blow-Up* (1967).

Bonhoeffer, Dietrich (1906-45) German Lutheran pastor and theologian. Influenced in his theology by BARTH, he was active in the anti-Nazi Resistance during World War II, was impris-oned in 1943 and hanged by the Gestapo in 1945. His posthumously published *Letters and Papers from Prison* (1955) are among the key spiritual writings of the 20th century.

Bonnard, Pierre (1867-1947) French painter and lithogra-pher. Bonnard's work is notable for being intensely colourful, especially in his interior work.

Borel, Emile (1871-1956) French mathematician and politi-cian. Borel's work in probability theory was highly innovative, resulting in the solution of problems previously intractable. He was a Socialist deputy (1924-36) and joined the French Resist-ance during World War II.

Borg, Bjorn (1956-) Swedish tennis player. He won five consecutive Wimbledon championship titles (1976-80) and remains one of the most respected tennis players in the world, notably for his great skill, modesty and criticism of ridiculously high prize money.

Borges, Jorge Luis (1899-1986) Argentinian short-story writer, poet and critic. Borges is regarded as one of the greatest South American writers, with a remarkable gift for creating short fictions with a beguiling metaphysical content. Collections of his stories include *Fictions* (1944, characteristically described as "games with infinity") and *The Aleph and Other Stories* (1971).

Born, Max (1882-1970) German nuclear physicist. He left Nazi Germany (1933) and became professor of natural philosophy at Edinburgh University (1936-63). With the German physicist **Walther Bothe** (1891-1957), he shared the Nobel prize for physics for his research into the statistical interpretation of quantum physics.

Bose, Sir Jagadis Chandra (1858-1937) Indian physicist and plant physiologist. His research into the response of animal and plant tissue to varied stimuli was particularly innovative. He also invented the crescograph, a device that automatically records plant movements.

Bose, Subhas Chandra (1897-1945) Indian nationalist leader. He was president of the Indian National Congress (1938-39) and, in collaboration with the Japanese during World War II, organized the Indian National Army to combat British rule in India.

Botha, Louis (1862-1919) South African general and statesman. As general of the Transvaal army, he led the Boer forces against the British during the Boer War. He supported the Allies during World War I, and became first prime minister of South Africa (1910-19).

Botha, P[ieter] W[illem] (1916-) South African politician. He was prime minister (1978-84) and introduced limited reforms of apartheid.

Botham, Ian (1955-) English cricketer. A talented all-rounder, he captained England (1980-81) and scored 5,057 runs in Test matches (including 14 centuries).

Bothe, Walther *see* **Born, Max**.

Boulanger, Nadia [Juliette] (1887-1979) French music teacher, composer and conductor. She was the first woman to conduct a symphony orchestra in London (for the Royal Philharmonic in 1937) and was a highly influential teacher of composition. Her pupils included COPLAND and MILHAUD.

Boulez, Pierre (1925-) French composer and conductor. A follower of SCHOENBERG, he developed a composition style based on total serialism and electronic instruments. He was director of the New York Philharmonic (1971-77).

Boult, Sir Adrian [Cedric] (1889-1983) English conductor. He was leader of the BBC Symphony Orchestra (1931-50) and the London Philharmonic Orchestra (1950-57). He published an autobiography, *My Own Trumpet* (1973).

Bowen, Elizabeth [Dorothea Cole] (1899-1973) Anglo-Irish novelist and short-story writer. Her novels, e.g. *The Hotel* (1927) and *The Heat of the Day* (1949), are studies of upper middle-class heroines trapped in complex and unhappy relationships. Other works include *Collected Stories* (1980).

Boycott, Geoffrey (1940-) English cricketer. He is regarded as one of England's greatest modern batsmen, He captained Yorkshire (1970-78) and played for England (1964-74, 1977-81), but his erratic and often highly controversial behaviour, e.g. in touring South Africa in 1982, prevented him becoming England's captain.

Bradman, [Sir] Don[ald George] (1908-) Australian cricketer. A brilliant batsman, he scored 117 centuries during the 1930s and 40s. He was Australian captain (1936-48). *See also* FRY, C.B.

Bragg, Melvyn (1939-) English novelist and broadcaster. His novels, frequently set in his native Cumberland, include *The Hired Man* (1969) and *A Place in England* (1970). He is best known as a television presenter of arts programmes.

Branagh, Kenneth (1961-) Irish-born British actor and director. He founded the Renaissance Theatre Company in 1986. His film production of *Henry V* (1990), in which he starred and also directed, was hailed by many critics as comparable with OLIVIER'S.

Brancusi, Constantin (1876-1957) Romanian sculptor (he became a French citizen just before his death). His sculptures, e.g. *Sleeping Muse* (1909), pioneered abstraction in sculpture.

Brando, Marlon (1924-) American actor. His screen performances in *The Men* (1950) and *On the Waterfront* (1954) were highly praised, the latter earning him an Oscar. He also won an Oscar for his role as the Mafia don in COPPOLA's *The Godfather* (1971), which , however, he refused to accept in protest at the oppression of Indians in the US. Other films in which he starred include BERTOLUCCI's *Last Tango in Paris* (1972) and *Apocalypse Now* (1979).

Brandt, Bill (1904-83) German-born British photographer. He became one of the best-known photojournalists of the 1930s for his compassionate images of the bleak lives of the poor in urban slums and mining communities.

Brandt, Willy [Ernst Karl Frahm] (1913-) German statesman. He was active in the German Resistance during World War II and became mayor of Berlin (1957-66) and chancellor of West Germany (1969-74) He was awarded the Nobel Peace Prize in 1971.

Braque, Georges (1882-1963) French painter. The term "Cubism" (*see* PICASSO) was coined in 1909 to describe his works. He also pioneered the use of collage in modern painting.

Brassaï [Gyula Halesz] (1899-1984) Hungarian-born French photographer and painter, whose photographs of Parisian lowlife and Bohemian society were highly praised in the 1930s. His books include *Paris by Night* (1933) and *Conversations with Picasso* (1964).

Brattain, Walter *see* **Shockley, William Bradford.**

Braudel, Fernand (1902-85) French historian. His best-known work, The Mediterranean *and the Mediterranean World* (1949), which focused on socioeconomic trends and the changing relationship between man and the environment rather than on politics or military events, has been very influential on historical studies.

Bream, Julian [Alexander] (1933-) English guitarist and lutenist, who is recognized as one of the finest modern classical guitar players. Several composers, e.g. BRITTEN, have written works for him.

Brecht, Bertolt (1898-1956) German dramatist and poet. A Marxist, he devised what he called an "epic" form of theatre, drawing from traditions such as music hall and popular ballads and using "alienation" devices, in order to illustrate that capitalism is evil and communism good. The plays include *Mother Courage* (1941) and *The Caucasian Chalk Circle* (1955).

Brendel, Alfred (1931-) Czech-born Austrian pianist, who became one of the world's leading concert pianists.

Bresson, Robert (1931-) French film director. His films, which include *The Trial of Joan of Arc* (1962) and *The Devil, Probably* (1977), are intellectual and complex explorations of religious faith from a Roman Catholic point of view.

Breton, André (1896-1966) French poet, essayist and critic. He became a surrealist in the early 1920s. His works include the novel *Nadja* (1928) and *Poems* (1948).

Brezhnev, Leonid Ilyich (1906-82) Soviet statesman. He helped organize KRUSHCHEV's downfall in 1964, and became general secretary of the Communist Party (1977-82) and Soviet president (1977-82). The period of his rule is now described as the "period of stagnation" in the USSR.

Brian, [William] Havergal (1876-1972) English composer, frequently described as "post-Romantic." His more than 30 works include the huge *Gothic Symphony* (1919-27) and five operas.

Bridge, Frank (1879-1941) English composer and conductor. He is best known for his chamber music, a few orchestral pieces, and for having been BRITTEN's teacher.

Bridges, Robert [Seymour] (1844-1930) English poet and critic. His works include *The Testament of Beauty* (1929). He was appointed poet laureate in 1913. Once highly regarded, the critical reputation of his work declined rapidly in the 1930s.

Brittain, Vera *see* **Williams, Shirley**.

Britten, [Edward] Benjamin [1st Baron Britten] (1913-76) English composer and pianist. A pupil of Frank BRIDGE, his works include the operas *Peter Grimes* (1945) and *A Midsum-*

mer Night's Dream (1960), chamber music, orchestral works and song cycles. His works are noted for their romantic lyricism, and a prominent theme is the clash between innocence and evil, as in the opera *Billy Budd* (1951). Many of his vocal works were written for his long-term companion, the tenor Peter PEARS. He was created a peer in 1976

Brook, Peter [Stephen Paul] (1925-) English stage and film director based in Paris. He is regarded as one of the finest experimental directors of the modern era, with productions such as his *Mahabharata* (1988), a nine-hour version of the Indian epic with a multi-cultural cast. His short book *The Empty Space* (1969) explains his theory of stagecraft.

Brooke, Rupert [Chawner] (1887-1915) English poet. He died of cholera while on his way to action in World War I. His war poems, included in *Collected Poems* (1918), were very popular with the public (for a while) with their idealized vision of the nobility of war.

Brooks, Mel [Melvin Kaminsky] (1926-) American comedian, film writer and director. He started his career as a scriptwriter for TV before turning to making fast-moving, irreverent comedy films, e.g. *Blazing Saddles* (1974), *Silent Movie* (1978, with MARCEAU in the only speaking role), and *Life Stinks* (1991). His wife is the actress **Anne Bancroft** [Anna Maria Italiano] (1931-) who is noted for her serious acting, e.g. in *The Miracle Worker* (1962), for which she won an Oscar, and *The Graduate* (1968), but who also appears to effect in her husband's films, e.g. *To Be or Not To Be* (1983).

Brown, Herbert *see* **Wittig, Georg**.

Brubeck, Dave (1920-) American jazz composer and pianist. He studied musical composition with SCHOENBERG and MIL-

HAUD, forming his "Dave Brubeck Quartet" in 1951. "Take Five" is his best-known composition.

Bruce, Lenny (1925-66) American comedian. Bruce's satirical and often scabrous humour made him a cult hero of the 1950s. He was imprisoned for obscenity in 1961, and banned from re-entering Britain in 1963. Drug addiction contributed to his death.

Buber, Martin (1878-1965) Austrian-born Jewish theologian and existentialist philosopher. A Hasidic scholar, Buber's philosophy, which centres on the relationship between man and God, has had a large impact on both Jewish and Christian theology. His works include *I and Thou* (1923) and *Eclipse of God* (1952).

Buchan, John [1st Baron Tweedsmuir] (1875-1940) Scottish novelist, statesman and historian. He wrote several best-selling adventure novels, e.g. *The Thirty-Nine Steps* (1915), *Greenmantle* (1916) and *Mr Standfast* (1919). He was created a peer in 1935, and was appointed governor-general of Canada (1935-40)

Buchman, Frank [Nathan Daniel] (1878-1961) American evangelist. He founded the Oxford Group and the longer-lived Moral Rearmament, which were intended to provide ideological alternatives to both capitalism and communism. His works include *The Oxford Group and its Work of Moral Rearmament* (1954) and *America Needs an Ideology* (1957).

Bukharin, Nikolai Ivanovich (1888-1938) Soviet statesman. One of the early Bolshevik leaders, he was appointed chairman of the Comintern in 1926, and supported STALIN against TROTSKY. He was denounced as a Trotskyite in the late 1930s and executed after a show trial. (The character of Rubashov in KOESTLER's novel *Darkness at Noon* is based on Bukharin.)

Bulganin, Nikolai Aleksandrovich (1895-1975) Soviet states-man. He became chairman of the council of ministers (1955-58), and drifted into obscurity in the late 1950s following his participation in a failed power play against KRUSHCHEV.

Bunche, Ralph Johnson (1904-71) American diplomat and UN official. The grandson of a slave, he became assistant professor of political science at Howard University, Washington, and became the first black to be awarded the Nobel Peace Prize, in 1950, for his attempt at reconciling Israel and the Arab states (1948-49).

Buñuel, Luis (1900-85) Spanish-born film director (settled in Mexico from 1947). His first films, *Un chien andalou* (1928) and *L'Age d'or* (1930), were made in collaboration with Salvador DALI, and are regarded as masterpieces of Surrealist cinema. Later films include *The Discreet Charm of the Bourgeoisie* (1972) and *That Obscure Object of Desire* (1977).

Burgess, Anthony [John Anthony Burgess Wilson] (1917-) English novelist, critic and composer. His novels include the still highly controversial futuristic fantasy of juvenile crime *A Clockwork Orange* (1962, filmed by KUBRICK in 1971), *Inside Mr Enderby* (1963), *Earthly Powers* (1980) and the autobiographical *Little Wilson and Big God* (1987).

Burgess, Guy (1911-63) English diplomat and spy. Recruited by Soviet Intelligence in the 1930s, he worked for MI5 during World War II and served with PHILBY at the British Embassy in Washington DC after the war. With his fellow agent, **Donald Maclean** (1913-83), he fled to the USSR in 1951.

Burnet, Sir Frank Macfarlane *see* **Medawar, Sir Peter Brian**.

Burra, Edward [John] (1905-76) English painter. His favourite medium was watercolour, and his style ranged from early naturalism with strong social comment to, in later years, a dark, private symbolism.

Burroughs, William S[eward] (1914-) American novelist. A friend of GINSBERG and KEROUAC, Burroughs became a heroin addict in the 1940s. His luridly obscene fiction, e.g. *Junkie* (1953) and *The Naked Lunch* (1959), features the squalid, nightmarish underworld of drug addiction.

Burton, Richard [Richard Jenkins] (1925-84) Welsh actor. Burton was regarded by his peers and the critics as one of the most talented actors of his generation. Films he starred in include *The Spy Who Came in from the Cold* (1965) and *Who's Afraid of Virginia Woolf?* (1966), the latter also starring Elizabeth TAYLOR, to whom he was married twice (1964-70, 1975-76).

Busby, Sir Matt[hew] (1909-) Scottish footballer and manager of Manchester United (1946-69). Many members of his highly regarded team of 1958 died in a plane crash at Munich. His rebuilt team of "Busby Babes" became the first English team to win the European Cup (1968).

Bush, Alan Dudley (1900-) English composer and pianist. A Marxist, his works include the operas *Wat Tyler* (1950) and *Joe Hill* (1970), several symphonies and choral works. He published his collected essays, *In My Eighth Decade*, in 1980.

Bush, George [Herbert Walker] (1924-) American Republican politician and 41st president of the US. The son of a wealthy senator, he served in the US Navy (1942-45) during World War II, becoming its youngest pilot, and flew in the Pacific theatre of operations. He became US ambassador to the UN (1971-73), special envoy to China (1974-75) and CIA director (1976). He campaigned against REAGAN for the Republican nomination in 1980 (describing Reagan's monetarist policy as "voodoo economics"), then served under him as vice-president (1980-88). His reputation was damaged by the Iran-Contragate scandal of 1987, and by persistent rumours of CIA involvement in drug running, but he was elected president in 1988, easily defeating the Democrat candidate, **Michael Dukakis** (1933-), governor of Massachusetts (1974-78, 1982-).

Buthelezi, Chief Gatsha (1928-) South African Zulu chief and politician. He helped found the paramilitary organization Inkatha, which is pledged to creating a multiracial democracy in South Africa, but which is claimed by its ANC opponents (*see* MANDELA) to be a major cause of strife in South Africa.

Butler, R[ichard] A[usten], [Baron] (1902-82) English Conservative politician. As minister of education (1941-45), he introduced the important Education Act of 1944. He was also chancellor of the exchequer (1951-55), home secretary (1957-62) and foreign secretary (1963-64). He was created a life peer in 1965, and published his memoirs, *The Art of the Possible*, in 1971. His failure to win leadership of the Conservative Party, most notably in 1963 when DOUGLAS-HOME became prime minister, surprised many commentators.

C

Cadbury, George (1839-1922) English businessman, social reformer and philanthropist. With his brother Michael Cadbury (1835-99) he established the village of Bournville, near Birmingham, for the Cadbury work force. The village came to be seen as a model by many modern architects and town planners.

Cage, John (1912-) American composer. Cage's experimental music, e.g. *Water Music* (1952), in which the pianist is required, among other things, to blow whistles under water, and *4 minutes 33 seconds* (1952), in which the performers remain silent and do not touch their instruments, has been derided and admired in about equal proportions.

Cagney, James (1899- 1986) American film actor. Cagney's performances as gangsters, e.g. in *The Public Enemy* (1931) and *Angels With Dirty Faces* (1938), resulted in him becoming one of the most imitated persons of the day ("You Dirty Rat," etc.). He won an Oscar for his performance in the musical, *Yankee Doodle Dandy* (1942).

Callaghan, [Leonard] James [Baron Callaghan of Cardiff] (1912-) British Labour statesman who succeeded Harold WILSON as prime minister (1976-79). After the passing of a vote of no confidence in his premiership in the House of Commons, he called a general election, which Labour lost, and he was replaced as Labour leader by Michael Foot. He published his memoirs, *Time and Chance*, in 1987.

Callas, Maria (1923-77) American-born Greek operatic soprano, renowned both for her marvellous voice and acting skills, which made her one of the most revered opera singers of the century.

Calvino, Italo (1923-87) Cuban-Italian novelist, essayist and critic. His early novels, e.g. *The Path of the Nest of Spiders* (1947), belonged in the Italian realist tradition, while his later, highly complex explorations of fantasy and myth, e.g. *Invisible Cities* (1972), have been compared to Latin American "magic realism."

Campbell, Sir Malcolm (1885-1948) English racing driver. He was awarded a knighthood in 1931, the year he set a land speed record of 246 mph, for his achievements in setting land and water speed records. His son, **Donald [Malcolm] Campbell,** (1921-67) held the English water speed record, at a speed of 276 mph, but he died on Lake Coniston while trying to break it.

Campbell, Mrs Patrick [Beatrice Stella Tanner] (1865-1940) English actress. She was regarded as one of the finest (and wittiest) actresses of her generation. Among the many roles she created was that of Eliza Doolittle in her friend Shaw's play *Pygmalion*.

Campbell, [Ignatius] Roy [ston Dunnachie] (1901-57) South African poet. His verse includes several fine lyric poems and scathing satires on the the literary establishment. Collections include *The Flaming Terrapin* (1924), *Adamastor* (1930) and *Flowering Rifle* (1939), the last causing great controversy with its praise of General Franco (Campbell fought on Franco's side in the Spanish Civil War).

Campbell-Bannerman, Sir Henry (1836-1908) British statesman. He was Liberal prime minister (1905-08), and played a major part in healing the rifts within the Liberal party following the Boer War.

Camus, Albert (1913-60) French novelist, essayist and dramatist, who is regarded as one of the leading Existentialist writers. His works, which portray man as helpless in the face of an uncaring, absurd universe, include the novels *The Outsider* (1942) and *The Plague* (1947). He joined the French Resistance during the war, and was awarded the Nobel prize for literature in 1957. His study of 20th-century totalitarianism, *The Rebel* (1953), led to a break with SARTRE, who disapproved of the work's condemnation of Communist tyranny.

Capa, Robert [André Friedmann] (1913-54) Hungarian photographer who became one of the best-known war photographers of the century, with his often dramatic pictures of battlefield incidents, particularly from the Spanish Civil War and the D-Day landings. He was killed by a mine in Vietnam.

Capek, Karel (1890-1938) Czech dramatist, novelist and essayist. His best-known play is *R.U.R.* (1920), which introduced the word "robot." With his brother **Josef Capek** (1887-1945), he wrote *The Insect Play* (1921), a prophetic satire on totalitarianism.

Capone, Al[phonse] (1899-1947) Italian-born American gangster. Capone, nicknamed "Scarface," established his powerful criminal empire of specializing in bootleg liquor, prostitution and extortion in Chicago during the prohibition era. He was eventually jailed for tax evasion and died of syphilis.

Capote, Truman (1924-84) American novelist and socialite. His works include light romances such as *Breakfast at Tiffany's*

(1958), and the bleak "faction" documentary novel *In Cold Blood* (1966), a chilling study of murder.

Capra, Frank (1897-1991) Italian-born American film director. Capra's comedies, e.g. *Mr Deeds Goes to Town* (1936) and *Mr Smith Goes to Washington* (1939), usually portray an ultimately successful struggle by a decent, everyday American against the flawed political system, and were enormously popular in the 1930s. His other films include *Arsenic and Old Lace* (1944) and *It's a Wonderful Life* (1946). His autobiography, *The Name Above the Title*, was published in 1971.

Cardin, Pierre (1923-) French couturier, who became one of the world's leading fashion designers, and designed clothes for both men and women.

Carnap, Rudolf (1891-1970) German-born American philosopher. Regarded as a leading logical positivist, he attempted to develop a formal language that would remove ambiguity from scientific language. His works include *Introduction to Semantics* (1942) and *The Logical Foundations of Probability* (1950).

Carné, Marcel (1909-) French film director. His films include *Les Visiteurs du soir* (1942) and the highly acclaimed theatrical epic *Les Enfants du paradis* (1944), both of which were filmed during the German occupation of France.

Carnegie, Andrew (1835-1919) Scottish-born American industrialist and philanthropist. Carnegie believed that personal wealth should be used for the benefit of all members of society, a view expounded in his *Gospel of Wealth* (1899). His benefactions, notably in the provision of public libraries, have been estimated at around £70 million.

Carter, Elliott [Cook] (1908-) American composer. His works include orchestral pieces, string quartets and cello and piano sonatas. They are regarded as intellectually rigorous and complex, using a wide variety of styles and techniques, from Renaissance music to serialism. His collected writings were published in 1977.

Carter, Jimmy [James Earl Carter] (1924-   ) American Democratic statesman and 39th president of the US (1977-81). A successful peanut farmer, he became governor of Georgia (1974-77) and defeated Gerald FORD in the 1976 presidential campaign. His administration made significant attempts at linking overseas trade with human rights issues. He was defeated by REAGAN in the 1980 presidential election.

Cartier-Bresson, Henri (1908-   ) French photographer and film director. His documentary black-and-white photographs were taken on the principle of what he called "decisive moments" of real-life action, without prior composition and preparation, and the full uncropped frame was sacrosanct. His books include *Europeans* (1955) and *Cartier-Bresson's France* (1971). In films, he was closely associated with RENOIR.

Cartland, Dame Barbara (1901-) English romantic novelist. Over 500 million copies of her upwards of 500 published novels have been sold, making her one of the best-selling authors of all time.

Caruso, Enrico (1873-1921) Italian tenor. Regarded as perhaps the most outstanding operatic tenor of all time, Caruso was also one of the first indisputably great singers to make recordings.

Carver, Raymond (1939-88) American poet and short-story writer. His works include *What We Talk About When We Talk About Love* (1981) and *Fire: Essays, Poems, Stories* (1984).

Cary, [Arthur] Joyce [Lunel] (1888-1957) Irish-born English novelist. His novels include *Mister Johnson* (1939) and *The Horse's Mouth* (1944).

Casals, Pablo (1876-1973) Spanish cellist, pianist and composer. Casals' recordings of Bach's cello suites and of the Dvorak cello concerto are particularly highly regarded.

Casement, Sir Roger [David] (1864-1916) British consular official and Irish nationalist. While working for the British colonial service, he exposed the repression of the people of the Congo by its Belgian rulers in 1904. Knighted in 1911, he adopted Irish nationalism shortly afterwards and was hanged for treason in London. The contents of his so-called "Black Diaries," revealing his hidden homosexual life, were leaked by the British government to discredit him.

Castro [Ruz], Fidel (1926-) Cuban statesman, prime minister (1959-76) and president (1976-). He overthrew BATISTA in a coup in 1959, and shortly afterwards announced his conversion to communism. Castro survived several attempts at his overthrow by exiled opponents and the CIA, e.g. the abortive Bay of Pigs invasion in 1961, but survived by becoming a client of the USSR. Soviet subsidies began to decrease in the late 1980s, and Castro's rule became more beleaguered.

Cavell, Edith [Louisa] (1865-1915) English nurse. She treated both German and Allied casualties in Brussels during the German occupation, and was executed by firing squad by the German authorities, who accused her of helping British soldiers to escape to Holland. Her execution was condemned worldwide.

Ceausescu, Nicolae (1918-89) Romanian dictator. He was secretary general of the Romanian Communist Party from

1969, and president of Romania from 1974. His pursuit of a foreign policy independent of the the Soviet Union resulted in his brutal domestic policies being ignored or played down by Western states. His regime was overthrown by dissident Communists in 1989, and he and his wife were executed by firing squad.

Céline, Louis Ferdinand (1894-1961) French novelist and physician. His masterpiece is *Journey to the End of the Night* (1932), a dark and pessimistic autobiographical account of the author's wartime and African experiences. A vicious anti-semite, Céline fled to Denmark after the Liberation of France, where he was imprisoned for several years.

Chabrol, Claude (1930-) French film director. He was one of the New Wave directors of the 1950s, and was strongly influenced by HITCHCOCK. His films include *Les Bonnes Femmes* (1960) and *Le Boucher* (1970).

Chadwick, Sir James (1891-1974) English physicist. He discovered the neutron in 1932, and was awarded the Nobel prize for physics in 1935.

Chagall, Marc (1889-1985) Russian-born French painter. Chagall's vividly coloured work features unusual compositions "of images that obsess me," often drawing on symbolism from Russian and Jewish folk art. Highlights of his work include 12 striking stained glass windows in a Jerusalem synagogue (1961) and decorations for the ceiling of the Paris Opera House (1964)

Chain, Sir Ernst Boris (1906-79) German-born British biochemist. He prepared penicillin for clinical use, and with FLOREY and Alexander FLEMING, shared the 1945 Nobel prize for physiology or medicine.

Chaliapin, Fyodor Ivanovich (1873-1938) Russian operatic bass singer. His performances, particularly in Russian operas such as Musorgsky's *Boris Godunov*, were widely regarded as definitive.

Chamberlain, [Arthur] Neville (1869-1940) British states-man and Conservative prime minister (1937-40). He pursued a policy of appeasement towards the totalitarian powers of Germany, Italy and Japan in the 1930s (Winston CHURCHILL being a notable opponent of the policy), which was abandoned when Germany invaded Poland in 1939. He died shortly after illness forced his resignation from Churchill's war cabinet.

Chandler, Raymond [Thornton] (1888-1959) American nov-elist and screenwriter. His detective novels, e.g. *Farewell, My Lovely* (1940), have been widely praised for their witty, street-wise dialogue.

Chanel, Coco [Gabrielle Bonheur Chanel] (1883-1971) French couturière and perfumer. She originated the thin, low-waist style for women's dresses, exemplified by the "little black dress," and launched a famous range of perfumes, notably Chanel No 5.

Chaplin, Sir Charlie [Spencer] (1889-1977) English comedi-an and film director. He made his film debut in M*aking a Living* (1914), in which he introduced the down-at-heel, gentleman-tramp character with a beguiling shuffle, bowler hat and cane, that became perhaps the most famous comic creation of the century. Other films include *City Lights* (1931) and *The Great Dictator* (1940). He was knighted in 1975.

Charles, Prince [Charles Philip Arthur George, Prince of Wales] (1948-) heir apparent to ELIZABETH II of the United Kingdom. His interest in alternative methods of healing and cultivation and concern for social harmony resulted in a campaign of vilification against him in Britain's tabloid press. Other notable concerns of his are town planning and vernacular architecture. He married **Lady Diana Spencer** (1961-) in 1981, and they have two children.

Charles, Ray [Ray Charles Robinson] (1930-) American singer, pianist and songwriter. Originally a blues/jazz singer, Charles became one of the most popular singers in the world with songs such as "I Can't Stop Loving You."

Charlton, Bobby [Robert Charlton] (1937-) English footballer. One of the "BUSBY BABES" and a survivor of the 1958 Munich air crash, Charlton became one of the most popular forwards of the 1960s, and was capped over 100 times for England. His brother **Jack Charlton** [John Charlton] (1935-), also an England international, became a national hero in Ireland following his steering of Ireland to the 1990 World Cup finals.

Charnley, Sir John (1911-82) English orthopedic surgeon. He invented an artificial hip joint, and developed methods of hip replacement surgery. He was knighted in 1977.

Charpentier, Gustave (1860-1956) French composer. His best-known work is the opera *Louise* (1900), for which he wrote both libretto and music, and which made him a rich man.

Cherenkov, Pavel Alekseievich (1904-) Soviet physicist. In the mid-1930s, he discovered the form of radiation known as Cherenkhov radiation, and was awarded the 1958 Nobel prize for physics.

Chernenko, Konstantin Ustinovich (1911-85) Soviet statesman. He was a protégé of BREZHNEV, who apparently wished Chernenko to succeed him as president. When ANDROPOV died, Chernenko was appointed his successor as general secretary of the Soviet Communist Party, and was elected state president in 1984. His death was seemingly brought on by emphysema.

Cherwell, Frederick Alexander Lindemann, Viscount (1886-1957) German-born British physicist. He was scientific adviser to CHURCHILL during World War II.

Cheshire, Sir [Geoffrey] Leonard (1917-) English philanthropist. He was awarded the Victoria Cross for completing over 100 bombing raids over Germany in World War II, and was the official British observer of the atomic bomb blast at Nagasaki. He subsequently founded the Cheshire Foundation Homes for the incurably sick. He married the philanthropist **Sue Ryder** [Baroness Ryder of Warsaw and Cavendish] (1923-) in 1959 He was knighted in 1991.

Chesterton, G[ilbert] K[eith] (1874-1936) English essayist, novelist, critic and poet. With his friend BELLOC, he became known as a gifted disputant for what they saw as the glory of old, rural Roman Catholic England. Chesterton's novels and "Father Brown" detective stories, e.g. *The Innocence of Father Brown* (1911), and the weirdly anarchic *The Man Who Was Thursday* (1908), are highly entertaining.

Chevalier, Maurice (1888-1972) French singer and film actor, who came to be seen as the archetypal romantic Frenchman throughout the world. His films include *Love Me Tonight* (1932) and *Gigi* (1958).

Chiang Ch'ing *or* **Jiang Qing** (1913-) Chinese Communist politician and actress. She married MAO as his third wife in 1939 and became the main force behind the savage purges of the Cultural Revolution in the late 1960s. After Mao's death, her power gradually waned, and she was arrested in 1976 with three confederates (the "Gang of Four") and charged with murder and subversion. She was sentenced to death in 1981, the sentence later being suspended.

Chiang Kai-shek *or* **Jiang Jie Shi** (1887-1975) Chinese general and statesman. He was president of China (1928-38, 1943-49), then, after losing the civil war to MAO TSE-TUNG and his Communist forces, fled the mainland to establish the nationalist republic of China in Formosa, of which he became president (1950-57).

Chichester, Sir Francis [Charles] (1901-72) English yachtsman and aviator. He made the first solo round-the-world voyage in his yacht *Gipsy Moth IV* (1966-67).

Chirico, Giorgio de (1888-1978) Greek-born Italian painter. His dreamlike pictures of open, deserted squares were hailed by the Surrealists as precursors of their own works in the early 1920s.

Chomsky, Noam [Avram] (1928-) American linguist, philosopher and political activist. His innovative work in linguistics is based on the principles that humans are born with an innate capacity for learning grammatical structures and that the linguist must distinguish between "deep" and "surface" grammar. Chomsky has also been a prominent spokesman for left-wing causes, and was a notable opponent of the Vietnam war.

Chou En-Lai *or* **Zhou En Lai** (1898-1976) Chinese Communist statesman. He was foreign minister (1949-58) and prime minister (1949-76) of the People's Republic of China. He advocated detente with the US in the early 1970s, and was regarded as a moderate during the chaos of China's Cultural Revolution in the late 1960s.

Christian X (1870-1947) king of Denmark (1912-47) and of Iceland (1918-44). During the Nazi occupation of Denmark

(1940-45), he resolutely opposed their demands for anti-semitic legislation, and was imprisoned in 1943 for speaking out against Nazi ideology.

Christie, [Dame] Agatha [Clarissa Mary] (1890-1976) English detective story writer, whose ingeniously plotted novels, e.g. *The Murder of Roger Ackroyd* (1926), established her as one of the greatest writers in the genre.

Churchill, Sir Winston [Leonard Spencer] (1874-1965) British Conservative statesman and writer. After an adventurous early life, which included action at the battle of Omdurman (1898) and escape from imprisonment by Louis BOTHA during the Boer War, he held several posts under both Liberal and Conservative governments. He opposed CHAMBERLAIN's policy of appeasement in the 1930s, and served as prime minister (1940-45) in World War II. His works include *The Second World War* (1948-54) and *History of the English-Speaking Peoples* (1956-58). He was awarded the Nobel prize for literature (1953).

Clair, René [René Lucien Chomette] (1898-1981) French film director. His films include the comedies *An Italian Straw Hat* (1928), *The Ghost Goes West* (1936) and *It Happened Tomorrow* (1944).

Clapton, Eric (1945-) English guitarist, who is widely recognized as one of the most influential rock guitarists. He played with the Yardbirds (1963-65) and the "super group" Cream (1966-68).

Clark, Jim (1936-68) Scottish racing driver. He was World Champion in 1963 and 1965, and was killed in a crash in West Germany. He won 25 Grand Prix events, and is one of the greatest racing drivers of all time.

Claudel, Paul [Louis Charles] (1868-1955) French poet, dramatist and diplomat. A devout Roman Catholic, his work includes the plays *Tidings Brought to Mary* (1912) and *The Satin Slipper* (1921). Volumes of poetry include *Five Great Odes* (1910).

Cleese, John [Marwood] (1939-) English comedy actor and writer. He was one of the main talents involved in the anarchic and highly influential TV comedy series, *Monty Python's Flying Circus* (1969-74). His own subsequent TV comedy series, *Fawlty Towers* (1975, 1979), was also highly successful, as was the film *A Fish Called Wanda* (1988).

Clemenceau, Georges [Eugène Benjamin] (1841-1929) French statesman. A leading left-winger, he was an outspoken critic of the French government's war policy in the early days of World War I. He became prime minister (1906-9, 1917-20). His forceful negotiation of the Versailles Treaty (1919) is believed by many to have led directly to World War II.

Cockcroft, Sir John Douglas (1897-1967) English nuclear physicist. With the Irish physicist **Sir Ernest [Thomas Sinton] Walton** (1903-), he produced the first laboratory splitting of an atomic nucleus, for which they shared the 1951 Nobel prize for physics.

Cockerell, Sir Christopher Sydney (1910-) English engineer. He invented the hovercraft, the prototype of which first crossed the English Channel in 1959.

Cocteau, Jean (1889-1963) French film director, novelist, dramatist, poet and critic. His experimental, surreal films include *The Blood of a Poet* (1932) and *Beauty and the Beast* (1945). The best known of his novels is *Les Enfants Terribles* (1929).

Colette [Sidonie Gabrielle Colette] (1873-1954) French novelist. Her novels, e.g. *Chéri* (1920) and *Gigi* (1944), are often erotic and display a strong sympathy for animals and the natural world.

Collingwood, R[obin] G[eorge] (1889-1943) English philosopher, historian and archaeologist. He was an authority on the archaeology of Roman Britain, and developed a historicist approach to philosophy in his *An Essay on Metaphysics* (1940). Other works include *The Principles of Art* (1937) and *Autobiography* (1939).

Collins, Michael (1890-1922) Irish nationalist politician. A prominent military leader of Sinn Fein, he helped negotiate the peace treaty with Great Britain in 1921 that established the Irish Free State, and was killed in an ambush.

Collins, Michael (1930-) *see* **Armstrong, Neil**.

Coltrane, John [William] (1926-67) American jazz saxophonist. A virtuoso on the tenor and soprano saxophones, he became one of the most influential and popular jazz musicians of his generation.

Compton, Arthur Holly (1892-1962) American physicist. He was a prominent researcher into X-rays, gamma rays and nuclear energy, and discovered the Compton effect. He was awarded the 1927 Nobel prize for physics.

Compton, Denis [Charles Scott] (1918-) English cricketer, who played for Middlesex and England (1937-57). Regarded as one of the best all-rounders ever in cricket (and a self-taught batter), he broke two records in 1947 by scoring 3,816 runs and 18 centuries in one season.

Compton-Burnett, Dame Ivy (1884-1969) English novelist.

Her novels, which are mostly in dialogue and feature the traumas of upper-middle-class Edwardian family life, include *Brothers and Sisters* (1925) and *Manservant and Maidservant* (1947).

Connery, Sean [Thomas] (1930-) Scottish film actor. He achieved worldwide fame in his role as the Ian FLEMING character James Bond in such movies as *Doctor No* (1962) and *Goldfinger* (1964). Connery gradually became recognized as one of the finest film actors of his time, and received an Oscar for his part as a tough Irish cop in *The Untouchables* (1987).

Connors, Jimmy (1952-) American tennis player. He was Wimbledon champion (1974. 1982) and US champion (1974, 1976, 1978, 1982, 1983).

Conrad, Joseph [Teodor Josef Konrad Korzeniowsky] (1857-1924) Polish-born English novelist (English was his third language, after Polish and French). He qualified as a master mariner in the British marine service in 1886. His novels and novellas, which often feature isolated or outcast characters in exotic settings, include *Almayer's Folly* (1895) and *Heart of Darkness* (1902).

Constantine, Learie Nicholas, Baron (1902-71) West Indian cricketer. Regarded as an exceptionally fine fielder, he was also an outstanding batsman and a dynamic bowler. He was created a life peer in 1969 for his services to race relations.

Coolidge, [John] Calvin (1872-1933) American Republican statesman. He became 30th president of the US (1923-29). His election was regarded as a stabilizing influence in American politics following years of political scandal. His encouragement of stock market speculation in the late 1920s may have contributed to the ensuing economic crash.

Cooper, Gary [Frank James Cooper] (1901-61) American film actor. He specialized in the tall, silent "integrity" type. His many films include *Mr Deeds Goes to Town* (1936), *Sergeant York* (1940) and *High Noon* (1952), the latter two winning him Oscars.

Copland, Aaron (1900-1990) American composer, pianist and conductor. His work includes the well-known ballet scores *Rodeo* (1942) and *Appalachian Spring* (1944). These and his other works, which include orchestral and chamber works and film scores, often incorporate elements and themes from traditional music such as folk songs.

Coppola, Francis Ford (1939-) American film director and screenwriter. He wrote the screenplay for *Patton* (1970), and subsequently became a very successful director with films such as *The Godfather* (1972) and *Apocalypse Now* (1979).

Corman, Roger (1926-) American film director and producer. Known primarily in the 1950s and 60s as a creator of cheap B movies, e.g. *She-Gods of Shark Reef* (1958), he also fostered the careers of many of the most prominent American directors and actors of the 70s and 80s, e.g. SCORSESE, NICHOLSON, COPPOLA and DE NIRO. His most highly regarded film is *The Masque of the Red Death* (1964). Corman also makes occasional guest appearances in films, e.g. as the FBI Director in *The Silence of the Lambs* (1990).

Cosgrave, W[illiam] T[homas] (1880-1965) Irish nationalist politician. He became first president of the Irish Free State (1922-32). His son **Liam Cosgrave** (1920-) became Fine Gael prime minister of the Republic of Ireland (1973-77).

Cousteau, Jacques [Yves] (1910-) French oceanographer. He invented the aqualung (1943) and developed techniques of underwater cinematography that, through films such as *The Silent World* (1956) and his long-running TV series, *The Undersea World of Jacques Cousteau* (1968-76), were highly influential in raising public awareness of the world's oceans.

Coward, Sir Noel [Pierce] (1899-1973) English dramatist, actor and composer. His witty, sophisticated comedies, e.g. *Private Lives* (1930) and *Blithe Spirit* (1941), were regarded as mildly shocking in their day. He also wrote several amusing songs, e.g. "Mad Dogs and Englishmen." His film roles include the leading role in the patriotic film *In Which We Serve* (1942), and a highly engaging cameo role in *Our Man in Havana* (1959).

Crawford, Joan [Lucille le Sueur] (1908-77) American film actress. She won an Oscar for her performance in *Mildred Pierce* (1945). The highlight of her later work is the macabre *What Ever Happened to Baby Jane?* (1962), in which she starred with Bette DAVIS.

Crick, Francis [Harry Compton] (1916-) English molecular biologist. With John WATSON, he discovered the structure of DNA, and was awarded the 1962 Nobel prize for physiology or medicine.

Crippen, Hawley Harvey (1862-1910) American doctor who poisoned his wife in London in 1910. He and his mistress, Ethel le Neve, disguised as a boy, fled to Canada, and were arrested on docking at Montreal after the ship's captain had radiotelegraphed their descriptions to Scotland Yard.

Cripps, Sir [Richard] Stafford (1889-1952) British Labour statesman. A leading left-winger, with a reputation for being a severe ascetic, he became chancellor of the exchequer (1947-50), and introduced a programme of high taxation and wage restraint to deal with Britain's economic problems.

Croce, Benedetto (1866-1952) Italian philosopher and statesman. He initially supported Mussolini, but after 1925 became a leading anti-fascist and advocate of liberal policies. His major work is *Philosophy of the Spirit* (1902-17).

Cronin, A[rchibald] J[oseph] (1896-1981) Scottish novelist and physician. His novels include *The Stars Look Down* (1935) and *Shannon's Way* (1948). His works formed the basis for the hugely popular 1960s TV series *Dr Finlay's Casebook*.

Crosby, Bing [Harry Lillis Crosby] (1904-77) American singer and actor. His relaxed, jazz-influenced style of singing or "crooning" made him one of the most popular and imitated singers of the century. His recording of BERLIN's "White Christmas" (1942) is often said to be the best-selling record of all time (Crosby had over 80 hits). He also made a series of highly popular "Road to..." series of comedy films with his friend Bob HOPE, e.g. *Road to Rio* (1947).

Crossman, Richard [Howard Stafford] (1907-84) English Labour politician. His revelatory diaries of ministerial life in Harold WILSON's 1960s cabinets were published in three volumes (1975-77), and provide valuable insight into the political life of the period.

cummings, e[dward] e[stlin] (1894-1962) American poet, novelist and artist. His autobiographical novel *The Enormous Room* (1922) describes his wrongful imprisonment for treason, and his subsequent experimental free verse and distinctive use of typography, e.g. *Collected Poems* (1938), influenced many other poets.

Curie, Marie (1867-1934) Polish-born French chemist. With her husband **Pierre Curie** (1859-1906), also a chemist, and the physicist **Antoine Henri Becquerel** (1852-1908), she was awarded the 1903 Nobel prize for physics for work on radioactivity, thus becoming the first woman to win a Nobel prize. She subsequently became the first person to win two Nobel prizes when her discovery of radium and polonium led to her being awarded the 1911 prize for chemistry.

Curtin, John Joseph Ambrose (1885-1945) Australian Labour statesman and prime minister (1941-45). He introduced several significant welfare measures, e.g. unemployment and sickness benefit.

Cushing, Harvey Williams (1869-1939) American neurosurgeon, who made significant contributions to neurosurgery, e.g. his identification of the adrenal gland disorder, Cushing's disease.

D

Dahl, Roald (1916-91) English author (of Norwegian parentage) known primarily for his entertaining children's stories, e.g. *Charlie and the Chocolate Factory* (1964) and collections of brutally funny poems. Stories for adults include the collection *Kiss, Kiss* (1960) and the autobiographical *Boy* (1984).

Daladier, Edouard (1884-1970) French socialist statesman. He was prime minister (1933, 1934, 1938-40) and signed the Munich Pact of 1938. He denounced the Vichy government in 1943, and was then imprisoned in Germany for the duration of the war.

Dalai Lama [Tenzin Gyatso] (1935-) Tibetan spiritual and temporal leader. He became the 14th Dalai Lama in 1940, and fled Tibet in 1959 following the Chinese invasion of his country in that year. He is widely respected throughout the world for his constant advocation of a peaceful solution, in line with Buddhist principles, to the brutal repression of his country by China. He was awarded the 1989 Nobel Peace Prize.

Dale, Sir Henry Hallett (1875-1968) English physiologist. He and **Otto Lowei** (1873-1961) were awarded the 1936 Nobel prize for physiology or medicine for their work on the chemical basis of nerve impulse transmission.

Dali, Salvador (1904-89) Spanish surrealist painter. Influenced by CHIRICO and FREUD, Dali became established as the leading surrealist painter by 1931, the year in which he painted his *The Persistence of Memory*, which includes his limp watch faces that remain the image most characteristic of his "dream photographs." He made two films with Buñuel, and published three volumes of autobiography, e.g. *Diary of a Genius* (1966).

Dallapiccola, Luigi (1904-75) Italian composer and pianist. Regarded as the leading Italian exponent of twelve-tone music, his works include the opera *Night Flight* (1937-39) and the ballet *Marsia* (1948). Much of his work, as in his *Songs of Prison* (1938-41), reflects his concern about political and spiritual repression.

Dam, [Carl Peter] Henrik (1895-1976) Danish biochemist. He was awarded the 1943 Nobel prize for physiology or medicine which he shared with the American biochemist **Edward Doisy** (1893-) for discovering vitamin K (in 1934).

D'Annunzio, Gabriele (1863-1938) Italian poet, novelist, dramatist and political adventurer. The sensuous imagery of much of his work has been widely admired. His novel, *The Flame of Life* (1900), created a public scandal with its thinly disguised description of his affair with the great French tragedian **Eleonora Duse** (1858-1924). His oratory was credited with Italy's joining the allies in World War I. He seized the city of Fiume in 1919, which he ruled until 1920. He became a supporter of Mussolini.

Darlan, Jean [Louis Xavier] François (1881-1942) French admiral and politician who became vice-premier of Vichy France under Pétain. He was assassinated by a French monarchist.

Darrow, Clarence Seward (1857-1938) American attorney. A strong opponent of capital punishment, he conducted many successful and highly publicized defences, notably of murderers and labour leaders, and became the US's most prominent defence counsel. His most famous case was the Tennessee trial of John T. Scopes, a schoolteacher charged with teaching Darwinism (he lost the case, but won a moral victory).

Davies, Marion *see* **Hearst, William Randolph.**

Davies, Sir Peter Maxwell (1934-) English composer. Heavily influenced by medieval music, his works include *Eight Songs for a Mad King* (1969) and the opera *Taverner* (1962-68, revised 1970). With BIRTWHISTLE, he founded the Pierrot Players (later called the Fires of London). Since 1970 he has been based in Orkney, where he frequently collaborates with the poet George Mackay Brown.

Davis, Bette [Ruth Elizabeth Davis] (1908-89) American actress, whose electrifying and commanding screen presence made her one of the most highly rated film actresses. Her films include *Of Human Bondage* (1934), *Dangerous* (1935), *Jezebel* (1938), the latter two earning her Oscars, *The Little Foxes* (1941) and *All About Eve* (1950). *See also* CRAWFORD.

Davis, Sir Colin [Rex] (1927-) English conductor. Noted particularly for his interpretations of Berlioz, he was conductor of the BBC Symphony Orchestra (1967-71).

Davis, Miles [Dewey] (1926-91) American jazz trumpeter, composer and bandleader. He joined the Charlie PARKER Quintet at the age of 19. He became the leading exponent of the "cool jazz" school with his subsequent groups, working with musicians such as COLTRANE.

Davis, Nancy *see* **Reagan, Ronald.**

Davis, Steve (1958-) English snooker player. He was the world's leading snooker player for most of the 1980s, renowned for his imperturbability during televised contests.

Davisson, Clinton Joseph *see* **Thomson, Sir George Paget**.

Dawes, Charles G[ates] (1865-1951) American banker. He devised the Dawes Plan of 1924 for German reparation payments after World War I. He was US vice-president (1925-29) and was awarded the 1925 Nobel Peace Prize.

Day, Doris [Doris Kappelhoff] (1924-) American film actress, famous for her light-hearted, girl-next-door image. her films include *Calamity Jane* (1953) and *The Pajama Game* (1957).

Day, Sir Robin (1923-) English broadcaster and journalist. He presented the popular TV current affairs programme *Question Time* (1979-89) and was a notably incisive interviewer of politicians.

Dayan, Moshe (1915-81) Israeli general and statesman. He commanded the Israeli forces during the Sinai invasion (1956) and was minister of defence during the Six Day War of 1967. He played an important part in the talks leading to the Israel-Egypt peace treaty of 1979, in which year he resigned from office in protest at what he perceived as BEGIN's intransigence towards the Arabs.

Day Lewis, Cecil (1904-72) Irish-born English poet. In the 1930s he was regarded as part of the "Auden generation" of left-wing poets, e.g. *The Magic Mountain* (1933). He became poet laureate in 1968. He also wrote detective novels under the pseudonym "Nicholas Blake," e.g. *A Question of Proof* (1935).

Deakin, Alfred (1856-1919) Australian statesman. He was prime minister (1903-04, 1905-08, 1909-10), and led the movement for Australian federation.

Dean, Christopher *see* **Torvill, Jayne**.

Dean, James [James Byron] (1931-55) American film actor. Dean became a cult figure in the 1950s for his portrayal of troubled, disaffected adolescence in films such as *East of Eden* (1955) and *Rebel Without a Cause* (1955). He died in a car crash.

Debussy, Claude [Achille] (1862-1918) French composer. Regarded as the founder of impressionism in music and one of the strongest influences on modern music, his works include the orchestral pieces *Prélude a l' après-midi d' un faune* (1894) and *La Mer* (1905), and the opera *Pelléas et Mélisande* (1902).

de Gaulle, Charles [André Joseph Marie] (1890-1970) French general, statesman and first president (1958-69) of the Fifth Republic. An opponent of the Vichy regime led by PÉTAIN, he fled to Britain in 1940, where he became the leader of the Free French forces. Elected president of the provisional government in 1945, he resigned in 1946 after disagreement over his executive powers (regarded by him as insufficient). He was asked to form a government in 1958, during the Algerian crisis, and was granted considerable power by the National Assembly following a referendum. He granted independence to France's colonies in Africa (1959-60), oversaw increased economic prosperity, fostered France's independent nuclear deterrent policy and strongly opposed the UK's entry into the Common Market. His party won a large majority in the election following the student riots of 1968. He resigned in 1969, after being defeated on constitutional reform.

De Forest, Lee (1873-1961) American electrical engineer. He invented the triode valve in 1907, and made significant contributions to the development of sound and picture transmission.

De Havilland, Sir Geoffrey (1882-1965) English aircraft

designer. He designed several famous aircraft, e.g. the Tiger Moth (1930) and the plywood Mosquito (1941) and the first commercial jet airliner, the De Havilland Comet (1952).

Deighton, Len [Leonard Cyril] (1929-) British thriller writer. His books include *The Ipcress File* (1962) and *Funeral in Berlin* (1965).

de Klerk, F[rederik] W[illem] (1936-) South African statesman. He succeeded BOTHA as leader of the ruling National party and president (1989) and continued the policy of dismantling apartheid, in 1990 legalizing the African National Congress and organizing MANDELA's release from prison.

De la Mare, Walter [John] (1873-1956) English poet and novelist. Much of his work was written for children, e.g. *Peacock Pie* (1913), and the loss of childhood innocence is a major theme in his work. The best of his work, e.g. the poetry collection *The Listeners* (1910) and the novel *Memoirs of a Midget* (1921), has a delicately eerie quality.

Delaunay, Robert (1885-1941) French painter. He founded the movement called "Orphism," which was the name given by the French poet **Guillaume Apollinaire** [Apollinaris Kostrowitzky] (1880-1918), to Delaunay's introduction of colour abstraction into his Cubist-style paintings. He influenced many other artists, notably KLEE.

Delius, Frederick (1862-1934) English composer. Heavily influenced by traditional folk tunes and drawing much of his inspiration from landscape, his work includes tone poems such as *Over the Hills and Far Away* (1895), the opera *A Village Romeo and Juliet* (1900-1901) and the variations for chorus and orchestra, *Appalachia* (1902). Sir Thomas BEECHAM was a notable champion of his work.

Delvaux, Paul (1897-) Belgian surrealist painter. Influenced by CHIRICO and MAGRITTE in the mid-1930s, he embarked on a series of paintings, e.g. *Phases of the Moon* (1939), depicting nude girls in dreamlike, architectural settings.

de Mille, Cecil B[lount] (1881-1959) American film producer and director. With GOLDWYN, he is credited with creating the mass movie industry of Hollywood. His films, e.g. *The Ten Commandments* (1923), were extravagantly produced epics that achieved enormous success throughout the world.

Dempsey, Jack [William Harrison Dempsey] (1895-1983) American boxer. An ex-miner who became one of the most popular boxers of his day, he was world heavyweight champion (1919-26).

Deng Xiao Ping *or* **Teng Hsiao-p'ing** (1904-) Chinese Communist statesman. Denounced in the Cultural Revolution of the late 1960s as a "capitalist roader" he was subsequently rehabilitated by CHOU EN-LAI in 1973. He went into hiding after his patron's death in 1976, fearing reprisals from MAO's widow, CHIANG CH'ING, then re-emerged as a powerful figure in the late 1970s. He introduced economic reforms and developed friendly relations with the West, but also sanctioned the Tiananmen Square massacre of dissident students.

De Niro, Robert (1943-) American actor, who is regarded as one of the finest modern screen actors, with a remarkable facility for submerging himself in a wide variety of roles. His films include *Taxi Driver* (1976), *King of Comedy* (1982), *The Godfather II* (1974) and *Raging Bull* (1980), the latter two films winning him Oscars.

Denning, Alfred Thompson, Baron (1899-) English judge. Regarded as having a notable concern for individual rights,

Denning was also responsible for several controversial judgments and was disinclined to rely on precedent. His books include *The Closing Chapter* (1983).

Derain, André (1880-1954) French painter. He was influenced by PICASSO and BRAQUE, and became one of the leading Fauvist painters.

Desai, [Shri] Morarji [Ranchhodji] (1896-) Indian statesman. He held several ministerial posts under NEHRU, founded the Janata party in opposition to Indira GANDHI's Congress Party, which he defeated in the 1977 general election, and served as prime minister (1977-79).

De Sica, Vittorio (1902-74) Italian film director and actor. His early films, e.g. *Bicycle Thieves* (1948), are regarded as among the finest Italian neo-realist films for their compassionate insight into the lives of the poor. *The Garden of the Finzi-Continis* (1971) won an Oscar for best foreign film.

De Valera, Eamon (1882-1975) American-born Irish statesman. He was sentenced to death by the British government for his part in the 1916 Easter Rising, but was reprieved after US intervention. He became president of Sinn Féin (1917-1926). He opposed the Anglo-Irish Treaty (1921), gave largely symbolic leadership to the anti-treaty forces during the civil war (1922-23), and was imprisoned (1923-24). He became prime minister (1932-48, 1951-54, 1957-59) and president (1959-73).

Devine, George [Alexander Cassady] (1910-66) English stage director and administrator. He became one of the most prominent influences on the British stage as artistic director of the English Stage Company at the Royal Court, and fostered the work of new wave dramatists such as OSBORNE and ARDEN.

de Vries, Hugo [Marie] (1848-1935) Dutch botanist and geneticist. He rediscovered the genetic principles first put forward by Mendel, and developed the theory of evolution through the mutation of genes.

Dewey, John (1859-1952) American philosopher and educational theorist. His philosophy was firmly in the pragmatist tradition, relying on the definition of knowledge as "successful practise" and truth as "warranted assessibility," a view developed in works such *The Quest for Certainty* (1929). He also published radical studies of education theory, e.g. *The School and Society* (1899).

Diaghilev, Sergei [Pavlovich] (1872-1929) Russian ballet impresario. His highly successful production of *Boris Godunov* in Paris (1908) led to the founding of his Ballet Russe de Diaghilev in 1911, based in Monte Carlo. He became one of the most influential ballet impresarios, drawing upon the talents of composers such as DEBUSSY and STRAVINSKY and artists such as PICASSO. He was much influenced by Isadora DUNCAN's dancing. *See also* FOKINE.

Diefenbaker, John George (1895-1979) Canadian Conservative statesman. He was prime minister (1957-63).

Dietrich, Marlene [Maria Magdelene von Losch] (1904-92) German-born American singer and film actress, notable for her strong sexual presence and husky, alluring voice. Her films include *The Blue Angel* (1930, the last film she made in Germany), *Shanghai Express* (1932), *The Devil is a Woman* (1935) and the comedy western *Destry Rides Again* (1939).

Dior, Christian (1905-57) French couturier. The extravagance of his New Look design of the late 1940s, with narrow waists and full pleated skirts, proved very popular in the austerity of the postwar period. He later designed the "Sack" dress.

Dirac, Paul Adrien Maurice (1902-84) English physicist. He devised a complete mathematical formulation of EINSTEIN's theory of relativity in *The Principles of Quantum Mechanics* (1930), in which he predicted the existence of antimatter. He shared the 1933 Nobel prize for physics with SCHRÖDINGER.

Disney, Walt[er Elias] (1901-66) American cartoonist and film producer. His cartoon films of the 1930s and 40s, e.g. *Snow White and the Seven Dwarfs* (1938) and *Bambi* (1942), achieved high critical and popular acclaim. Mickey Mouse and Donald Duck are two of his most famous cartoon creations. He built Disneyland amusement park in California (1955), and planned Disney World in Florida (1971).

Djilas, Milovan (1911-) Yugoslav politician. An early associate of TITO, he became vice-president of Yugoslavia (1953-54) and was purged in 1954. He was subsequently imprisoned in 1956 for supporting the Hungarian uprising. He was released in 1966, and "rehabilitated" in 1989. His books include *The New Order* (1957) and *Memoir of a Revolutionary* (1973).

Dobell, Sir William (1899-1970) Australian portrait and landscape painter. His prizewinning portrait of fellow artist Joshua Smith resulted in a stormy debate between those who supported a more conventional approach to portraiture and the "moderns." A legal battle ensued, which Dobell won.

Dobzhansky, Theodosius (1900-75) Russian-born American geneticist. His seminal studies of genetic variation, described in *Genetics and the Evolutionary Process* (1970), linked Darwin's evolutionary theory with Mendel's heredity laws.

Doenitz, Karl *see* **Dönitz, Karl.**

Doisy, Edward *see* **Dam, Henrik.**

Dolci, Danilo (1924-) Italian social reformer. Described as the "GANDHI OF ITALY," he built schools and community centres in poverty-stricken Sicily, in the teeth of fierce opposition from an unholy alliance of church, state and Mafia. He was imprisoned in 1956 for leading a famous "strike in reverse," organizing the unemployed to repair a road. His books include *Report from Palermo* (1956) and *A New World in the Making* (1965).

Dollfus, Engelbert (1892-1934) Austrian statesman. A devout Roman Catholic, he became leader of the Christian Socialist Party and was elected Chancellor (1932-34). He opposed the German Anschluss and was assassinated by Austrian Nazis.

Dolmetsch, Arnold (1858-1940) French-born British musician and instrument maker. He pioneered the revival of early music played on copies of original instruments.

Domar, Evsey *see* **Harrod, Sir Henry Roy Forbes.**

Domingo, Placido (1941-) Spanish tenor who studied in Mexico City. He is regarded as one of the finest modern operatic tenors for his sophisticated vocal technique and considerable acting ability.

Dönitz or **Doenitz, Karl** (1881-1980) German admiral. He was commander of the German navy (1943-45). As head of the Nazi state following HITLER's suicide, he surrendered unconditionally to the Allies, and was sentenced at Nuremberg to ten years imprisonment for war crimes.

Donleavy, J[ames] P[atrick] (1926-) American-born Irish novelist. His works include *The Ginger Man* (1955), a comedy of undergraduate life in Dublin, and *The Beastly Beatitudes of Balthazar B* (1968).

Dos Passos, John [Roderigo] (1896-1970) American novelist. His masterpiece is his huge trilogy of American life, *U.S.A.*, comprising *The 42nd parallel* (1930), *1919* (1932) and *The Big Money* (1936).

Doyle, Sir Arthur Conan (1859-1930) Scottish novelist, short-story writer and physician. His most famous creation is the amateur detective Sherlock Holmes, who solves mysteries by a mixture of deduction and intuitive perception. The stories include the collection, *The Adventures of Sherlock Holmes* (1892), and *The Hound of the Baskervilles* (1902).

Douglas-Home, Sir Alec [Baron Home of the Hirsel] (1903-) Scottish Conservative politician. He became the 14th Earl of Home in 1951, renouncing his title in 1963 to contest (and win) the seat of Kinross after succeeding MACMILLAN as prime minister. (The furore over his completely unexpected emergence as party leader resulted in reform of the Tory leadership election process.) After leading the Conservatives to defeat in the 1964 general election, he was replaced by HEATH.

Dreiser, Theodore [Herman Albert] (1871-1945) American novelist. His early novels, e.g. *Sister Carrie* (1904), are grim naturalistic works with a deterministic view of human behaviour. His later novels, and documentary works such as *America is Worth Saving* (1941), are more optimistic, reflecting his transition from nihilism to socialism. His masterpiece is the doom-laden narrative *An American Tragedy* (1925).

Dreyer, Carl [Theodor] (1889-1968) Danish film director. His films, e.g. *The Passion of Joan of Arc* (1928), are concerned with spirituality and martyrdom. His film *Day of Wrath* (1943), which depicts 17th-century witch-hunts, was made during the German occupation of Denmark, of which it was widely seen as an allegory (Dreyer escaped to Sweden).

Dubcek, Alexander (1921-) Czech statesman. As first secretary of the Communist Party (1968-69), he introduced the political reforms of the "Prague Spring" of "socialism with a human face," which ended with the Russian invasion of 1968. From 1970, he worked as a forestry inspector and lumber yard clerk. Following the "Velvet Revolution," which brought HAVEL to the presidency, he was appointed chairman of the federal assembly (1989).

Dubuffet, Jean (1901-85) French painter. He devised the concept of "Art Brut" in reaction against "museum art," and made paintings assembled from bits of rubbish, broken glass, etc. His collected works were published in 1967.

Duchamp, Marcel (1887-1968) French-born American painter and sculptor. The most famous of his early works is the Cubist-style painting *Nude Descending a Staircase* (1912). He was also one of the early pioneers of Dadaism, and introduced the concept of the "found object" after settling in New York in 1915.

Dufy, Raoul (1877-1953) French painter and designer. His early work was much influenced by MATISSE and Fauvists such as DERAIN. The best known of his works are the bright, colourful paintings of the 1920s, often of seascapes, regattas or racetracks.

Dukakis, Michael *see* **Bush, George.**

Dulles, John Foster (1888-1959) American Republican states-man and lawyer. He was secretary of state (1953-59) under EISENHOWER, and developed the confrontational foreign policy of "brinkmanship" in the Cold War against the USSR.

Du Maurier, Dame Daphne (1907-89) English novelist and short-story writer. Several of her very popular works, e.g. *Jamaica Inn* (1936) and *Rebecca* (1938) have been filmed. Her gift for creating an atmosphere of menace, as in the haunting story "Don't Look Now" (also made into a very successful film) is especially good filmed.

Duncan, Isadora (1878-1927) American dancer and choreographer. She was encouraged in her early career by Mrs Patrick CAMPBELL, and developed a free, interpretative style of dancing that was very influential on the development of modern dance (e.g. on DIAGHILEV). Her ardent feminism and unconventional lifestyle alienated many of her contemporaries. Her life was dogged by tragedy; both of her children died in a car crash. A film of her life, *Isadora*, starring Vanessa REDGRAVE, was made in 1968.

Dunsany, Edward John Moreton Drax Plunkett, 18th Baron (1878-1957) Anglo-Irish novelist, dramatist and short-story writer. The best of his work, e.g. the fantasy stories in the *Book of Wonder* (1912), is rated a good bit above the usual ruck of "Celtic Twilight" fantasy. His readership and critical reputation increased sharply with the rise of the fantasy market in the 1960s.

du Pré, Jacqueline (1945-87) English cellist. She became recognized as one of the world's finest cellists in the 1960s. She married Daniel BARENBOIM in 1967, with whom she frequently performed. Her performing career came to an end in 1973, after she developed multiple sclerosis. Although confined to a wheelchair, she pursued an active teaching career until her death, and gave an acclaimed series of TV masterclasses.

Durkheim, Emile (1858-1917) French sociologist. Regarded as one of the most influential figures in modern sociology, his work was in the Positivist tradition of the 19th-century philosopher, Auguste Comte. He saw the "collective social mind" as the basis for all morality, with religion being seen as society's way of formulating its ideals. His works include *The Rules of Sociological Method* (1895) and *Suicide* (1897).

Durrell, Lawrence [George] (1912-90) English poet, novelist and travel writer. His masterpiece is the series of sexual and linguistically elaborate novels comprising the Alexandria Quartet, i.e. *Justine* (1957), *Balthazar* (1958), *Mountolive* (1958) and *Clea* (1960).

Dürrenmatt, Friedrich (1921-) Swiss dramatist, novelist and critic. His plays, e.g. *The Physicists* (1963), exemplify his belief that the world is a chaotic mess, which cannot be sorted out but which equally cannot be accepted for what it is. He has also written several bizarre and ironic detective novels, e.g. *The Pledge* (1958).

Duse, Eleonora *see* D'ANNUNZIO, GABRIELE.

Duvalier, François (1907-71) Haitian president (1957-71). Known as Papa Doc, Duvalier's tyrannical rule of Haiti was based on a duality of fear through his supposed Voodoo powers, and, more realistically, his murderous "civil militia" gangs of "Tonton Macoutes." He was excommunicated by the Roman Catholic church (1960-66) and was succeeded by his son, **Jean-Claude Duvalier ("Baby Doc")** (1951-), who was turned out of office in free elections in 1986.

Dylan, Bob [Robert Allen Zimmerman] (1941-) American folk/rock singer and songwriter. Influenced by Woody GUTHRIE, he became the most prominent "protest" folksinger in the 1960s with songs such as "The Times They Are A-Changin'". He later took up rock music, for which he was never forgiven by many of his fans, who got a further shock when he became a born-again Christian in 1979. His lyrics are very highly regarded by some critics. *See also* BAEZ.

Earhart, Amelia (1898-1937) American aviator. She was the first woman to make a solo flight across the Atlantic (1932), after which she became a celebrity. She disappeared on a flight across the Pacific while attempting a round-the-world flight.

Eastman, George (1854-1932) American inventor of photographic equipment and philanthropist. His invention of the Kodak roll-film camera, which was cheap and easy-to-use, revolutionized the photographic industry, as did his development of colour photography in the late 1920s. He gave away more than 100 million dollars to various charities and institutions.

Eccles, Sir John Carew (1903-) Australian neurophysiologist. He shared the 1963 Nobel prize for physiology or medicine for his work on nerve impulses.

Eco, Umberto (1932-) Italian critic and novelist. Works such as *A Theory of Semiotics* (1972) established him as a leading literary critic. His best known work of fiction is the medieval philosophical whodunit, *The Name of the Rose* (1981).

Eddington, Sir Arthur Stanley (1882-1944) English astronomer and physicist. A lifelong Quaker who emphasized the fundamental strangeness of the universe, he published several popular and highly readable books explaining such topics as EINSTEIN's theory of relativity, e.g. *Mathematical Theory of*

Relativity (1923) and *The Expanding Universe* (1933). He also did important work on the nature of the stars, e.g. *The Internal Constitution of the Stars* (1926).

Eden, [Robert] Anthony, 1st Earl of Avon (1897-1977) British Conservative statesman. He served several terms as foreign minister and was prime minister (1955-57). He resigned from office following the Suez Crisis, when British and French occupation of Egypt after NASSER'S NATIONALIZATION of the Suez Canal received worldwide condemnation.

Edward VII (1841-1910) king of Great Britain and Ireland (1901-10). Queen Victoria's oldest son, his short reign had been preceded by many decades as the leader of fashionable society. He was noted for his charm and was popular with the public. He was succeeded by GEORGE V.

Edward VIII *see* **Windsor, Duke of**.

Edward, Prince *see* **Elizabeth II**.

Ehrenburg, Ilya Grigorievich (1891-1967) Soviet novelist and journalist. He was known primarily for his anti-Western works, e.g. the novel *The Fall of Paris* (1941), and for his war reporting, until the publication of his novel, *The Thaw* (1955), which was the first post-Stalin work to criticize Stalinism.

Ehrlich, Paul (1854-1915) German bacteriologist. He did significant research into immunology and chemotherapy, and developed a cure for syphilis (1910). He was awarded the 1908 Nobel prize for physiology or medicine.

Eichmann, [Karl] Adolf (1906-62) Austrian Nazi leader and war criminal. He was instructed by HITLER in 1942 to bring about the "Final Solution," i.e. the extermination of Europe's Jews, and oversaw the deportation of Jews to death camps. He was captured by US forces at the end of the World War II, but escaped to Argentina, from where he was abducted by Israeli agents in 1960. He was tried for crimes against humanity by the Israelis, and executed.

Eijkman, Christiaan (1858-1930) Dutch physician. He discovered that beriberi is caused by nutritional deficiency. His research led to the discovery of "essential food factors," i.e. vitamins. He shared the 1929 Nobel prize for physiology or medicine with Sir Frederick HOPKINS.

Einstein, Albert (1879-1955) German-born physicist and mathematician. His formulations of the special theory of relativity (1906) and general theory of relativity (1916), and research into quantum theory, mark him as one of the greatest of all thinkers. He was awarded the 1921 Nobel prize for physics. Being Jewish and a pacifist, he was forced to flee Nazi Germany in 1933, and became a US citizen in 1940.

Eisenhower, Dwight D[avid] (1890-1969) American general and Republican statesman, known as "Ike." He became supreme commander of the Allied forces in 1943, and 34th president of the US (1953-60). During the Cold War, he adopted a more conciliatory approach to that favoured by DULLES. His memoirs include *Mandate for Change* (1963) and *Waging Peace* (1965).

Eisenstadt, Alfred (1898-) German-born American photographer. He became one of the world's leading photojournalist in the 1930s, when he pioneered the use of the Leica camera for capturing "storytelling moments." His books include *Witness to Our Time* (1966).

Eisenstein, Sergei Mikhailovich (1898-1948) Soviet film director. He served with the Red Army (1918-20) during the

Civil War and became one of the most influential directors of all time with films such as *Battleship Potemkin* (1925) and *October* (1928), in which he deployed his theory of montage through skilful cutting .

Elgar, Sir Edward [William] (1857-1934) English composer. A devout Roman Catholic, he became recognized as the leading British composer with works such as the *Enigma Variations* (1899) and the oratorio *The Dream of Gerontius* (1900). He composed many other well-known works, e.g. the five *Pomp and Circumstance* marches (1903-30) and the *Cello Concerto* (1919).

Eliot, T[homas] S[tearns] (1888-1965) American-born English poet and critic, whose early work was much influenced by his friend POUND. His early poetry, e.g. *The Waste Land* (1922), is concerned with the breakdown of civilized values in the postwar "Jazz Era." He also wrote verse dramas, e.g. *The Family Reunion* (1939), and published critical works, e.g. *The Sacred Wood* (1920).

Elizabeth II (1926-) queen of the United Kingdom from 1952. The daughter of GEORGE VI. She married Prince PHILIP in 1947, and has four children: Prince CHARLES, Princess **Anne** (1950-), Prince **Andrew** (1960-) and Prince **Edward** (1964-). She is regarded as the most formal of all modern European monarchs. Her main personal interests are those traditionally associated with upper-class country life, especially horse racing.

Ellington, Duke [Edward Kennedy Ellington] (1899-1974) American jazz composer, pianist and bandleader. Regarded as one of the finest jazz composers, his some two thousand works include "Mood Indigo," "Sophisticated Lady" and "Creole Love Call." His various bands, composed of some of the finest instrumentalists, toured widely.

Ellis, [Henry] Havelock (1859-1939) English physician and sexologist. His seven-volume *Studies on the Psychology of Sex* (1897-1928, revised edition 1936) were very influential in bringing the discussion of sexual matters into the realm of open debate (although the work was banned in Britain, except for doctors, until 1953).

Elton, Charles Sutherland (1900-) English ecologist. His field studies of animal communities in their environments raised awareness of the ability of animals to adapt to changing habitats, and popularized such terms as "ecological niche." His works include *The Pattern of Animal Communities* (1966).

Éluard, Paul [Eugène Grindel] (1895-1952) French poet. He was part of the Surrealist movement until the late 1930s, and joined the Communist Party in 1942. He joined the French Resistance during the German Occupation, when his anti-Nazi poems were secretly circulated to raise morale. His postwar poetry, e.g. *The Phoenix* (1951), is more personal and lyrical.

Empson, Sir William (1906-84) English poet and critic. His *Seven Types of Ambiguity* (1930, written while he was studying mathematics at Cambridge) is regarded as a modern classic of literary criticism for its witty insights.

Engler, [Gustav Heinrich] Adolf (1844-1930) German botanist. His taxonomic classification of plants in works such as *Syllabus of Plant Names* (1892) was used as a standard reference for many years by biologists.

Epstein, Sir Jacob (1880-1959) American-born British sculptor of Russian-Polish descent. Much of his work for public commissions, e.g. *Ecce Homo* (1934), was widely derided and attacked for indecency. His portrait busts, e.g. of EINSTEIN and SHAW, were, in contrast, highly praised.

Erlanger, Joseph (1874-1965) American physiologist. With **Herbert Spencer Gasser** (1888-1963), he shared the 1944 Nobel prize for physiology or medicine for their work on nerve fibres and the transmission of nerve impulses.

Ernst, Max (1891-1976) German-born French painter. He was a leading member of both the Dada and surrealist movements. He pioneered the use of collage and photomontage, and developed "frottage" (pencil rubbings on a variety of surfaces). Birds and frozen, petrified cities are prominent subjects in his work.

Erté [Romain de Tirtoff] (1892-1990) Russian-born French designer and fashion illustrator, who became one of the most notable exponents of Art Deco style. His designs appeared in magazines such as *Harper's Bazaar* and were used by ZIEGFELD in his "follies."

Escoffier, Georges Auguste (1846-1935) French chef, who is regarded as one of the greatest chefs of all time. He invented Peach Melba in honour of Dame Nellie MELBA.

Evans, Sir Arthur John (1851-1941) English archaeologist. His excavations of the palace of Knossos in Crete resulted in the rediscovery of Minoan civilization (so named by Evans after the legendary king Minos).

Evans, Dame Edith [Mary Booth] (1888-1976) English actress, notable for her command of a wide variety of roles. She created the role of Lady Utterword in SHAW's *Heartbreak House* (1921), and gave a definitive performance as Lady Bracknell in WILDE's *The Importance of Being Earnest*. Her most notable film role was as a lonely old lady in *The Whisperers* (1967).

Evans, Sir Geraint [Llewellyn] (1922-) Welsh baritone, who became one of Britain's best known and popular operatic baritones, with a worldwide reputation for his skill and warmth.

Eysenck, Hans [Jürgen] (1916-) German-born British psychologist. Eysenck has been a notable critic of FREUD's theory of psychoanalysis, which he regards as having insufficient basis in empirically derived evidence. His controversial views on the role of genetic factors in determining intelligence are expressed in his *Race, Intelligence and Education* (1971).

F

Fairbanks, Douglas [Douglas Elton Ullman] (1883-1939) American film actor and producer, who became one of the leading stars of silent films, starring in such swashbucklers as *The Mark of Zorro* (1920). Mary PICKFORD was his second wife (1920-36). His son, **Douglas Fairbanks Jr** (1909-), was also an actor starring in swashbucklers, notably *The Prisoner of Zenda* (1937). His first wife was Joan CRAWFORD.

Falla, Manuel de (1876-1946) Spanish composer and pianist. His works include the ballet *The Three-Cornered Hat* (1919), the puppet opera *Master Peter's Puppet Show* (1923), song cycles and concertos.

Farouk, King *see* **Nasser, General Abdel**

Fassbinder, Rainer Werner (1946-82) German film director. His films include *The Bitter Tears of Petra Von Kant* (1972), *Fear Eats the Soul* (1974) and *The Marriage of Maria Braun* (1979). Fassbinder was influenced by GODARD's political commitment, and his films do show the underside of the German "economic miracle," but his analysis of oppression is by no means simplistic.

Faulkner, William [Harrison] (1897-1962) American novelist. His first novel, *Soldier's Pay* (1926), was written with Sherwood ANDERSON's encouragement. His most famous series of works, e.g. *The Sound and the Fury* (1929), deals with political, social, racial and sexual tensions within a fictional Mississippi county, Yoknapatawpha.

Fauré, Gabriel [Urbain] (1845-1924) French composer and organist. His works include the haunting *Requiem* (1887), around a hundred lyrical songs such as "Après un Rêve," orchestral and piano pieces.

Fawcett, Dame Millicent [Millicent Garrett] (1847-1929) English feminist. She became first president of the National Union of Women Suffrage Societies (1897-1919), and opposed the more militant tactics of PANKHURST. Her works include *Political Economy for Beginners* (1870) and *Women's Suffrage* (1912).

Fellini, Federico (1920-) Italian film director. His best-known film is *La Dolce Vita* (1960), a cynical portrayal of Roman high society. Other films include *81/2* (1963), an autobiographical work containing fantasy sequences, *Fellini's Roma* (1972) and *Amarcord* (1974).

Fermi, Enrico (1901-54) Italian-born American physicist. With his Jewish wife, he fled to the US in 1938 after being awarded the Nobel prize for physics for his work on radioactive substances and nuclear bombardment. He built the first nuclear reactor at Chicago in 1942.

Ferrier, Kathleen (1912-53) English contralto. She created the title role in BRITTEN's *Rape of Lucretia* (1946), and sang at the first Edinburgh Festival in MAHLER's *Song of the Earth* under Bruno WALTER, who became a close friend and described her as "one of the greatest singers of all time." Her tragically short singing career ended with her death from cancer.

Fermor, Patrick Leigh (1915-) English travel writer and soldier. His exploits in World War II included the organization of the Cretan Resistance and the capture of a German general. His highly regarded travel books include *Mani* (1958) and *Between the Woods and the Water* (1986).

Feydeau, Georges (1862-1921) French dramatist, noted for his bedroom farces, e.g. *Hotel Paradise* (1956).

Feynman, Richard (1918-88) American physicist. He shared the 1965 Nobel prize for physics for his work in quantum electrodynamics.

Fields, Dame Gracie [Grace Stansfield] (1898-1979) English singer and comedienne, whose image was "Our Gracie," the earthy, straightforward Northern lass. Her 1930s films, e.g. *Sally in Our Alley* (1931) and *Sing As We Go* (1934), were very popular in England.

Fields, W. C. [William Claude Dukenfield] (1880-1946) American comedian, noted for his hard drinking, red nose, gravel voice and antipathy to children and animals. He worked in vaudeville before appearing regularly in ZIEGFELD's *Follies* (1915-21) and many films, e.g. *My Little Chickadee* with Mae WEST (1940). He was a notable Mr Micawber in *David Copperfield* (1934).

Finney, Albert (1936-) English actor. His portrayal of the rebellious young working-class hero of the film *Saturday Night and Sunday Morning* (1960), with its mocking attitude to authority and realistic approach to sex, had a strong impact on British cinema.

Firbank, [Arthur Annesley] Ronald (1886-1926) English novelist. His weird and exotic works, characterized by oblique dialogue and fantastic characters, include *Valmouth* (1919) and *Concerning the Eccentricities of Cardinal Pirelli* (1926).

Fischer, Bobby [Robert James Fischer] (1943-) American chess player. He became a grandmaster at 15, and was the first US player to win the world championship (1972) when he won a hotly debated contest against Boris SPASSKY. He became the best-known chess player in the history of the game, partly because of his undoubted genius, but also because of his bizarre charges against opponents, e.g. that he was being bugged.

Fitzgerald, Ella (1918-) American jazz singer, whose highly praised vocal range, rhythmic subtlety and clarity of tone made her one of the most popular singers of her day. She toured widely, notably with BASIE, ARMSTRONG and ELLINGTON.

Fitzgerald, F[rancis] Scott [Key] (1896-1940) American novelist and short-story writer. His works are moralistic fables of extravagance and glamour set against the background of 1920s "Jazz Age" High Society. His novels include *The Great Gatsby* (1925) and *Tender is the Night* (1934).

Flagstad, Kirsten (1895-1962) Norwegian soprano, noted for her roles in Wagner's operas. She is regarded as one of the finest Wagnerian singers of all time.

Flaherty, Robert [Joseph] (1884-1951) American documentary film director. His films include e.g. *Nanook of the North* (1922), about an Eskimo family, and *Man of Aran* (1934), about life on the west coast Irish island of Aran. Although undoubtedly somewhat romantic in his view of his subjects, Flaherty's work set high standards for all following documentary film makers.

Fleming, Sir Alexander (1881-1955) Scottish bacteriologist. He discovered the antiseptic qualities of the bactericidal enzyme lysozome (1922), and made one of the most important medical discoveries ever when he noticed the antibacterial qualities of the substance he dubbed "penicillin." He shared the 1945 Nobel prize for physiology or medicine with CHAIN and FLOREY.

Fleming, Ian [Lancaster] (1908-64) English novelist. His series of novels featuring the British secret agent James Bond (*see* CONNERY), *Live and Let Die* (1954) and *Goldfinger* (1964), were enormous popular successes and have all been filmed. The novels have been criticized by some for being slick and amoral in their treatment of sex and violence.

Florey, Howard Walter, Baron (1898-1968) Australian pathologist. He shared the 1945 Nobel prize for physiology or medicine with Sir Alexander FLEMING and CHAIN for their work on penicillin.

Flynn, Errol [Leslie Thomas Flynn] (1909-59) Australian-born American film actor. His starring roles, in the swashbuckling tradition of FAIRBANKS, included *Captain Blood* (1935) and *The Sea Hawk* (1940), earned him considerable popularity, which was somewhat dimmed in Britain following *Objective Burma* (1944), a film that failed to note any British participation. Flynn was a legendary womaniser and drinker (*see also* NIVEN). The last film he worked on was a ridiculous documentary tribute to Fidel CASTRO, *The Cuban Rebel Girls* (1959).

Foch, Ferdinand (1851-1929) French general and marshal of France (1918). He was given command of the Allied forces in March 1918, and, always a believer in attack, led the Allies to victory following the arrival of US troops in July 1918.

Fokine, Michel (1880-1942) Russian-born American ballet dancer and choreographer. He choreographed The Dying Swan for PAVLOVA, and, with DIAGHILEV in Paris, created a new comprehensive style of ballet, in which all the elements, dance, music, costume and *mise en scène*, formed a coherent whole. He became a US citizen in 1932.

Fonda, Henry (1905-82) American film actor. His performances in such films as John FORD's *Young Mr Lincoln* (1939) and *The Grapes of Wrath* (1940), earned him great accolades. Fonda became seen as the epitome of "decent" America, a man determined to set injustices right. He won an Oscar for his part in *On Golden Pond* (1981), in which he starred with his daughter, **Jane [Seymour] Fonda** (1937-). Her early film career began with insignificant bimbo roles, but she won recognition as a fine actress in films such as *They Shoot Horses Don't They?* (1969) and *Klute* (1971), the latter earning her an Oscar. She braved public disfavour in the 1960s with her outspoken opposition to the Vietnam war and espousal of radical causes, and subsequently became known primarily as a fitness fanatic with her bestselling "workout" videos and books.

Fonteyn, Dame Margot [Margaret Hookham] (1919-91) English ballerina. Regarded as one of the finest classical ballerinas of the century, she partnered NUREYEV at the age of 43.

Foot, Michael [Mackintosh] (1913-) British Labour politician. A leading left-winger, pacifist and CND member, he was secretary of state of employment (1974-76) and leader of the House of Commons (1976-79), and succeeded CALLAGHAN as leader of the Labour Party 1980-83). After losing the 1983 election, Foot resigned as leader and was succeeded by KINNOCK. His many books include biographies of Swift and BEVAN.

Ford, Ford Madox [Ford Hermann Hueffer] (1873-1939) English novelist, poet and critic. His most important works are the novels *The Good Soldier* (1915) and the tetralogy *Parade's End* (published in one volume 1950). Ford founded the *Trans-

atlantic Review in 1924, and gave generous encouragement to many writers.

Ford, Gerald R[udolph] (1913-   ) American Republican statesman and 38th president of the US (1974-77). He replaced AGNEW as NIXON's vice-president in 1973, becoming president the following year, after Nixon's impeachment and resignation. Ford's controversial decision to grant Nixon a free pardon was widely condemned. He barely retained the Republican presidency nomination from REAGAN's challenge, and was defeated by CARTER in the 1977 election.

Ford, Henry (1863-1947) American car designer and manufacturer. His Model T Ford, first introduced in 1908, was enormously successful (around 15 million sold) and its production line manufacture, a standard product available in any colour "as long as it's black"), became a role model for much of industry.

Ford, John [Sean Aloysius O'Feeney] (1895-1973) American film director. He is regarded as one of the greatest of all directors for his epic and poetic vision of history, particularly that of the American West, e.g. *Stagecoach* (1939) and *The Searchers* (1956), both starring John WAYNE. Ford's vision of America is expressed strongly in *Young Mr Lincoln* (1939) and *The Grapes of Wrath* (1940), both starring the actor who most exemplified Ford's sense of fundamental American decency, Henry FONDA. Ford's other films include *The Informer* (1935), *How Green Was My Valley* (1941) and *The Quiet Man* (1952).

Forman, Milos (1932-) Czech film director, resident in the US since since 1968. His Czech films include *A Blonde in Love* (1965) and *The Fireman's Ball* (1967). He settled in the US following the ending of the Prague Spring (*see* DUBCEK). His American films include the very successful black comedy *One*

Flew Over the Cuckoo's Nest (1975) and *Amadeus* (1988), the latter being mostly filmed in Prague.

Forster, E[dward] M[organ] (1879-1970) English novelist and critic. His novels, e.g. *The Longest Journey* (1907) and *Howard's End* (1910), are mainly concerned with moral and ethical choices, and the personal relationships of educated, middle-class people.

Fowler, H[enry] W[atson] (1858-1933) English lexicographer. The second of his two books on English usage, *A Dictionary of English Usage* (1926), was for many years the standard work on the subject.

Fowles, John (1926-) English novelist. The film rights to his first book, *The Collector* (1963), a creepy psychological study of a butterfly collector turned kidnapper, were sold while the book was still in proof stage. His next two novels, *The Magus* (1966) and *The French Lieutenant's Woman* (1969), established him as a major novelist.

Franck, James (1882-1964) German-born American physicist. With the German physicist **Gustav Ludwig Hertz** (1887-1975), he shared the 1925 Nobel prize for physics for work on the quantum theory, notably on the effects produced from bombarding atoms with electrons.

Franco, Francisco (1892-1975) Spanish general and dictator. He led the right-wing rebellion against the Spanish Republican government during the Spanish Civil War (1936-39). He became leader of the Fascist Falange Party in 1937, and ruled Spain from 1939 until his death. He nominated Prince JUAN CARLOS as his successor.

Frank, Anne (1929-45) German-born Dutch Jewish girl. Her journal describing her and her family's experiences while hiding from the Nazis in occupied Amsterdam was published by the family's sole survivor, her father, in 1947. The family were captured in August 1944, and Anne died in Belsen. Her diary is one of the most moving accounts of the terrible suffering of the Jewish people during the war, and was filmed in 1959 as *The Diary of Anne Frank*.

Franklin, Rosalind Elsie (1920-58) British chemist. Her X-ray crystallography research into DNA contributed to the discovery of its structure by James WATSON and CRICK.

Fraser, [John] Malcolm (1930-) Australian Liberal statesman. He was installed as caretaker prime minister (1975-83) following GOUGH's dismissal, and won the ensuing 1975 election by a large majority.

Frayn, Michael (1933-) English dramatist and novelist, noted for his dry, sardonic humour. Representative novels include *The Tin Men* (1965), a satire on robotics, and *A Very Private Life* (1968), a futuristic, anti-utopian fantasy. His plays include *Noises Off* (1982), which uses the conventions of farce to send up theatrical life.

Frazer, Sir James George (1854-1941) Scottish scholar and anthropologist, whose study of religious customs and myth, *The Golden Bough* (1890-1915), influenced FREUD and many 20th-century writers, e.g. T. S. ELIOT and James JOYCE.

Frege, [Friedrich Ludwig] Gottlob (1848-1925) German mathematician and philosopher. His work received little recognition in his own time, but he is now regarded as having laid the foundations for both modern mathematical logic and the philosophy of language.

French, Sir John [Denton Pinkstone], [1st Earl of Ypres] (1852-1925) English field marshal. He commanded the British

Expeditionary Force in France (1914-15). He was replaced as commander by HAIG. He became Lord Lieutenant of Ireland (1918-21) during the Anglo-Irish War.

Freud, Lucian (1922-) German-born British painter. The grandson of Sigmund FREUD, renowned for his nudes and portraits, often painted from odd angles and in an unsettling, extreme-realist style.

Freud, Sigmund (1856-1939) Austrian psychiatrist, who founded psychoanalysis. His works, which include *The Interpretation of Dreams* (1900) and *The Ego and the Id* (1923) have been enormously influential on 20th-century thought. The main tenet of Freudian theory is that neuroses and dreams are repressed manifestations of sexual desire, which is often incestuous, as in the "Oedipus Complex." His stress on the importance of sex was rejected by ADLER and JUNG. His daughter **Anna Freud** (1895-1982) pioneered child psychology in the UK. Her works include *Beyond the Best Interests of the Child* (1973).

Friedman, Milton (1912-) American economist. His controversial monetarist theory of economics, which is based on the thesis that inflation is caused by too much money flowing through an economy, and on the primacy of market forces and consumer choice and the need for minimal government intervention, became the dominant economic theory of the 1980s, even in ex-communist countries, despite much dissent from all quarters ("voodoo economics"—George BUSH). Friedman's many works include *Inflation: Causes and Consequences* (1963). He was awarded the 1976 Nobel prize for economics.

Frisch, Karl von (1886-1982) Austrian zoologist and ethologist who discovered that bees communicate information on food sources and direction by "dancing" and that they orientate themselves by the direction of light. He shared the 1973 Nobel prize for physiology or medicine with LORENZ and TINBERGEN.

Frisch, Max (1911-) Swiss novelist and dramatist. His works include the BRECHT-influenced plays *The Fire Raisers* (1962) and *Andorra* (1961), and the novels *I'm Not Stiller* (1954) and *Homo Faber* (1957)

Frisch, Otto Robert (1904-79) Austrian-born British nuclear physicist. He and his aunt, Lise Meitner, discovered nuclear fission, and their work led directly to the invention of the atom bomb, the development of which Frisch worked on at Los Alamos. He wrote the cheerily entitled *Meet the Atoms* (1947).

Frisch, Ragnar *see* **Tinbergen, Jan.**

Fromm, Erich (1900-80) German-born American psychoanalyst and social philosopher. Combining elements of Marxism with FREUD's psychoanalysis, Fromm's work is based on the principle that social and economic factors determine human behaviour. His works include *Psychoanalysis and Religion* (1950) and *The Art of Loving* (1956).

Frost, Robert [Lee] (1874-1963) American poet. His quiet, lyrical poems, e.g. "Stopping By Woods on a Snowy Evening," have been much admired. Several critics have noted the dark, enigmatic nature of much of his symbolism.

Fry, C[harles] B[urgess] (1872-1956) English sportsman, regarded as one of the greatest all-round sportsmen ever. He played for England in athletics, cricket and soccer, played in an FA Cup final for Southampton and, like BRADMAN, hit six consecutive centuries. He was offered the throne of Albania, but declined. His autobiography is *Life Worth Living* (1939).

Fry, Christopher (1907-) English dramatist, whose verse dramas, such as *A Phoenix Too Frequent* (1946) and *The Lady's*

Not for Burning (1949), were popular with both critics and public.

Fuchs, [Emil Julius] Klaus (1911-88) German-born British physicist. He began work on British atom-bomb research in 1941, becoming a British citizen in 1942, and subsequently worked on the Los Alamos Manhattan project (1943-46). He was jailed in 1950 for 14 years for passing details of atom-bomb research to the Soviet Union, and on his release in 1959 settled in East Germany.

Fuchs, Sir Vivian Ernest (1908-) English explorer and scientist. He led the Commonwealth Trans-Antarctic Expedition (1955-58), which made the first overland crossing of Antarctica, reaching the South Pole in January 1958.

Fugard, Athol (1932-) South African dramatist, whose plays explore the tragedy of racial tension caused by apartheid in South Africa. His works include *Boesman and Lena* (1968) and *Sizwe Bansi is Dead* (1972).

Fuller, [Richard] Buckminster (1895-1983) American architect and engineer. He invented the "geodesic dome," a lightweight framework consisting of a set of polygons in the shape of a shell, the best known of which was the US pavilion at the 1967 Montreal exhibition.

Furtwängler, Wilhelm (1886-1954) German conductor. He became one of the most popular conductors in Europe in the 1920s and early 30s, particularly for his highly charged interpretations of Wagner. His popularity outside Germany declined rapidly from the late 1930s, due to his accommodation with the Nazi regime.

G

Gable, [William] Clark (1901-60) American film actor. His rugged good looks, sardonic wit and easygoing charm made him one of the most popular film stars of his day. He was voted "King of Hollywood" in 1937. His films include *It Happened One Night* (1934), *Mutiny on the Bounty* (1935) and *Gone With the Wind* (1939), in which he played Rhett Butler to Vivien LEIGH's Scarlett O'Hara. His last film was the downbeat *The Misfits* (1960), in which he starred opposite Marilyn MONROE.

Gabo, Naum [Naum Neemia Pevsner] (1890-1977) Russian-born American sculptor. He is regarded as one of the founding fathers of the Constructivist movement in Russia. He also produced innovative kinetic and non-figurative sculptures out of substances such as transparent plastic.

Gabor, Dennis (1900-79) Hungarian-born British engineer. He was awarded the 1971 Nobel prize for physics for his invention (in 1947) of the hologram.

Gaddafi *or* **Qaddafi, Moammar al-** (1942-) Libyan statesman and military dictator. Influenced by NASSER, Gaddafi took power in a coup in 1969, and became president in 1977. Regarded almost universally as an unpredictable and often dangerous leader, Gaddafi has openly supported terrorist groups around the world, such as the IRA and Spanish fascists, in what he sees as a holy war against "imperialism" and "zionism."

Gagarin, Yuri [Alekseevich] (1934-68) Soviet cosmonaut, who became, in 1961, the first man in space, when his Vostok satellite circled the earth. He died in a plane crash.

Gaitskell, Hugh [Todd Naylor] (1906-63) British Labour politician. He was regarded as being on the right of his party, having introduced, as chancellor of the exchequer (1950-51), national health service charges, which resulted in BEVAN's and WILSON's resignations. He became Labour Party leader (1955-63). His sudden death was followed by Harold Wilson's election to leadership of the Labour Party.

Galbraith, John Kenneth (1908-) Canadian-born American economist and diplomat. He has been notably critical of the wastefulness of capitalist society in its deployment of resources in activities such as creating consumer needs for superfluous products. His works include *The Affluent Society* (1958) and *The New Industrial State* (1967). He was American ambassador to India (1961-63).

Gallup, George Horace (1901-84) American statistician. He developed the opinion poll into a sophisticated device, the "Gallup Poll," for testing public opinion, most notably on elections. He founded the American Institution of Public Opinion in 1935. His books include *Public Opinion in a Democracy* (1939).

Galsworthy, John (1867-1933) English novelist and dramatist. His plays, which are realistic dramas attacking social injustices, include *Strife* (1909) and *Justice* (1910). Public furore over the latter resulted in UK prison reform. His novels include the Forsyte saga trilogy, *The Man of Property* (1906), *In Chancery* (1920) and *Awakening* (1920).

Galway, James (1939-) Irish flautist, regarded as one of the finest flautists of the modern era. Equally at home in modern, classical, baroque and (in his early days) the war music of the Orange flute bands, he became a well-known figure through his televised appearances in the 1960s and 70s.

Gandhi, Indira (1917-84) Indian stateswoman and prime minister. The daughter of NEHRU, she became prime minister (1966-77) of India. She instituted a state of emergency in 1975, and lost the ensuing 1977 general election. Her second term of office as prime minister (1980-84) saw much ethnic strife. After ordering Indian soldiers to seize the Sikh Golden Temple at Amritsar, which was occupied by Sikh Punjab separatists, she was assassinated by her Sikh bodyguards. Her son **Rajiv** (1944-91) became prime minister in 1984, and was killed in a suicide bomb attack (the bomber, a woman, was generally assumed to be a Tamil separatist) during the 1991 election.

Gandhi, Mahatma [Mohandas Karamchand Gandhi] (1869-1948) Indian nationalist statesman and spiritual leader ("Mahatma" means "Great Soul"). A passionate advocate of non-violent resistance, Gandhi's long campaign against British rule in India, using tactics of civil disobedience through passive resistance and hunger strikes, had great influence on world public opinion. He also struggled for reconciliation between Hindus and Moslems, and championed the cause of the Hindu Harijan caste of "untouchables." He was assassinated by a Hindu extremist, in the wake of India's independence and partition.

Garbo, Greta [Greta Lovisa Gustafson] (1905- 90) Swedish-born American film actress. Noted for her austere and remote beauty ("What one sees in other women drunk, one sees in Garbo sober"—TYNAN), her films include *Queen Christina*

(1933) and *Ninotchka* (1939). She probably never said "I want to be alone," but she lived in seclusion (in New York) from 1951 to her death.

García Lorca, Federico *see* **Lorca, Federico García**.

Garland, Judy [Frances Gumm] (1922-69) American film actress and singer. She became one of the most loved child stars of the cinema with her performance as Dorothy in *The Wizard of Oz* (1939), and later starred in such films as *Easter Parade* (1948) and *A Star is Born* (1954). She died of drink and drug abuse. Her daughter, **Liza Minnelli** (1946-), became a star in the 1970s with films such as *Cabaret* (1972).

Gasser, Herbert Spencer *see* **Erlanger, Joseph**.

Gaudier-Brzeska, Henri [Henri Gaudier] (1891-1915) French sculptor. He moved to London in 1912, where he became a leading avant-garde artist and a signatory of the Vorticist Manifesto. He was killed in the trenches during World War I.

Gaulle, Charles de *see* **de Gaulle, Charles**.

Gavaskar, Sunil Manohar (1949-) Indian cricketer. He was captain of India ((1978-83, 1984-85). He was dubbed the "Little Master" for his skill (and stature) and scored 34 test centuries.

Gell-Mann, Murray (1929-) American physicist. He introduced the concept of "strangeness" and the quark hypothesis into physics (the word "quark" is taken from JOYCE's *Finnegans Wake*), and was awarded the 1969 Nobel prize for physics for his research into particle physics. He predicted the existence of the omega-minus particle in his book, *The Eightfold Way* (1964), the title of which refers to the Buddhist path to Nirvana.

Genet, Jean (1910-86) French dramatist and novelist. His works, include the plays *The Maids* (1947) and *The Balcony* (1950), and the novels, e.g. *Our Lady of the Flowers* (1944) and *Querelle de Brest* (1947), are often based on Genet's underworld experiences.

Gentile, Giovanni (1875-1944) Italian philosopher and politician. He collaborated with CROCE on both philosophical study and politics, but developed his own variant of idealism, called "actualism," in which only the act of thought is real. He became a long-term supporter of MUSSOLINI and Fascist minister and was assassinated by partisans in Florence.

George V (1865-1936) king of Great Britain and Northern Ireland and Emperor of India (1910-36). He was the second son of EDWARD VII, and changed the surname of the Royal Family from Saxe-Coburg to Windsor in 1917. He was a very popular monarch, noted particularly for his radio broadcasts. His eldest son was the Duke of WINDSOR, his second GEORGE VI.

George VI (1895-52) king of Great Britain and Northern Ireland (1936-1952) and emperor of India (1936-1947). He was the second son of GEORGE V, and succeeded to the throne following the Duke of WINDSOR's abdication. He achieved great popularity, particularly during World War II. His death was believed by his family to be have been brought on by the pressure of becoming king. He was succeeded by his eldest daughter, ELIZABETH II.

Gershwin, George [Jacob Gershovitz] (1898-1937) American composer and pianist. He and his brother, the lyricist **Ira Gershwin** (1896-1983), created several very popular musicals, e.g. *Lady Be Good* (1924) and *Funny Face* (1927). Their black opera, *Porgy and Bess*, (1935) was initially poorly received but soon became acknowledged as a masterpiece of American music. Gershwin was much influenced by jazz, as in his best-known orchestral work *Rhapsody in Blue* (1924).

Getty, J[ean] Paul (1892-1976) American industrialist and art collector, renowned for his wealth, miserliness and acquisition of works of art. He made his money in oil (he also inherited 15 million dollars from his father), and was a billionaire by the late 1960s. The J. Paul Getty Museum in Malibu, California, houses his art collection.

Giacometti, Alberto (1901-66) Swiss sculptor and painter. He became a surrealist in 1930, and broke with the movement in 1935. Influenced by SARTRE's existentialism, he began producing his famous thin, elongated, spidery figures, e.g. *Pointing Man* (1947).

Giap, Vo Nguyen (1912-) Vietnamese general. He led the Viet Minh army against the French and commanded the North Vietnamese army against the US during the Vietnam War. His works on military strategy include *People's War, People's Army* (1961).

Gide, André (1860-1951) French novelist. Brought up a strict Protestant, he decided he was homosexual after reading Oscar Wilde. His novels, e.g. *Fruits of the Earth* (1897) and *Strait is the Gate* (1909), are short, fascinating studies of sexual and social self-deception.

Gielgud, Sir [Arthur] John (1904-) English stage and film actor and producer. Regarded as one of the leading Shakespearian actors of the century, Gielgud, like OLIVIER, also slipped effortlessly into the acting roles required by such dramatists as PINTER. His late appearances in several Hollywood films were regarded as unfortunate by many, although he won an Oscar for *Arthur* (1980).

Gierek, Edward (1913-) Polish Communist statesman. He became leader of the Polish United Workers Party following GOMULKA's resignation in 1971. He presided over increasing industrial unrest and the rise of Solidarity (*see* WALESA) and was forced to resign in 1980.

Gill, [Arthur] Eric [Rowton] (1882-1940) English sculptor, engraver, typographer and writer. He converted to Roman Catholicism in 1913, and his religious beliefs were profoundly influential in his work, which includes *The Stations of the Cross* carvings for Westminster Cathedral (1914-18) and the *Prospero and Ariel* sculpture (1931) for Broadcasting House. His books include *Art* (1934) and *Autobiography* (1940).

Gillespie, Dizzy [John Birks Gillespie] (1917-) American jazz trumpeter and bandleader, renowned as a virtuoso trumpeter and and for his "bop" sessions with Thelonius MONK and Charlie PARKER.

Ginsberg, Allen (1926-) American poet, regarded as the leading poet of the 1950s "beat generation." His poem *Howl* (1956) includes the claim that Ginsberg's friends were the "best minds" of the 50s. Ginsberg saw drugs and sex as a liberation, and had much influence on the hippy culture of the 1960s.

Giscard d'Estaing, Valéry (1926-) French statesman. He served as minister of finance under DE GAULLE (1962-66) and POMPIDOU (1969-74) and was elected president (1974-81) following the latter's death. He was defeated in the 1984 presidential election by MITTERAND.

Glashow, Sheldon *see* **Weinberg, Steven**.

Glass, Philip (1937-) American composer. He studied under BOULANGER and SHANKAR and became one of the leading avant-garde composers of the 1970s, noted for his deep interest in

Eastern harmonies and use of repeated motifs. His works include *Einstein on the Beach* (1976) and *Akhnaton* (1984) and the score for the film *Mishima* (1985).

Godard, Jean-Luc (1930-) French film director. Regarded as one of the most influential New Wave French film directors of the 1950s, his films include *Breathless* (1959) and *Week-End* (1967).

Goddard, Robert Hutchings (1882-1945) American physicist. He produced the first successful liquid-fuelled rocket in 1926.

Gödel, Kurt (1906-78) Austrian-born American logician and mathematician. His demonstration of the "undecidability" of mathematics, "Godel's theorem," shows the existence of undecidable elements in arithmetic systems.

Goebbels, [Paul] Joseph (1897-1945) German Nazi politician. He joined the Nazi Party in 1924, becoming head of its propaganda section in 1929 and minister of enlightenment and propaganda (1933-45). A ferocious anti-semite, Goebbels drew much of the inspiration for his propaganda techniques from the Bolsheviks. He followed HITLER's suicide with his own, after shooting his wife and children.

Goering, Hermann *see* **Göring, Hermann.**

Golding, William [Gerald] (1911-) English novelist. His first novel, *The Lord of the Flies* (1954), describes the reduction to savagery of a group of schoolboys stranded on an island. This and his second novel, *The Inheritor* (1955), a bleak parable of man's inhumanity, established Golding's reputation as a master novelist.

Goldman, Emma (1869-1940) Russian-born American anarchist. She was imprisoned several times for agitating against employers and for advocating such measures as resistance to the draft. She was deported to the USSR in 1919 and returned in 1924. Her works include an autobiography, *Living My Life* (1931).

Goldschmidt, Richard Benedikt (1878-1958) German-born American geneticist, noted for his theory that the pattern and chemical composition of the chromosome molecule determines heredity, rather than the qualities of the individual genes.

Goldschmidt, Victor Moritzz (1888-1947) Swiss-born Norwegian geneticist. He drew on advances in geology, chemistry and mineralogy to create the modern discipline of geochemistry.

Goldwyn, Samuel [Samuel Goldfish] (1882-1974) Polish-born American film producer. Goldwyn became one of the founders of the Hollywood movie business, with DE MILLE and others, with *The Squaw Man* (1914), and formed Metro-Goldwyn-Mayer with L. B. Mayer (1885-1957) in 1924. Among the films he produced are *Wuthering Heights* (1939) and *The Secret Life of Walter Mitty* (1947). His "Goldwynisms" are mostly apocryphal, e.g. "You can include me out."

Gollancz, Sir Victor (1893-1967) English publisher and philanthropist. He became a successful publisher in the 1930s, notably of crime fiction, with highly distinctive yellow wrappers on his books. He founded the Left Book Club in 1936, using authors such as KOESTLER and ORWELL, which became a strong influence on left-wing politics. A noted humanitarian, he campaigned for Jewish refugees before the war, and organized aid to Germany after it. His books include *My Dear Timothy* (1952) and *From Darkness to Light* (1959).

Gomulka, Wladyslaw (1905-82) Polish Communist statesman. He was general secretary of the Polish United Workers Party (1943-48) but was imprisoned in 1951 for lack of enthusiasm for Soviet dominance of his country. He served again as general secretary (1956-70) and was forced to resign in 1971.

Goodman, Benny [Benjamin David] (1909-86) American jazz clarinetist and bandleader. In the 1930s he became one of the first white jazz bandleaders to break racial taboos and hire black players. A highly popular musician, he became known as the "King of Swing."

Gorbachev, Mikhail Sergeevich (1931-) Soviet Communist statesman. He became general secretary of the Soviet Communist party in 1985 in succession to ANDROPOV, and soon began instituting his policies of *glasnost* (openness) and *perestroika* (reconstruction), which resulted in far-reaching social and political reforms that changed Soviet and world history irrevocably. He became "executive president" in 1990, with wide-ranging powers, facing strong opposition from radicals such as YELTSIN and from hard-line Communists. His powers were insufficient to withstand the break-up of the USSR, and he resigned in December 1991.

Göring *or* **Goering, Hermann [Wilhelm]** (1893-1946) German Nazi politician and military leader. An ace fighter pilot during World War I, he joined the Nazi Party in 1922, becoming head of the SA storm troops in 1923. He served HITLER as Prussian prime minister, minister of the interior and air minister (1933-45), organizing the rebuilding of the Luftwaffe.

Gorky, Arshile [Vosdanig Manoog Adoian] (1904-48) Armenian-born American painter. Originally a surrealist, his style, characterized by vibrant colours and sinuous, fluid lines, developed into an abstract approach that was influential on the New York Action school of painters.

Gorky *or* **Gorki, Maxim** [Aleksey Maximovich Peshkov] (1868-1936) Russian novelist, dramatist and short-story writer. His best-known works are the autobiographical trilogy *Childhood* (1913), *Among People* (1915) and *My Universities* (1923), and the play *The Lower Depths* (1902). A firm communist, he helped formulate the doctrine of socialist realism in the USSR in the 1930s.

Gorton, Sir John Grey (1911-) Australian Liberal statesman. He was Liberal prime minister (1968-71), and resigned in 1971 following his defeat on a vote of confidence.

Grace, W[illiam] G[ilbert] (1848-1915) English cricketer and physician. One of the first English cricketers to become a national institution, he began playing first-class cricket (for Gloucestershire) in 1864, and had scored a hundred centuries by 1895. He was also noted for his cunning gamesmanship.

Graham, Billy [William Franklin Graham] (1918-) American evangelist. He was ordained a Southern Baptist minister in 1940. His evangelical crusades began in Los Angeles in 1949, and were subsequently taken all over the world, including Eastern Europe. Despite being the friend and confidant of figures such as RIchard NIXON, Graham's personal integrity has never been disputed.

Graham, Martha (1894-1991) American dancer and choreographer. Regarded as one of the main founders of modern dance, with a distinctively angular and dramatic approach based on strict physical control, she founded her own troupe in 1929, and subsequently founded the Martha Graham School of Contemporary Dance in New York.

Grahame, Kenneth (1859-1932) Scottish author. He wrote three children's books, *The Golden Age* (1895), *Dream Days*

(1898) and (his masterpiece) *The Wind in the Willows* (1908).

Grainger, Percy [Aldridge] (1882-1961) Australian-born American pianist and composer. Like his friends Grieg and DELIUS, Grainger was a notable enthusiast for folk songs, on which many of his own works are based, e.g. *Molly on the Shore* and *Country Gardens*.

Gramsci, Antonio (1891-1937) Italian politician and Marxist theorist. He helped found the Italian Communist Party in 1921, and became its leader in 1924. MUSSOLINI's Fascists banned the party in 1926, and Gramsci spent the next 11 years of his life in prison, being released shortly before his death. Gramsci's prison writings are regarded as among the most important works of socialist theory for their postulation of such concepts as his theory of the all-pervading hegemony of a dominant class in society.

Grant, Cary [Archibald Alexander Leach] (1904-86) English-born American film actor. Handsome, debonair and suave, Grant became one of Hollywood's leading stars in light comedy roles such as *Bringing Up Baby* (1938) and *His Girl Friday* (1940) and in performances in HITCHCOCK thrillers, e.g. *Notorious* (1946) and *North by Northwest* (1959).

Granville-Barker, Harley (1877-1946) English dramatist, producer and critic. The best of his plays are the naturalistic dramas *The Voysey Inheritance* (1905) and *Waste* (1907). His productions of Shakespeare broke new ground in their concern for textual authenticity and disdain for over-elaborate sets. His *Prefaces* to Shakespeare's plays were published in four volumes, 1927-45).

Grappelli, Stephane (1908-) French jazz violinist. With Django REINHARDT, he was a founder of the Quintette de Hot

Club de France, which became the leading European jazz group. He is still regarded as the finest jazz violinist ever.

Grass, Günter [Wilhelm] (1927-) German novelist, dramatist and poet. His works include the novel *The Tin Drum* (1959), a grimly comic satire on the collapse of the Third Reich as seen through the eyes of a boy, and *The Plebians Rehearse the Uprising*, a satire on BRECHT's dramatic and political theories.

Graves, Robert [von Ranke] (1895-1985) English poet, novelist and critic. His works include his classic autobiographical account of World War I soldiering, *Goodbye to all That* (1929), several great love poems, e.g. "She Tells Her Love While Fast Asleep," and historical novels such as *I, Claudius* and *Claudius the God* (both 1934).

Green, Henry [Henry Vincent Yorke] (1905-73) English novelist. His strange, highly original novels, e.g. *Living* (1929), *Loving* (1945) and *Back* (1946), are noted for their fluid and confident use of the rhythms and expressions of ordinary speech, and have been highly praised by his contemporaries, e.g. WAUGH.

Greene, [Henry] Graham (1904-1991) English novelist. He converted to Roman Catholicism in 1926, and his religious beliefs play an important part in his fictional world, the so-called "Graham Greeneland," a seedy, exotic world of spiritually tainted not-quite heroes. Regarded as one of the greatest modern novelists, his division of his work into "entertainments," e.g. *Brighton Rock* (1938), and "serious" works, e.g. *The Heart of the Matter* (1948) is generally disregarded.

Greer, Germaine (1939-   ) Australian feminist, writer and broadcaster. Her controversial study of the oppression of women in male-dominated society, *The Female Eunuch* (1970), established her as the foremost feminist writer of the 1970s. Later books, e.g. *Sex and Destiny: the Politics of Human Fertility* (1984) display a radical reappraisal of her earlier views.

Grierson, John (1898-1972) Scottish documentary film director and producer, described as the "father of British documentary" for such films as *Drifters* (1929), about the North Sea herring fleet, and *Night Mail* (1936), made for the GPO film unit, where his collaborators included AUDEN and BRITTEN.

Griffith, Arthur (1871-1922) Irish nationalist leader. He founded Sinn Fein in 1905, and (with Michael COLLINS) signed the Anglo-Irish Treaty of 1921. He became the first president of the Irish Free State in 1922, following DE VALERA's resignation, and died in office.

Griffith, D[avid] W[ark] (1875-1948) American film director and producer. He made over 150 films (mostly one-reelers) before directing his two greatest films, *The Birth of a Nation* (1915) and *Intolerance* (1916). (The latter was necessary after the first, which celebrated the Ku Klux Klan.) Griffith's great skill with such techniques as rapid cutting, soft-focus and fadeouts was highly influential on other film-makers. In 1919, he founded United Artists with CHAPLIN, FAIRBANKS and PICKFORD.

Gris, Juan [[José Victoriano Gonzalez] (1887-1927) Spanish painter. He settled in Paris in 1906, where he became an associate of PICASSO and BRAQUE, and one of the leading Cubist painters. He later designed stage sets for DIAGHILEV.

Gromyko, Andrei Andreyevich (1909-89) Soviet statesman and diplomat. He was Soviet foreign minister (1957-1985) and a Politburo member (1973-89). Noted for his austerity and bleak demeanour, Gromyko adapted effortlessly to each stage of relations with the West, from Cold War through 1970s detente to the GORBACHEV era. He became a fittingly ceremonial head of state (1985-88) as the old order crumbled.

Gropius, Walter (1883-1969) German-born American architect and designer. He founded and directed (1919-28) the highly innovative Bauhus school of architecture and applied arts. Criticized by the Nazis, he moved to the UK in 1934, and emigrated to the US in 1937.

Grosz, George (1893-1959) German-born American artist, best known for his bitterly satirical drawings attacking German militarism and capitalism. He fled to the US in 1932, becoming a citizen in 1938. His later work consists largely of romantic oil paintings.

Guevara, Che [Ernesto Guevara] (1928-67) Argentinian-born Communist revolutionary. He joined Fidel CASTRO's forces in the Cuban revolution (1956-59), becoming one of Castro's closest associates. He subsequently led a guerrilla group in Bolivia, where he was killed by government troops. In poster form, he became something of an icon for disaffected Western youth in the late 1960s.

Guinness, Sir Alec (1914-) English stage and film actor. Regarded as one of the most versatile actors of his generation, he appeared as a modern-dress Hamlet in Tyrone GUTHRIE's 1939 production, and became a household name through films such as the comedy *Kind Hearts and Coronets* (1949), and the war epic *The Bridge on the River Kwai* (1957). His role as the mystic warrior in *Star Wars* (1977) and its follow-ups reputedly earned him more than all of his previous films put together.

Gulbenkian, Calouste Sarkis (1869-1955) Turkish Armenian-born British financier, industrialist, diplomat and philanthropist. He made his fortune in oil deals in the Middle East and endowed the Gulbenkian Foundation for the arts and sciences.

Gurdjieff, George Ivanovich (1877-1949) Russian mystic. He attracted disciples to his supposedly Sufi-based regime of spiritual enlightenment through physical discipline. His works include the posthumously published *Meetings with Remarkable Men* (1963).

Guthrie, Sir [William] Tyrone (1900-71) English actor and theatrical producer. His productions included a controversial *Hamlet* (1939) in modern dress starring GUINNESS, and several important Shakespeare productions, notably at the Shakespeare Festival in Stratford, Ontario.

Guthrie, Woody [Woodrow Wilson Guthrie] (1912-67) American folksinger and writer. His songs, which attack racial bigotry and the economic exploitation of the poor and immigrants, include "This Land is Your Land" and "Pastures of Plenty," and were a strong influence on such 1960s "protest" singers as BAEZ and DYLAN. He published an autobiography, *Bound for Glory* (1943).

Haber, Fritz (1868-1934) German chemist, inventor of the Haber process, who was awarded the 1918 Nobel prize for chemistry. He died while fleeing Germany en route to the UK.

Hahn, Kurt (1886-1974) German educationalist. An admirer of the English "public" system, he fled Germany in 1934 and established a school at Gordonstoun that emphasized physical education and self-reliance. The school's pupils have included Prince PHILIP and Prince CHARLES. The latter will not be sending his sons there.

Hahn, Otto (1879-1968) German physical chemist. With MEITNER and others, he undertook significant research into radioactive elements by bombarding uranium with slow neutrons, which led to the discovery of nuclear fission. He was awarded the 1944 Nobel prize for chemistry.

Haig, Douglas, 1st Earl (1861-1928) British field marshal. In World War I he was appointed commander in chief of the British forces on the western front (1915-18). The terrible losses of soldiers under his command—the Somme offensive of 1916 resulted in 90,000 British dead—led to fierce criticism of his tactics. FOCH assumed overall leadership of the Allies in 1918. In 1921, Haig founded the British Legion to ameliorate the plight of ex-servicemen and their families.

Haile Selassie [title of Ras Tafari Makonnen] (1892-1975) emperor of Ethiopia (1930-36, 1941-74). He lived in Britain during the occupation of his country by Italy (1936-41). In the early 1960s, he helped establish the Organization of African Unity in Addis Ababa. The famine of 1973 created unrest, which led to Selassie's deposition in the military coup that resulted in MENGISTU's rise to power. Selassie is worshipped as a god by the Rastafarian cult.

Haitink, Bernard [Johann Herman] (1929-) Dutch conductor, renowned as an interpreter of Bruckner and MAHLER. He has been a regular conductor at Glyndebourne and Covent Garden and was created an honorary KBE in 1977.

Haldane, J[ohn] B[urdon] S[anderson] (1892-1964) Scottish biochemist and philosopher. He made significant contributions to the study of enzymes and genetics, and wrote several popular books on science, e.g. *Science and Ethics* (1928) and *Science in Everyday Life* (1939). A Marxist, he joined the Communist Party in 1938, resigning in 1956 in disgust at LYSENKO's pseudo-science.

Hall, Sir Peter [Reginald Frederick] (1930-) English stage director and theatre manager. He was director of the Royal Shakespeare Company (1960-68) and of the National Theatre (1973-88). His *Diaries* (1983) are required reading for the history of the modern British stage.

Hammarskjöld, Dag [Hjalmar Agne Carl] (1905-61) Swedish secretary general of the the United Nations (1953-61). His period of office was a turbulent one, and he died in a plane crash during the Congo crisis. He was posthumously awarded the 1961 Nobel Peace Prize.

Hammerstein II, Oscar (1895-60) American songwriter and librettist, best known for his musicals written with Richard RODGERS, e.g. *South Pacific* (1949) and *The Sound of Music* (1959).

Hammett, [Samuel] Dashiell (1894-1961) American novelist. Like CHANDLER, he wrote realistic crime novels, based on his own experiences as a Pinkerton detective. His best known are *The Maltese Falcon* (1930) and *The Thin Man* (1932).

Hammond, Dame Joan (1912-) New Zealand operatic soprano. Her recording of PUCCINI's *Turandot* was the first classical record to sell over a million copies.

Hampton, Lionel (1913-) American jazz vibraphonist and bandleader. Hampton began his career with Benny GOODMAN's bands in the late 1930s, and became renowned for his exuberant personality and gift for bringing skilled musicians together in bands of his own.

Hancock, Tony [Anthony John Hancock] (1924-68) English comedian. His radio series, *Hancock's Half Hour*, co-starring the English comic actor **Sid James** (1913-76) and scripted by Alan Simpson and Ray Galton, became one of the most popular BBC comedy radio shows ever. The series transferred successfully to television (1956-61), and several films starring Hancock followed, e.g. *The Rebel* (1961). Hancock's comedy persona of a lugubrious misfit closely matched his true personality. His career went into decline, and he killed himself.

Hardie, [James] Keir (1856-1915) Scottish Labour politician. He was the first leader of the parliamentary Labour Party (1906-07). A committed pacifist, he withdrew from politics following the failure of the Left throughout Europe to oppose World War I.

Hardy, Godfrey Harold (1877-1947) English mathematician, noted for his work on analytic number theory. His books include *A Mathematician's Apology* (1940) and *Bertrand Russell and Trinity* (1942).

Hardy, Oliver *see* **Laurel, Stan**.

Hardy, Thomas (1840-1928) English novelist, short-story writer and poet. His novels are set for the most part in his native Dorset, his "Wessex." The greatest of these are *Far from the Madding Crowd* (1874), *The Return of the Native* (1878), *Tess of the D'Urbervilles* (1891) and *Jude the Obscure* (1896). Censorship of his novels by magazines led to him abandoning the novel form for poetry. He is now ranked, with ELIOT and YEATS, as one of the three great modern poets in English.

Harlow, Jean [Harlean Carpentier] (1911-37) American film actress who became one of the screen's main sex symbols of the 1930s, with her tough, wise-cracking "platinum blonde" image. The films include *Hell's Angels* (1930) and *Red Dust* (1932).

Harriman, W[illiam] Averall (1891-1986) American diplomat. He was the main negotiator of the nuclear test-ban treaty of 1963, between the US, UK and USSR, and led the US delegation at the Vietnam peace talks. He was also governor of New York (1955-58).

Harris, Sir Arthur Travers (1892-1984), nicknamed "Bomber Harris" for his advocacy of heavy bombing raids on German cities during World War II. Despite much dissent about its morality—and military wisdom—the policy lasted (with CHURCHILL's muted support) from 1942 to the firebombing of Dresden in 1944.

Harris, Frank (1856-1931) Irish-born Anglo-American writer and editor, whose best-known work is *My Life and Loves* (1922-27), an entertaining, sexually explicit and thoroughly unreliable autobiography.

Harrison, George (1943-) English singer-songwriter. He played lead guitar for the Beatles (1962-70). His songs with the group include "With a Little Help From My Friends" (i.e.

drugs) and "Something." Harrison's work displays a fascination with Eastern religions and mysticism, e.g. "My sweet Lord." He organized the "Concert for Bangladesh" of 1971, the first great rock charity show, and provided the financial backing for several Monty Python films.

Harrod, Sir Henry Roy Forbes (1900-78) English economist, noted for his model of economic growth, the Harrod-Domar model of economic growth, so-called because the Polish-born American economist **Evsey Domar** (1914-) formulated the model independently.

Hart, Lorenz [Milton] (1895-1943) American lyricist. His collaborations—around thirty in all—with the composer Richard RODGERS include *The Boys From Syracuse* (1938) and *Pal Joey* (1940).

Hartley, L[eslie] P[oles] (1895-1972) English novelist, whose best-known works are the Eustace and Hilda trilogy, i.e. *The Shrimp and the Anemone* (1944), *The Sixth Heaven* (1946), and *Eustace and Hilda* (1947), and *The Go-Between* (1953), a subtle portrayal of social and sexual intrigue in Edwardian England.

Hartnell, Sir Norman [Bishop] (1901-79) English couturier. He became court dressmaker in 1938. He designed the WRAC uniform, several functional "utility" designs in the postwar period, and Queen ELIZABETH's coronation robes.

Hasek, Jaroslav (1883-1923) Czech novelist and short-story writer. His masterpiece is The Good Soldier Svejk (1925), based on his own experiences in the Austro-Hungarian army. He also served in the Bolshevik Red Army as a political commissar.

Haughey, Charles [James] (1925-) Irish Fianna Fáil politician. He became prime minister of the Republic of Ireland (1979-81,

1982 and 1988-92). Regarded by many observers as the supreme living example of a machine politician, his political career has been a notably controversial one. He was acquitted of complicity in alleged gunrunning in the 1970s, and after a series of scandals in the 1980s was forced to resign in 1992.

Havel, Vaclav (1936-) Czech dramatist and statesman. His plays of the 1960s and 70s, e.g. *The Garden Party* (1963), satirized the brutality and corruption of Czech communism. Following the brief spell of artistic expression during the "Prague Spring," he was imprisoned for several years after the Soviet invasion of 1968. He was a spokesman for Charter 77, the civil rights movement, and was elected his country's president.

Hawke, Robert [James Lee] (1929-) Australian trades unionist and Labor statesman. After establishing a solid Labor Party base as an advocate for the trades union movement, he became an MP in 1980, and became prime minister after his party's victory in the 1983 election. He resigned in 1992.

Hawking, Stephen William (1942-) English physicist. He has suffered from amyotrophic lateral sclerosis, a rare crippling nervous disease, since the early 1960s, and is confined to a wheelchair. Widely regarded as perhaps the greatest physicist since EINSTEIN, his research into the theory of black holes has been highly acclaimed. His book explaining his theories, *A Brief History of Time* (1988), has had enormous sales.

Hawkins, Coleman (1904-69) American jazz tenor saxophonist. His recording of the ballad "Body and Soul" (1939) was regarded as a model of the "swing" style by his peers.

Hawks, Howard (1896-1977) American film director and producer. His films include a classic "gangster" movie, *Scarface* (1931), *To Have and Have Not* (1944), starring BOGART and

BACALL, *The Big Sleep* (1946), again starring Bogart, two great westerns, *Red River* (1948) and *Rio Bravo* (1959), starring John WAYNE, and the comedy, *Gentlemen Prefer Blondes* (1953), with Marilyn MONROE.

Hayek, Friedrich August von (1899-1992) Austrian-born British economist. A leading member of the Austrian school of economics, he opposed the theories of KEYNES, supporting instead free-market policies and opposing government economic management. His books include *The Pure Theory of Capital* (1941) and *The Road to Serfdom* (1944). He shared the 1974 Nobel prize for economics with MYRDAL.

Healey, Denis [Winston] (1917-) English Labour politician. He was chancellor of the exchequer (1974-79) and deputy leader of his party (1980-83). Widely regarded as one of the most impressive modern British politicians, his unexpected defeat by Michael FOOT in the 1980 Labour leadership election has been seen by some as costing Labour the subsequent general election.

Heaney, Seamus [Justin] (1939-) Irish poet and critic. Brought up a Roman Catholic in Northern Ireland, Heaney now lives and works in the Republic of Ireland. His collections of poetry include *Death of a Naturalist* (1966) and *Station Island* (1984). He is regarded by many critics as the finest Irish poet since YEATS.

Hearst, William Randolph (1863-1951) American newspaper publisher and politician. In the late 1920s he owned more than twenty-five daily newspapers, most of them noted for their sensationalism, and had become a Hollywood mogul, producing several features starring his mistress, the actress **Marion Davies** (1897-1961). He served as congressman for New York

(1903-07) and built a spectacular castle at San Simeon in California. Orson WELLES' film, *Citizen Kane* (1941), is a thinly fictionalized account of Hearst's life.

Heath, Edward [Richard George] (1916-) British Conservative statesman and prime minister (1970-74). His period of office was marked by much industrial strife, particularly by miners' strikes, and he lost two general elections in 1974. A fervent pro-European, he negotiated Britain's entry into the Common Market in 1973, and lost the leadership of his party to THATCHER, after which he became an outspoken critic of his successor's social and economic policies. He has also been an active and influential figure in world politics. An intensely private man, he is also noted for his devotion to music and sailing.

Heaviside, Oliver (1850-1925) English physicist and electrical engineer. Independently of the Irish-American physicist **Arthur Edwin Kennelly** (1861-1939), he predicted the existence of the ionosphere, an ionized gaseous layer in the atmosphere, in 1902.

Heidegger, Martin (1889-1976) German philosopher. He is usually described as an existentialist, despite his disclaimer of the label. His major work is *Being and Time* (1927), a dense and highly obscure work that classifies modes of being and examines human existence. He declared his support for HITLER in 1933, and, through concepts such as "angst," had a great deal of influence on existentialists such as SARTRE.

Heifetz, Jascha (1901-87) Lithuanian-born American violinist. He became a US citizen in 1924, and his flamboyant and expressive interpretation of music from Bach to WALTON has been widely acclaimed.

Heisenberg, Werner Karl (1901-76) German theoretical physicist. He was awarded the 1932 Nobel prize for physics for his work on quantum theory. He dismissed Nazi attacks on EINSTEIN, but remained in Germany during World War II. His "uncertainty principle" states that the uncertainty of our knowledge of the values of subatomic variables means that the values cannot be measured simultaneously.

Heller, Joseph (1923-) American novelist. His experiences as a bombardier during World War II formed the basis for his first novel, Catch-22 (1961), a grim, surrealist satire on military life and logic. Subsequent novels include *Something Happened* (1974) and *Picture This* (1988).

Helpmann, Sir Robert (1809-86) Australian ballet dancer, choreographer and actor. His choreographic work includes *Miracle in the Gorbals* (1944) and *Yugen* (1964). He was the first male principal of the Sadler's Wells Ballet (1933-50), and appears in the ballet films, *The Red Shoes* (1948) and *Tales of Hoffman* (1951).

Hemingway, Ernest [Millar] (1898-1961) American novelist and short-story writer, whose laconic narrative style, with its "tough guy" dialogue and macho values, made a big impression on his contemporaries. Major novels include *A Farewell to Arms* (1929), based on his own experiences as an ambulance driver in World War I, and *For Whom the Bell Tolls* (1940), based on his reporting experiences during the Spanish Civil War. He settled in Cuba in 1945, which was the setting for *The Old Man and the Sea* (1952). He was awarded the Nobel prize for literature in 1954. He committed suicide in the US in 1961. *A Moveable Feast* (1964) is an account of life in the expatriate American community in Paris in the 1920s.

Hendrix, Jimi [James Marshall Hendrix] (1945-70) American rock guitarist, singer and songwriter. With his trio, the Jimi Hendrix Experience, he became perhaps the most influential rock guitarist of the 1960s with his loud, exuberant style, e.g. in his *Purple Haze* album. He died of alcohol and drug abuse.

Henson, Jim [James Maury Henson] (1936-90) American puppeteer and film producer. His TV educational series for preschool children, *Sesame Street*, featuring an engaging cast of "muppets," has won wide acclaim since its appearance in 1969. *The Muppet Show* (1976-81), featuring Kermit the Frog and Miss Piggy among others, also achieved enormous viewing figures in over 100 countries. A later series for adults, *The Storyteller* (1987) marked a new, sadly curtailed departure in his extraordinary work. He also made several less critically well-received films, e.g. *Labyrinth* (1986).

Henze, Hans Werner (1926-) German composer. Henze's works, which often reflect his enthusiasm for left-wing causes, include the operas *Elegy for Young Lovers* (1961) and *The Bassarids* (1965), both with librettos by AUDEN, and *We Come to the River* ((1975), with libretto by BOND. Other works include the oratorio *The Raft of the Medusa* (1968), a tribute to Che GUEVARA, and symphonies and chamber works.

Hepburn, Katharine (1909-) American film and stage actress, noted for her wit and versatility. She had a long personal and acting relationship with Spencer TRACY, her co-star in *Woman of the Year (1942)* and *Guess Who's Coming to Dinner?* (1967). The latter won her an Oscar, as did *Morning Glory* (1933), *The Lion in Winter* (1968) and *On Golden Pond* (1981).

Hepworth, Dame [Jocelyn] Barbara (1903-75) English sculptor. She became one of Britain's leading abstract sculptors in the

1930s, noted for her strong, often monumental carving. Her second husband was Ben NICHOLSON.

Herbert, Sir A[lan] P[atrick] (1890-1971) English writer and politician. He was Independent MP for Oxford University (1935-50), and campaigned for reform of the divorce laws. A prolific writer, his works include a collection of mock law cases, *Misleading Cases in the Common Law* (1927), the novel *The Water Gipsies* (1930), and the librettos for several musical revues.

Hertz, Gustav Ludwig *see* **Franck, James.**

Hertzog, James Barry Munnik (1866-1942) South African statesman. He founded the Nationalist Party (1913) and advocated noncooperation with Britain during World War I. He became prime minister (1924-39) and founded the Afrikaner Party in 1941.

Herzog, Werner (1942-) German film director. His films include *Aguirre, Wrath of God* (1973), *Wozzeck* (1979) and *Fitzcarraldo* (1982). Bizarre enterprises, e.g. the building of an opera house up the Amazon in *Fitzcarraldo*, are a notable feature of his films.

Heseltine, Michael *see* **Thatcher, Margaret Hilda.**

Hess, Dame Myra (1890-1965) English pianist. She was also a much acclaimed concert pianist and an influential teacher. Her transcriptions of baroque music, particularly her version of Bach's "Jesu, Joy of man's Desiring," were very popular.

Hess, [Walter Richard] Rudolf (1894-1987) German Nazi politician. An early supporter of HITLER, he joined the Nazi Party in 1920 and became its deputy leader (1934-41). In 1941, on the eve of Hitler's invasion of Russia, he flew to Scotland, apparently in the hope of negotiating peace terms with Britain.

He spent the rest of his life imprisoned. In 1946 he was transferred to Spandau jail in Berlin.

Hess, Victor Francis (1883-1964) Austrian-born American physicist. He shared the 1936 Nobel prize for physics with the American physicist **Carl David Anderson** (1905-) for his research into cosmic rays.

Hesse, Hermann (1877-1962) German-born Swiss novelist, short-story writer and poet. His fiction reflects his fascination with oriental mysticism, spiritual alienation and worldly detachment. His novels, which were blacklisted by the Nazis in 1943, include *Steppenwolf* (1927) and *The Glass Bead Game* (1943). He was awarded the Nobel prize for literature in 1946.

Heston, Charlton [John Charlton Carter] (1923-) American film and stage actor. Renowned principally for his physique, noble profile and commanding presence in such epics as *The Ten Commandments* (1956) and *Ben Hur* (1959), Heston had few screen opportunities to display his considerable acting skills, which appear in WELLES' *Touch of Evil* (1958) and the grimly realistic western *Will Penny* (1967).

Heyerdahl, Thor (1914-) Norwegian anthropologist. His practical demonstration of his theory that South Americans emigrated to Polynesia on rafts of balsa wood, described in his book *The Kon-Tiki Expedition*, caught the public imagination and the book became a huge bestseller. Heyerdahl subsequently launched similar expeditions, e.g. a voyage by raft in 1970 from Morocco to the West Indies.

Hilbert, David (1863-1943) German mathematician. He made significant contributions to the study of several fields of mathematics, e.g. to number field theory and algebraic geometry.

Hillary, Sir Edmund [Percival] (1919-) New Zealand explorer and mountaineer. He and the Tibetan sherpa, **Tenzing Norgay** (1914-86), made the first ascent of Mount Everest in 1953. His other exploits include an overland trek to the South Pole in 1958.

Himmler, Heinrich (1900-1945) German Nazi leader. He was chosen by HITLER to head the SS in 1929, and by 1936 was in command of the German police structure. Through his secret police, the Gestapo, he organized repression first in Germany then in occupied Europe, and oversaw the construction of the Nazi concentration and death camp system and the attempted genocide of the Jews. He committed suicide after his capture by British troops.

Hindemith, Paul ((1895-1963) German composer and violist. The Nazis banned his works for their dissonance and "impropriety," and he settled in the US in 1939. A highly prolific composer, his works include operas, symphonies, song cycles, ballet and chamber music.

Hindenburg, Paul von Beneckendorff und von (1847-1934) German field marshal and statesman. He shared command of the German forces in World War I (1916-18) , and became president of Germany (1925-34). He defeated HITLER in the presidential election of 1932, but was persuaded to appoint Hitler chancellor in 1933, after which Hindenburg was a cipher president.

Hines, Earl [Kenneth] "Fatha" (1903-83) American jazz pianist, bandleader and songwriter. He became one of the most influential jazz pianists of the 1930s and 40s, renowned for his virtuoso solos and exuberant style.

Hirohito (1901-89) Japanese emperor. He became emperor in 1926 and ruled Japan as a divinity until her defeat in 1945, after which he became a constitutional monarch, known primarily for his marine biology research.

Hiss, Alger (1904-) American state department official. A highly respected public servant, he was jailed (1950-54) for spying for the USSR. Controversy continues over his conviction.

Hitchcock, Sir Alfred (1899-1980) English film director, based in Hollywood from 1940, whose suspenseful thrillers have long been regarded as masterpieces. His films include *Blackmail* (1929), *The Thirty-Nine Steps* (1935), *Rebecca* (1940), *Notorious* (1946) and *Psycho* (1960). In the last film, against all precedent, Hitchcock kills off the heroine in the notorious shower scene long before the end of the film.

Hitler, Adolf (1889-1945) Austrian-born German dictator. A failed artist in Vienna before World War I, and a highly decorated soldier by the end of the war, he co-founded the National Socialist Workers' Party in 1919, and was jailed for nine months following his part in the failed Munich coup of 1923, during which time he wrote *Mein Kampf* ("my struggle"), a lurid and viciously anti-semitic "testament" of his belief in the superiority of the Aryan race. He was appointed chancellor by HINDENBURG in 1933 and consolidated his brutal regime through HIMMLER's Gestapo. He allied himself temporarily with STALIN in 1939, in which year he invaded Poland, beginning World War II. He invaded Russia in 1941 and killed himself in Berlin in 1945 with Russian troops a few blocks away. Hitler's war resulted in *c*.40 million dead.

Ho Chi Minh [Nguyen That Tan] (1890-1969) Vietnamese statesman. A Marxist nationalist, he led the Viet Minh forces, with US help, against the occupying Japanese during World War II, and became president of Vietnam (1945-54), during which time he led his forces to victory against French colonial rule. He became president of North Vietnam (1954-69) after the country's partition at the 1954 Geneva conference. In the ensuing civil war (1959-75), he supported the Viet Cong guerrillas in the south with the North Vietnamese army (*see* GIAP).

Hockney, David (1937-) English painter and etcher. His work attracted wide acclaim while he was still a student, and he was soon being hailed as a light, witty master of Pop Art. He settled in California in the early 1960s, where his "swimming-pool" paintings, e.g. *A Bigger Splash*, display a fascination for water. Other works, depicting male figures, were described by Hockney as "propaganda for homosexuality." He became very involved with photography in the 1980s, and is now established as one of the world's leading representational painters.

Hodgkin, Sir Alan Lloyd (1914-) English physiologist. With **Sir Andrew Fielding Huxley** (1917-) and Sir John Carew ECCLES, he shared the 1963 Nobel prize for physiology or medicine for research into nerve impulses.

Hodgkin, Dorothy Mary Crowfoot (1910-) English chemist. She was awarded the 1964 Nobel prize for chemistry for her work on the molecular structures of penicillin, insulin and vitamin B12.

Hofstadter, Robert *see* **Mossbauer, Rudolf Ludwig**.

Hogan, Ben [William Benjamin Hogan] (1912-) American golfer. Regarded as one of the greatest ever golfers, he won over 60 US tournaments. Despite being badly injured in a car crash in 1949, he recovered and won all the major world championships of 1953.

Holiday, Billie "Lady Day" [Eleanora Holiday] (1915-59) American jazz singer. She became one of the most influential jazz singers of her time, with her sad, elegiac and subtle interpretations of popular songs. She sang with several bands, e.g. GOODMAN's and BASIE's, and appeared in several films, e.g. *New Orleans* (1947), the latter also featuring ARMSTRONG. Her life was a tragic one, and she died of heroin addiction.

Holly, Buddy [Charles Hardin] (1936-59) American rock singer, songwriter and guitarist. One of the most influential of all rock singers, his band, the Crickets, was the first to use the soon to be standard line-up of lead, rhythm and bass guitars, with drums. His songs include several standards, e.g. "That'll Be the Day" and "Peggy Sue." He died in a plane crash.

Holst, Gustav [Theodore] (1874-1934) English composer of Swedish descent. His works include operas, e.g. *The Boar's Head* (1924), choral music, e.g. *Ode to Death* (1919), and orchestral music, such as the *St Paul's Suite for Strings* (1913) and his best-known composition, *The Planets* (1917). His own favourite work was the mood-piece *Egdon Heath* (1927), inspired, like much of his music, by the English landscape and by Thomas HARDY.

Holyoake, Sir Keith Jacka (1904-83) New Zealand statesman. He served as National Party premier (1957, 1960-72) and became governor general (1977-80).

Honecker, Erich (1912-) East German Communist politician. He became first secretary of the Socialist Unity Party in 1971, and became effective leader of the East German state following ULBRICHT's death in 1973. He was appointed head of state in 1976, and fell from power in 1989 following the wide social unrest that followed GORBACHEV's statement that the USSR would no longer intervene in East German affairs. Severely ill with kidney cancer, he was charged in 1990 with treason and corruption.

Honegger, Arthur (1892-1955) French composer (of Swiss parentage). One of the group of Parisian composers dubbed Le Six (including MILHAUD), his works include the oratorio *King David* (1921), ballet music, symphonies, film scores and the intriguing orchestral work *Pacific 231* (1924), a musical portrait of a train.

Hoover, Herbert [Clark] (1874-1964) American Republican statesman and 31st president of the US (1929-33). He was appointed by Woodrow WILSON to oversee food relief for Europe after World War I. He succeeded COOLIDGE as president in 1929, and was widely perceived as failing to cope with the crisis of the Great Depression, which began later that year, and was heavily defeated by ROOSEVELT in the 1932 election.

Hoover, J[ohn] Edgar (1895-1972) American public servant and founder of the Federal Bureau of Investigation (1924-1972). He transformed the FBI into a highly effective federal crime-fighting force in the 1930s, but also used his organization's considerable powers against anyone perceived as "radical" in politics. He developed a vast network of surveillance and infiltration by dedicated agents, the latter factor reputedly having the curious effect of greatly increasing the efficiency of the American Communist Party.

Hope, Bob [Leslie Townes Hope] (1903-) English-born American comedian and film actor, renowned for his snappy wisecracks. His long association with Bing CROSBY includes the "Road" films, e.g. *The Road to Morocco* (1942).

Hopkins, Sir Frederick Gowland (1861-1947) English biochemist. He shared the 1929 Nobel prize for physiology or medicine with EIJKMAN for his discovery of "accessory food factors," which came to be called vitamins.

Hopper, Edward (1882-1967) American artist. Regarded as the foremost realist American painter, his paintings, which often depict isolated characters in urban scenes, e.g. *Nighthawks*, have a still, introspective and often mysterious quality that is quite distinct from any other artist's work. Hopper's work, never very fashionable, is now seen as having been unjustly obscured by the wave of abstract work from the 1950s on.

Housman, A[lfred] E[dward] (1859-1936) English poet and scholar. His poetic output was small, comprising *A Shropshire Lad* (1896), *Last Poems* (1922) and *More Poems* (1936).

Howard, Sir Ebenezer (1850-1928) English town planner. Influenced by the visionary ideals of American social reformers such as Ralph Waldo Emerson, Howard introduced the concept of the Garden City, as in his book *Garden Cities of Tomorrow* (1902), with its description of urban communities (limited to populations of around 30,000) surrounded by green belts. Letchworth and Welwyn Garden City in England are based on his concept.

Howe, Sir Geoffrey *see* **Major, John**.

Hoyle, Sir Fred (1915-) English astronomer, mathematician, broadcaster and writer. He became the main proponent of the "steady state" theory of the universe, which holds that the universe is basically unchanging (as opposed to the big-bang theory). He also proposed that life on earth is of extraterrestrial origin, and has written several science fiction novels, e.g. *The Black Cloud* (1957) and children's books.

Hubble, Edwin Powell (1889-1953) American astronomer. His discovery of galactic "red shift" and other research established the recession of the galaxies and, consequently, the theory of the expanding universe.

Hughes, Howard [Robard] (1905-76) American industrialist, aviator and film producer. He greatly extended his inherited oil wealth and produced two classic films, *Hell's Angels* (1930) and *Scarface* (1932), and the offbeat western, *The Outlaw* (1941). He also made several epic flights, including a record round-the-world trip. Hughes became increasingly eccentric after sustaining bad injuries in a plane crash in 1947 and went into seclusion in 1966, running his vast business empire behind a predominantly Mormon ring of "protectors." Wild rumours, and a hoax "authorized" biography resulted from his seclusion.

Hughes, Ted [Edward James Hughes] (1930-) English poet, noted for his violent poetic imagery drawn from the natural world, as in *The Hawk in the Rain* (1957) and *Crow* (1970). He was married (1956-63) to the American poet, Sylvia PLATH. He was appointed poet laureate in 1984.

Hussein, [Ibn Talal] (1935-) king of Jordan. He succeeded his mentally ill father in 1953. He lost the West Bank of his country to Israel after the Six Day War of 1967, and has trod an uneasy diplomatic line between friendship with the West and his efforts on behalf of the Palestinians (who form the majority in his country). His position became critical during the Gulf War of 1991, when he came under strong pressure within his country to give military support to Saddam HUSSEIN.

Hussein, Saddam (1937-) Iraqi dictator. He became president of Iraq in 1979, and quickly established a reputation for ruthlessness in the suppression of his opponents within and without the Ba'ath Party. He was given much Western support in his brutal war of attrition against Iraq (1980-88) despite incontrovertible proof of his genocidal campaigns against Iraqi Kurds. After his invasion of Kuwait in 1990, UN forces (predominantly US) forced his withdrawal in the Gulf War of 1991.

Husserl, Edmund (1859-1938) German philosopher. He founded and became the leading philosopher of phenomenology, the school of philosophy that centres on knowledge of consciousness, rather than the empirical world of "things." His works include *Ideas* (1913).

Huston, John [Marcellus] (1906-87) American film director (Irish citizen from 1964). His films include several classics, such as *The Maltese Falcon* (1941), *The Treasure of the Sierra Madre* (1947), both starring BOGART, and *The Man Who Would Be King* (1975). His last film, *The Dead* (1987), from a short story by JOYCE, starred his daughter, the actress **Anjelica Huston** (1951-).

Hutton, Sir Leonard (1916-) English cricketer. A Yorkshire player throughout his long career, he scored a century in his first Test match, against Australia. He became the first professional player to captain England regularly (1952-54).

Huxley, Sir Andrew Fielding *see* **Hodgkin, Sir Alan Lloyd**

Huxley, Sir Julian [Sorell] (1887-1975) English biologist. He became one of Britain's best-known scientists and humanists, with works such as *The Science of Life* (with H. G. WELLS, 1931), *Evolutionary Ethics* (1947) and *Towards a New Humanism* (1957). He was the first director-general of UNESCO (1946-48). His brother, **Aldous [Leonard] Huxley** (1894-1963) was a novelist, short-story writer and essayist. His early novels and stories, e.g. Crome Yellow (1921) and Point Counter Point (1928) depict the brittle world of 1920s English intellectual life. His masterpiece is Brave New World (1932), a chilling fable of a future totalitarian state. His nonfiction works include *The Doors of Perception* (1954) and *Heaven and Hell* (1956), in which he records the spiritual insights he claims to have received from taking hallucinogenic drugs.

Ibarruri, Gomez, Dolores ("La Pasionara") (1895-1989) Spanish Communist politician. A journalist, she was elected to parliament in 1936, and became world-famous for her slogan "They shall not pass" (borrowed from PETAIN) during the Spanish Civil War. She lived in exile in the USSR (1939-77) and was re-elected to the Spanish parliament in 1977.

Ibn Saud, Abdul Aziz (1880-1953) king of Saudi Arabia. He became the first king of Saudi Arabia (1932-53), and negotiated terms with American oil companies after the discovery of oil in his country (1938), thus becoming a very wealthy man. He had well over a hundred wives and was succeeded by one of his many sons.

Ilyushin, Sergei Vladimirovich (1894-1977) Russian aircraft designer. He designed many planes, notably bombers and passenger aircraft.

Ionesco, Eugène (1912-) Romanian-born French dramatist. His plays, regarded as masterpieces of the Theatre of the Absurd, include *The Old Soprano* (1950), *The Lesson* (1951) and *Rhinoceros* (1959). Ionesco's hatred of of both left and right totalitarianism resulted in him becoming an isolated figure in French intellectual circles.

Ireland, John Nicholson (1879-1962) British composer. Like DELIUS and HOLST, he was much influenced by English poetry, his works including several song cycles to words by HARDY, HOUSMAN and others. His other works, which were often inspired by a mystical reverence for English landscape, include a piano concerto and the orchestral tone poem, *The Forgotten Rite* (1913).

Ironside, William Edmund, 1st Baron (1880-1959) Scottish soldier. His early adventurous exploits included dangerous secret service work in the Boer War (1899-1902). (John BUCHAN used him as the model for the adventurer Richard Hannay.) He became chief of the General Staff at the outbreak of World War II.

Isherwood, Christopher [William Bradshaw] (1904-) English-born American novelist and dramatist. His best-known works are the novels *Mr Norris Changes Trains* (1932) and *Goodbye to Berlin* (1939), the latter forming the basis for the film *Cabaret* (1972). He also wrote works in collaboration with AUDEN, e.g. the verse drama *The Ascent of F6* (1936).

Issigonis, Sir Alec (1906-88) Turkish-born (of Greek ancestry) British car designer, settled in Britain from the early 1920s. He began working at Morris Motors in 1936, and designed the Morris Minor, over a million of which were sold between 1948-71. His other famous design was the Mini Minor, of which over 5 million have been sold since its appearance in 1959.

Ives, Charles Edward (1874-1954) American composer. His works, which are frequently experimental but based firmly within the American tradition, include five symphonies, chamber music, including the well-known piano sonata, the *Concord Sonata*, and orchestral works.

Jackson, Glenda (1936-) English actress. Jackson's reputation as an actress, starring in stage, film and TV with equal facility, was established by the mid-1960s and continues apace. Highlights include the films *Women in Love* (1969), *Sunday, Bloody Sunday* (1971) and *Stevie* (1978), and *The Return of the Soldier* (1982). She became Labour member of parliament for Hampstead in 1992.

Jackson, Jesse (1941-) American Democrat politician, sometimes called "Revd." He was ordained a Baptist minister in 1968 and became one of Martin Luther KING's aides, subsequently claiming to have cradled the dying King in his arms. He founded what he termed a "Rainbow Coalition" of blacks and other minority groups and campaigned twice for the Democratic presidential nomination, in 1984 and 1986.

Jackson, Michael [Joe] (1958-) American pop singer. The youngest of five brothers (the others are Jackie, Jermaine, Marion and Tito) who as children formed the Jackson 5, a rock soul group popular in the late 1960s and the 70s. Michael became a solo performer in the late 70s, appearing in the film *The Wiz* (1978), an all-black version of *The Wizard of Oz*. He became very successful with young teenagers in the early 80s, exploiting the development of pop videos, as in *Thriller* (1982), and undergoing plastic surgery.

Jacob, François *see* **Monod, Jacques-Lucien**.

Jagger, Mick [Michael Philip Jagger] (1943-) English singer and songwriter, and lead singer with the Rolling Stones rock group, the original members of which, with Jagger, were the guitarist and co-writer with Jagger of many of their songs, **Keith Richard** (1943-), bass guitarist **Bill Wyman** (1936-), drummer **Charlie Watts** (1941-) and guitarist **Brian Jones** (1944-69). Their carefully marketed image of "Satanic Majesties," and involvement with drugs, ensured high levels of publicity for the group. Several of the Jagger/Richard songs, e.g. the ballad "Ruby Tuesday," have become pop standards. Jagger is also regarded as one of the finest white rock/blues singers of his generation.

James, Henry (1843-1916) American-born British novelist, short-story writer and critic. James settled in England in 1869 and became a British citizen in 1914, after the outbreak of World War I. Much of his work is concerned with the contrast between American innocence and the older, wiser European culture, e.g. *Daisy Miller* (1879), and with the minutiae of Edwardian upper-class life, e.g. *The Spoils of Poynton* (1897).

James, M[ontague] R[hodes] (1862-1936) English scholar and ghost-story writer. His stories, e.g. *Ghost Stories of an Antiquary* (1904), are a mix of dry, scholarly wit with a horrifically reticent undertone of supernatural terror.

James, P. D. [Phyllis Dorothy James White] (1920-) English novelist. Her crime novels, particularly those starring her poet/ policeman, Inspector Dalgleish, e.g. *Death of an Expert Witness* (1977) and *A Taste for Death* (1986), have been much admired for their wit.

James, Sid *see* **Hancock, Tony**.

Janácek, Leos (1854-1928) Czech composer. His works, heavily influenced by Czech folk music and culture, include the operas *The Cunning Little Vixen* (1924) and *The House of the Dead* (1928) and two highly regarded string quartets (1923, 1928).

Jeans, Sir James [Hopwood] (1877-1946) English physicist and astronomer. He wrote several books for the popular market explaining modern scientific theory, e.g. *The Mysterious Universe* (1930) and *The New Background of Science* (1933) and made contributions to the study of quantum theory and stellar evolution.

Jellicoe, John Rushworth, 1st Earl (1859-1935) English admiral. He was badly wounded during the Boxer Rising of 1900 in Peking, where he served as head of an overland naval expedition. He was appointed Naval commander in chief at the outbreak of World War I and commanded the British fleet at the Battle of Jutland (1916). He was governor-general of New Zealand (1920-24).

Jenkins, Roy [Baron Jenkins of Hillhead] (1920-) Welsh Labour and Social Democrat politician. As Labour home secretary (1965-67) he introduced significant liberalizing reforms in the law, e.g. on homosexuality. With Shirley WILLIAMS, David OWEN and William Rodgers, the so-called "Gang of Four," he resigned from the Labour Party in 1981 to found the Social Democratic Party. He was SDP member for Glasgow Hillhead (1982-87).

Jiang Jie Shi *see* **Chiang Kai-shek**.

Jiang Qing *see* **Chiang Ch'ing**.

Jinnah, Mohammad Ali (1876-1948) nationalist leader and Pakistani statesman. He joined the Indian Muslim League in

1916, and worked towards peaceful cooperation between Muslim and Hindu nationalists. By 1940, however, despite GANDHI's urging of national unity, Jinnah was convinced of the need for Indian partition into Hindu and Muslim states. He became the first governor-general of Pakistan (1947-48).

John XXIII [Angelo Giuseppe Roncalli] (1881-1963) Italian pope (1958-63). He convened the Second Vatican Council in 1962, which recommended significant liberalizing changes in Roman Catholic practice and liturgy. He was a notable proponent of ecumenicalism and of detente between East and West, as expressed in his encyclical, *Pacem in Terris* of 1963.

John, Augustus [Edwin] (1878-1961) Welsh painter. By the beginning of the 20th century, he had acquired a reputation for both superb draughtsmanship and for his mildly shocking "bohemian" lifestyle. He later became known as a portraitist of the good and the great, e.g. HARDY. His sister, **Gwen John** (1876-1939), who became something of a recluse after her conversion to Roman Catholicism in 1913, was also a painter.

John, Elton [Reginald Kenneth Dwight] (1947-) English pop and rock musician. John was particularly popular in the 1960s and 70s with hit songs such as "Daniel" and "Don't Go Breaking My Heart."

John Paul II [Karel Jozef Wojtyla] (1920-   ) Polish pope (1978-) Noted for his courage and resistance to both Nazis and Communists, he had been appointed a cardinal in 1967, and gave shrewd and successful advice to his church throughout the growing unrest in Poland. In 1978 he became the first Polish pope and first non-Italian pope for 450 years. His primacy has been notable for both his wide travels throughout the world and for his his conservatism in matters such as abortion and the celibacy of the priesthood. He survived an assassination attempt in 1981. Also a dramatist and poet, his works include *The Future of the Church* (1979) and *Collected Poems* (1982).

Johns, Jasper (1930-) American painter, sculptor and printmaker. His work, especially his use of everyday images such as the stars and stripes, was very influential on later Pop Artists such as WARHOL.

Johns, W[illiam] E[arl] (1893-1968) English World War I bomber pilot and writer of 96 adventure stories featuring ace pilot Biggles (Sergeant Bigglesworth) and his chums Algy and Ginger. The first Biggles book was *The Camels are Coming* (1932); many of the other titles begin "*Biggles Flies (East, West, etc.)*. In all, he published 169 books, 11 of which feature a staunchly feminist World War II version of Biggles, "Worrals of the WAAF." A fine adventure story writer, with a fair share of tolerance and humour, his works remain popular with children.

Johnson, Amy (1903-41) English aviator. She was the first woman to fly solo from England to Australia (1930). Her other records include a solo flight from London to Cape Town (1936). She was lost, presumed drowned, after baling out over the Thames Estuary while serving as an Transport Auxiliary pilot in World War II.

Johnson, Jack (1878-1946) American boxer. He became the first black to win the world heavyweight title (1908-15). His reign as champion inspired the phrase "Great White Hope," which was applied to any white boxer thought capable of beating Jackson, who, with his controversial and uncompromising lifestyle, never attracted much white affection or support.

Johnson, Lyndon B[aines] (1908-73) American Democrat

statesman. Following KENNEDY's assassination in 1963, he became the 36th president of the US (1963-69). His time in office was a troubled one, and the increasing unpopularity of the Vietnam War and Civil Rights agitation overshadowed what he called his "Great Society" reforms, especially in the fields of medical aid for the poor and aged, and in education.

Joliot-Curie, Irène (1897-1956) French physicist, daughter of Marie and Pierre CURIE. With her physicist husband, **Frédéric Joliot-Curie** (1900-58), she shared the 1935 Nobel prize for chemistry for their discovery of artificial radioactivity. Both died of cancer, caused by lifelong exposure to radioactivity.

Jolson, Al [Asa Yoelson] (1886-1950) Russian-born American singer and actor. The son of a rabbi, Jolson became famous for his "black face" minstrel songs, e.g. "Mammy" and "Sonny Boy." He starred in the first full-length movie with sound, *The Jazz Singer* (1927).

Jones, Bobby [Robert Tyre Jones] (1902-71) American golfer. Regarded as one of the greatest golfers of all time, Jones won many major championships, before retiring at the age of 28, still an amateur. In 1930, he won the US and British Opens and the US and British amateur tournaments, a feat unlikely to be repeated.

Jones, Brian *see* **Jagger, Mick.**

Jones, Chuck [Charles Jones] (1912-) American cartoon director. His most famous creation is Bugs Bunny, the laconic, subversive rabbit with the catchphrase, "What's Up, Doc?" Jones has won two Oscars for his work.

Jones, Daniel (1881-1967) English phonetician. His *English Pronouncing Dictionary* (1917) includes a description of "Received Pronunciation" that, notably through the medium of the

BBC, became the standard against which everyday speech was measured.

Joplin, Scott (1868-1917) American pianist and composer. Joplin's "ragtime" compositions, e.g. *The Entertainer* and *Maple Leaf Rag* (1899), became enormously popular in the US, with *Maple Leaf Rag* alone selling over a million copies of sheet music. Longing to be accepted as the first black composer of "serious" music, Joplin grew depressed by the failure of his two operas, and died in a mental home.

Josephson, Brian David (1940-) Welsh physicist. He shared the 1973 Nobel prize for physics for his discovery of the "Josephson effect" on electric currents in superconductors.

Joyce, James [Augustine Aloysius] (1882-1941) Irish novelist and short-story writer. Educated in Jesuit schools and at Dublin University, he left Ireland in 1902, returning briefly twice. His works include a verse collection, *Chamber Music* (1907), the short-story collection *Dubliners* (1914), and two great novels, *Portrait of the Artist as a Young Man* (1914-15) and *Ulysses* (1922), the last being one one of the key novels of the century. His other main work, *Finnegans Wake* (1939), uses Joyce's formidable repertoire of punning and allusive language in an attempt at creating an effect of all actual and possible human experience.

Joyce, William (1906-46) American-born British traitor (of Anglo-Irish descent). An ex-member of MOSLEY's British Union of Fascists, he formed his own pro-Nazi party in 1937, and fled to Germany in 1939, where he broadcast rabid Nazi propaganda to Britain, soon being dubbed "Lord Haw-Haw" by the British public for his affected upper-class accent. he was executed for treason in 1946.

Juan Carlos I (1938-) king of Spain from 1975. Nominated by FRANCO in 1969 as his successor, Juan Carlos carefully steered his country towards democracy and respectability after Franco's death in 1975, despite two attempted coups.

Jung, Carl Gustav (1875-1961) Swiss psychiatrist. He began his career as a follower of FREUD, but split with him after challenging his concentration on sex. Jung's theory of the "collective unconscious," a sort of vast reservoir in the unconscious mind filled with memories and instincts common to all humans, and his use of the term "archetype" to denote an image or symbol drawn from this store, has been highly influential. His relationship with the Nazi regime in the 1930s is still a matter of intense debate.

K

Kádár, János (1912-89) Hungarian politician. He fought with the Communist partisans during World War II and became minister of internal affairs in 1948. Imprisoned (1951-54) for "TITOism," he joined NAGY's government during the Hungarian Revolution of 1956, but formed a puppet pro-Soviet government after the Soviet invasion. He served as prime minister (1956-58, 1961-65) and was first secretary of the Communist Party (1956-88). He served a brief period as party president in 1988, being dismissed shortly before his death.

Kafka, Franz (1883-1924) Prague-born German novelist and short-story writer. His novels *The Trial* (1925) and *The Castle* (1926), and several of his short stories, notably "Metamorphosis," are established classics of 20th-century literature. The atmosphere of his fiction, in which characters are often trapped in bureaucratic totalitarianism, is oddly prophetic of the coming era (many of his family were to die in Hitler's camps). His unfinished novel, *Amerika* (1927), is a surprisingly light-hearted CHAPLINesque affair set in the US (which he never visited).

Kaldor, Nicholas, Baron (1908-86) Hungarian-born British economist. A highly influential economist in the 1960s, particularly in the WILSON administrations, Kaldor advocated expenditure taxes rather than income taxes and was a notable critic of monetarism. His books include *The Scourge of Monetarism* (1982).

Kandinsky, Wassily (1866-1944) Russian-born French painter. One of the leading expressionist painters, he co-founded (with KLEE and MARC) the *Blaue Reiter* ("Blue Rider") group in 1912, and is regarded as the first major abstract artist. His thesis, *On the Spiritual in Art* (1912), was a highly influential work.

Kapitza, Peter Leonidovich (1894-1984) Russian physicist. He was awarded the 1978 Nobel prize for physics, and made notable contributions to the study of cryogenics. He was dismissed from his post as director of the Institute of Physical Problems in 1946 for refusing to work on the atom bomb, but was reinstated in 1955.

Karajan, Herbert von (1908-89) Austrian conductor. By the mid-1930s he was regarded as a brilliant, if dictatorial, conductor of symphonies and operas, whose recordings, notably of Beethoven's symphonies, are held by some critics to be definitive. His membership of the Nazi party from 1933 on is claimed by his admirers, rather unconvincingly, to have been simply a "career move."

Karamanlis, Konstantinos (1907-) Greek politician. He served as prime minister (1955-63), after which he left Greece, returning on the collapse of the military junta to serve again as premier (1974-80), and subsequently became president (1980-85).

Karpov, Anatoly Yegenyevich (1951-) Russian chess player. After FISCHER refused to defend his title, Karpov became world champion by default (1975-85), being displaced by KASPAROV in 1985, in the longest-ever world match (48 games over six months).

Kasparov, Gary [Gary Weinstein] (1963-) Russian chess player. He became world champion in 1985 after defeating

KARPOV in a long, exhausting contest. His autobiography, *Child of Change* (1987), depicts himself as a product of GORBACHEV's new glasnost era.

Kaunda, Kenneth [David] (1924-) Zambian politician. He became president of Zambia when his country became independent in 1964. Regarded as a relatively benign dictator by many in the West, his rule was shaken in the continent-wide wave of agitation for reform that followed the release of MANDELA in 1990. Kaunda's opaque philosophy of "African humanism" is expressed in such works as *A Humanist in Africa* (1966).

Kazan, Elia [Elia Kazanjoglous] (1909-) Turkish-born American film and stage director. His films include *On the Waterfront* (1954), *East of Eden* (1954) and *Splendour in the Grass* (1962).

Kazantzakis, Nikos (1885-1957) Greek novelist, poet and dramatist. His best-known work is the novel *Zorba the Greek* (1946).

Keaton, Buster [Joseph Francis Keaton] (1895-1966) American film comedian and director. Widely regarded as one of the all-time great comedians of the cinema, with his "deadpan" expression and remarkable acrobatic skill, his silent comedy films include *The Navigator* (1924) and *The General* (1926).

Keeler, Christine *see* **Profumo, John Dennis.**

Keller, Helen [Adams] (1880-1968) American writer. She became deaf and blind when 19 months old, and was taught to read and write by the partially sighted Anne Sullivan. Her books include *The Story of My Life* (1902).

Kelly, Gene [Eugene Curran Kelly] (1912-) American dancer, choreographer and film director. Noted for his athleticism and witty dancing style, his films include the musicals *On the Town* (1949) and *Singin' in the Rain* (1952). His "straight" acting films include, notably, *Inherit the Wind* (1960).

Kelly, Grace [Patricia] (1929-82) American film actress. Her films include *High Noon* (1952), *High Society* (1956) and *Rear Window* (1954). She married **Prince Rainier III** (1923-) of Monaco in 1956, and gave up her career.

Kendrew, Sir John Cowdery (1917-) English biochemist. With the Austrian-born British chemist **Max Ferdinand Perutz** (1914-), he shared the 1962 Nobel prize for biochemistry for work on the molecular structure of the protein myoglobin.

Kennedy, John Fitzgerald (1917-63) American Democratic politician, who became 35th president of the US (1961-63). He was the first Roman Catholic and the youngest man elected to the presidency. His brief period of office, cut short by his assassination in Dallas, was subsequently seen by many as a period of hope and social reform, with most of his "New Frontier" legislation being implemented by Lyndon JOHNSON. He gave half-hearted support for the CIA-backed Bay of Pigs invasion of CASTRO's Cuba in 1961, and forced KHRUSCHEV to withdraw Soviet missiles from Cuba in 1962. His brother **Robert [Francis] Kennedy** (1925-68) became attorney general (1961-64) and senator for New York (1965-68) and furthered civil rights legislation, and was assassinated. Another brother, **Edward [Moore] Kennedy** (1932-), became a (Massachusetts senator in 1962, and was widely regarded as a future president until the "Chappaquidick" incident of 1969, in which a girl passenger in his car was drowned in circumstances that remain obscure.

Kennelly, Arthur Edwin *see* **Heaviside, Oliver.**

Kenyatta, Jomo (*c*1889-1978) Kenyan politician. He was jailed for six years (1952-58) for his leadership of the Mau-Mau rebellion. He became prime minister of Kenya on independence in 1963 and president (1964-78).

Kerenski, Alexsandr Feodorovich (1881-1970) Russian revolutionary leader. A member of the Social Democratic Party's liberal wing, he became prime minister of the Russian provisional government of 1917, but was unable to unite the squabbling democratic factions and was deposed by LENIN's Bolsheviks in the October Revolution. He fled to France, and lived in the US from 1946. His works include *The Kerensky Memoirs* (1966).

Kern, Jerome [David] (1885-1945) American composer and songwriter. A highly prolific writer of music and songs, he had a huge influence on the American musical tradition with works such as the operetta *Show Boat* (1927), in which the songs were integral parts of the dramatic action rather than merely decorative. He wrote over a thousand songs for the stage and for movies in collaboration with, among others, WODEHOUSE and HAMMERSTEIN.

Kerouac, Jack [Jean-Louis Kerouac] (1922-69) American novelist. One of the "Beat generation" (*see* GINSBERG), his most popular work is the semi-autobiographical novel *On the Road* (1957), a meandering, episodic account of the ramblings across America of a young writer and his friend. His other works include *The Dharma Bums* (1958) and volumes of poetry.

Kertesz, André (1894-1985) Hungarian-born American photographer, notable for his documentary photographs of Paris during the 1920s, which were highly praised for their insight into the city's architecture and people. One of the first photographers to fully exploit the possibilities of the small Leica cameras, his work was influential on both BRASSAI and CARTIER-BRESSON.

Keynes, John Maynard, 1st Baron (1883-1946) English economist. His work, *The Economic Consequences of the Peace* (1919), foretold the terrible consequences that would follow from the Allies demand for war reparations from Germany. In his *General Theory of Employment, Interest and Money* (1936), he argued that unemployment was curable through macroeconomic management of monetary and fiscal policies, and advocated the creation of employment through government schemes (which influenced ROOSEVELT'S "NEW DEAL" policies). He was one of the so-called "Bloomsbury Group" of intellectuals (*see* WOOLF).

Khomeini, Ayatollah [Ruholla] (1900-89) Iranian religious leader. A prominent member of the Iranian Shiite Muslim opposition to the Shah of Iran (*see* PAHLAVI) from the early 1960s, he became *de facto* head of the Iranian state after the revolution of 1979. He established a theocratic dictatorship that crushed all dissent, and declared his intention of "exporting" the Shiite revolution to other Islamic countries, thus ensuring Western support for Saddam HUSSEIN in the ruinous Iran-Iraq War (1980-88). He further aroused Western anger by proclaiming a death sentence against Salman RUSHDIE in 1989.

Khrushchev, Nikita Sergeyevich (1894-1971) Soviet politician. Following the death of STALIN, whose protégé he was, he became first secretary of the Communist Party (1953-64) and condemned Stalin's crimes and "cult of personality" in his speech (not officially published until 1989) to the party congress of 1956. He became prime minister (1958-64) and promoted peaceful co-existence with the West, where his blunt peasant ways aroused as much admiration as anger. He was deposed in 1964 in the Kremlin coup that brought BREZHNEV to power.

Kim Il Sung (1912-) North Korean marshal and Communist politician. He became prime minister (1948-72) and president (1972-) of North Korea, establishing a rigorous and increasingly isolated dictatorship, based on Stalinist policies, and a notorious personality cult of himself as the "great leader." His son and proclaimed successor, **Kim Jong Il** (1942-), is officially titled the "dear leader."

King, Billie Jean (1943-) American tennis player. Regarded as one of the finest women players ever, she won a record twenty Wimbledon titles between between 1965 and 1980.

King, Martin Luther, Jr (1929-68) American civil rights leader and Baptist minister. Influenced by GANDHI's policy of nonviolent resistance, he organized opposition to segregationist policies in the Southern US. Over 200,000 people took part in his "March on Washington" in 1963, when he made his "I have a dream" speech. He was awarded the 1964 Nobel Peace Prize, and was assassinated in 1968. *See also* Jesse JACKSON.

King, William Lyon Mackenzie (1874-1950) Canadian Liberal statesman. He became leader of the Liberal party (1919-48) and prime minister (1921-26, 1926-30, 1935-48). He was also an authority on industrial relations, and wrote *Industry and Humanity* (1918).

Kinnock, Neil [Gordon] (1942-) Welsh Labour politician. He became MP for Bedwelty in 1970, and established a reputation as a spokesman for left-wing policies such as unilateral nuclear disarmament and abolition of the House of Lords. Elected leader of the Labour Party in 1983 in succession to FOOT, he gradually moderated his policies and had great success in marginalizing the hard left of the party. Attacked by Conservatives and Marxists alike for being a turncoat, Kinnock had by the late 1980s re-established the Labour Party as a mainstream electable force.

Kinsey, Alfred Charles (1894-1956) American sexologist and zoologist. He published two controversial studies of American sexual behaviour, *Sexual Behavior in the Human Male* (1948) and *Sexual Behavior in the Human Female* (1953). His evidence that sexual behaviour was much more diverse than generally supposed was initially disbelieved, then gradually accepted as authoritative. His trust in the honesty of his interviewees, however, remains open to question.

Kipling, [Joseph] Rudyard (1865-1936) Indian-born English short-story writer, poet and novelist. Born in Bombay, he was sent home to be educated, then returned to India where he soon made a name for himself as a journalist and caustic observer of Anglo-Indian society. He returned to England in 1889, where he achieved celebrity status with his poems of army life, *Barrack-Room Ballads* (1892). Subsequent works include two novels, *The Light That Failed* (1890) and *Kim* (1901), collections of short stories, e.g. *Debits and Credits* (1926) children's books, e.g. *The Jungle Books* (1894-95) and *Rewards and Fairies* (1910), and many great poems.

Kissinger, Henry [Alfred] (1923-) German-born American statesman. He became NIXON's adviser on national security affairs (1968-73) and shared the 1973 Nobel Peace Prize with the North Vietnamese negotiator **Le Duc Tho** (1911-) for the treaty ending US involvement in Vietnam. (His policy for winning the war through attrition was a complete failure, with the bombing of Cambodia in 1969-70 resulting in the victory of the Maoist Khmer Rouge.) He became secretary of state (1973-76), fostered détente with the Soviet Union and China, and helped negotiate peace between Israel and Egypt in 1973.

Kitchener of Khartoum, [Horatio] Herbert, 1st Earl (1850-1916) Anglo-Irish field marshal and statesman. He crushed the Dervish revolt in the Sudan at Omdurman (with a savagery condemned by CHURCHILL) and was commander in chief of the British forces during the Boer War of 1901-2, and of the British forces in India (1902-09). He was appointed secretary for war in 1914, and had mobilized Britain's largest-yet army by the time of his death by drowning when his ship hit a mine off Orkney.

Klee, Paul (1879-1940) Swiss painter and etcher. With KANDINSKY and MARC, he was a member of the German *Blaue Reiter* ("Blue Rider") group of expressionist artists, and developed a style of mainly abstract work characterized by doodle-like (technically very sophisticated) drawings.

Klemperer, Otto (1885-1973) German-born conductor. By the late 1920s he was established as a great interpreter of both classical and contemporary works (e.g. Beethoven, his friend MAHLER, and JANÁČEK). Being Jewish, he fled to the US in 1933, where he became director of the Los Angeles Symphony Orchestra, and a US citizen in 1936. He was director of the Budapest Opera (1947-50) and became an Israeli citizen in 1970.

Kodály, Zoltan (1882-1967) Hungarian composer. Like his friend BARTOK, with whom he collaborated on a plan for a

Hungarian folk-music archive, he was much influenced by the traditional music of his country. His works include the comic opera *Hary Janos* (1926) and the *Galanta Dances* (1933).

Koestler, Arthur (1905-83) Hungarian-born British author and journalist. While reporting on the Spanish Civil War he was imprisoned and sentenced to death by FRANCO as a Communist agent (which he in fact was), was reprieved and eventually settled in England in 1940. His masterpiece, and one of the greatest of all political novels, is *Darkness at Noon* (1940), which describes the trial and execution (under STALIN's regime) of an old Bolshevik called Rubashov, who is a fictional composite of several real victims of Stalin, notably BUKHARIN.

Koffka, Kurt *see* **Köhler, Wolfgang**.

Kohl, Helmut (1930-) German Christian Democrat statesman. He became chancellor of West Germany (1982-90) and became the first chancellor of reunited Germany after his CDU party won the all-Germany general election of 1990.

Köhler, Wolfgang (1887-1967) Estonian-born American psychologist. With the German psychologist **Kurt Koffka** (1886-1941) he founded the Gestalt school of psychology. His works include *Gestalt Psychology* (1929).

Kokoschka, Oskar (1886-1980) Austrian-born painter and dramatist. One of the leading expressionist painters, noted particularly for his landscapes and portraits, he fled to Britain in 1938, becoming a British citizen in 1947.

Kolff, Willem Johan (1911-) Dutch-born American physician. He invented the kidney dialysis machine in 1943, invented the artificial kidney in 1975 and also made significant contributions to cardiovascular surgery.

Korda, Sir Alexander [Sandor Kellner] (1893-1956) Hungarian-born British film director and producer. He settled in Britain in 1930. He directed *The Private Life of Henry VIII* (1933, with a memorable performance by Charles LAUGHTON), and produced *Things To Come* (1936) and one of the greatest of all films, WELLES' *The Third Man* (1949).

Kornberg, Arthur (1918-) American biochemist. He shared the 1959 Nobel prize for physiology or medicine with **Severo Ochoa** (1905-) for his discovery of the DNA enzyme polymerase.

Kosygin, Alexsei Nikolaeyvich (1904-80) Soviet statesman. A notable long-distance survivor in Soviet politics, He became prime minister (1964-80) of the Soviet Union after KHRUSHCHEV's overthrow, resigning in 1980.

Krebs, Sir Hans Adolf (1900-81) German-born British biochemist. He shared the 1953 Nobel prize for physiology or medicine with **Fritz Lipmann** (1899-1986) for his work on metabolic cycles, particularly his discovery of the Krebs Cycle.

Kreisler, Fritz (1875-1962) Austrian-born American violinist and composer. ELGAR's violin concerto was dedicated to him, and he became one of the most popular violinists of his day. He became a US citizen in 1943. His own compositions include the operetta *Apple Blossoms* (1919).

Krupp, Alfried Alwin Felix (1907-67) German industrialist. He took control of the Krupp industrial empire in 1943 by dispensation from HITLER, following the collapse into senility of his father **Gustav Krupp** (1870-1950). He was imprisoned in 1947 for using slave labour in his factories, but was freed in 1951. He subsequently helped develop Germany's economic postwar economy, and only agreed to pay compensation to some of his ex-slave labourers in 1959.

Kubrick, Stanley (1928-) American film director and producer. His films include the anti-war classic *Paths of Glory* (1957), the black nuclear war comedy *Dr Strangelove* (1963), the innovative science fiction classic *2001: A Space Odyssey* (1968), and the still highly controversial *A Clockwork Orange* (1971).

Kundera, Milan (1929-) Czech novelist. His masterpiece is *The Unbearable Lightness of Being* (1985), a poignant love story set against the background of repression that followed the Russian invasion of Czechoslovakia in 1968.

Kurosawa, Akira (1910-) Japanese film director. His films include the samurai classics *The Seven Samurai* (1955) and *Yojimbo* (1961), (remade in the west as *The Magnificent Seven* and *A Fistful of Dollars*), and samurai versions of *Macbeth*, titled *Throne of Blood* (1957, T. S. ELIOT's favourite film), and *King Lear*, titled *Ran* (1985). Like John FORD, whom he much admired—Ford to Kurosawa: "You like rain, don't you?"; Kurosawa: "You do know my films!"—Kurosawa was happiest with the epic form, and also had a "family" of actors he used regularly, e.g. the great Toshiro Mifune.

Kuznets, Simon (1901-85) Russian-born American economist and statistician. He was awarded the 1971 Nobel prize for economics for his research into economic growth and social change, e.g. the "Kuznets cycle" of twenty-year economic cyclical movement. His works include *National Income and its Composition* (1941).

L

Laing, R[onald] D[avid] (1927-89) Scottish psychiatrist. He became a counterculture guru in the 1960s with his view, expressed in such books as *The Divided Self* (1960) and *The Politics of the Family* (1976), that mental illness was not something to be "treated" but should rather be encouraged by his "anti-psychiatry" as a fulfilling experience, and argued that schizophrenia was an appropriate response to the real madness of the family group and society.

Lambert, Constant (1905-51) English composer and conductor. Known primarily as a composer of ballet music, including, for Diaghilev, *Romeo and Juliet* (1926), he also wrote several jazz-influenced orchestral works, e.g. *The Rio Grande* (1929), a work for chorus, orchestra and piano.

Lampedusa, Giuseppe di (1896-1927) Italian novelist. His best-known work is *The Leopard* (1958), which describes the decline of aristocratic society in Sicily following the island's annexation by Garibaldi in 1860.

Lancaster, Sir Osbert (1908-86) English cartoonist and author of several satirical studies of British architecture, e.g. *Progress at Pelvis Bay* (1936) and *Draynefleete Revealed* (1949). He also invented the "pocket cartoon" while working for *The Daily Express*, which often featured some acid comment on current affairs by the upper-class Maud Littlehampton.

Land, Edwin Herbert (1909-) American physicist and inventor of the Polaroid Land camera, the ability of which to take instant, developed photographs added a new dimension to photography, giving immediate records of objects and events. Land is also noted for his research into the nature of vision, particularly of colour.

Landau, Lev Davidovich (1908-68) Russian physicist. He was awarded the 1962 Nobel prize for physics, for his research into theories of condensed matter.

Landsteiner, Karl (1868-1943) Austrian-born American pathologist. He discovered the major human blood groups (A, O, B, AB in 1901 and M and N in 1927), which resulted in the development of blood transfusions. He was awarded the 1930 Nobel prize for physiology or medicine.

Lane, Sir Allen (1903-70) English publisher. He founded Penguin Books in 1935, which became one of the most successful—and most imitated—publishing concerns of the century. Initially Penguin specialized in cheap paperback reprints of novels (at sixpence each). Subsequent diversifications included the "Penguin Specials" on current affairs, Penguin Classics and Puffin children's books.

Lang, Fritz (1890-1976) Austrian-born American film director, notable for three classic German films, *Metropolis* (1926), *M* (1931) and *The Testament of Dr Mabuse* (1932). He was offered the job of running the German film industry by GOEBBELS, but fled to the the US in 1933 rather than work for the Nazis (he later claimed that *Dr Mabuse* was an attack on Nazism). He directed many fine films in the US, e.g. the grim film noir, *The Big Heat* (1953).

Lange, David Russell (1942-) New Zealand Labour politician. He became leader of the Labour Party in 1983, and won the 1984 general election decisively on an anti-nuclear defence policy, which led to angry confrontations with other Western powers, notably France and the US. Lange was re-elected in 1987, but resigned, due to ill health, in 1989.

Lange, Dorothea (1895-1965) American photographer. Her uncompromising documentary studies of the poverty and suffering of migrant workers during the Depression in the 1930s were highly praised and brought the plight of her subjects into stark public focus.

Langmuir, Irving (1881-1957) American chemist. He was awarded the 1932 Nobel prize for chemistry for his work on surface properties. He also developed the gas-filled tungsten lamp and the atomic hydrogen welding process.

Langtry, Lily [Emilie Charlotte le Breton] (1853-1929) English actress, nicknamed the "Jersey Lily." One of the great beauties of her day, she became the mistress of the Prince of Wales (later EDWARD VII). She published her (discreet) *Memoirs* in 1925.

Lankester, Sir Edwin Ray (1847-1929) English zoologist. He helped found the Marine Biological Association in 1884, and made important contributions to the study of embryos and protozoa. His works include *Treatise on Zoology* (1900-09).

Lansbury, George (1859-1940) English Labour politician, noted for his support for women's suffrage and pacifism. He became the first commissioner of works (1929-31) in Ramsay MACDONALD's administration, and became leader of his party (1931-35) when MacDonald joined the National Government. He resigned when the Labour Party opted for sanctions against fascist Italy in 1935, rather than compromise his pacifist principles. He published his autobiography, *My Life*, in 1928. His daughter, **Angela Lansbury** (1925-) became a film actress in the 1940s, appearing in such films as *Gaslight* (1944), *The Manchurian Candidate* (1962) and *Bedknobs and Broomsticks* (1972).

Lardner, Ring (1885-1933) American journalist and short-story writer, whose stories of American low life, e.g. *What of It?* (1925), are noted for their cynical wit.

Larkin, Philip [Arthur] (1922-85) English poet. His early verse, e.g. *The North Ship* (1945), shows the influence of YEATS. His later, far greater poems, owe more to the influence of HARDY, but LARKIN's later voice, as became apparent in *The Less Deceived* (1955), is all his own: a dark, sardonic lyricism combined with disconcertingly colloquial turns of phrase. Two further volumes, *The Whitsun Weddings* (1964) and *High Windows* (1972), established him as one of the greatest of all modern English poets. He also wrote two novels, *Jill* (1946) and *A Girl in Winter* (1947), and a collection of essays on jazz, *All What Jazz?* (1970).

Larwood, Harold (1904-) English cricketer. His use of "bodyline" tactics in the 1932-33 tour of Australia created great controversy, injuring (seriously) two Australian batsmen and causing diplomatic tension in relations between Australia and the UK. After the war, he emigrated to Australia where he settled very happily. He published two volumes of memoirs, *Bodyline* (1933) and *The Larwood Story* (1965).

Lasdun, Sir Denys Louis (1914-) English architect. Influenced by LE CORBUSIER, his buildings include the University of East Anglia (1968) and the National Theatre (1976). His books include *Architecture in an Age of Scepticism* (1984).

Lasker, Emanuel (1868-1941) German chess player. His reign as world champion (1894-1921), is still a record. Being Jewish, he was forced to flee Nazi Germany in 1933.

Laski, Harold [Joseph] (1893-1950) English political scientist and socialist propagandist. He joined the staff of the London School of Economics, becoming a professor in 1926. He made his public commitment to Marxism in the early 1930s, and was a highly influential spokesman for Marxism through his position as teacher, writer and Labour Party power-broker (he was party chairman 1945-46), and through his friendships with politicians such as ROOSEVELT. He was, however, widely distrusted, not just by the right but by many non-communists on the Left (ORWELL detested him). His works include *The Rise of European Liberalism* (1936).

Lauda, Niki [Nikolas Andreas Lauda] (1949-) Austrian racing driver. He was world champion driver in 1975, 1977 and 1984, and suffered dreadful injuries in the 1976 German Grand Prix. He retired in 1985.

Lauder, Sir Harry [Hugh MacLennan] (1870-1950) Scottish music-hall comedian and singer, who made an international career out of his Scottish comedy routines and songs, e.g. "Roamin' in the Gloamin" and "Stop Your Tickling, Jock." Although often reviled in Scotland as a shrewd propagator of the dual myth of the mean Scot in an impossibly romanticized setting of kilts and heather, his status as one of the last great music hall stars is secure.

Laughton, Charles (1899-1962) English-born American stage and film actor, renowned for his larger-than-life performances in films such as *The Private Life of Henry VIII* (1932), *Mutiny on the Bounty* (1935) and *The Hunchback of Notre Dame* (1939).

Laurel, Stan [Arthur Stanley Jefferson] (1890-1965), English-born American comedian, and **Oliver Hardy** (1892-1957) American comedian. Laurel began his career on the English music-hall stage (understudying CHAPLIN at one point), and Hardy performed with a minstrel troupe before going into films. They formed their Laurel (thin, vacant and bemused one) and Hardy (fat, blustering one) partnership in 1929, and made some very funny films, e.g. *Another Fine Mess* (1930).

Laval, Pierre (1883-1945) French statesman. He first entered politics as a socialist, becoming a senator in 1926 and prime minister (1931-32, 1935-36), while gradually moving to the right. He became PÉTAIN's deputy in 1940, was ousted later that year, and served again as prime minister (1942-44), when he sided openly with the Germans. He was executed for treason in 1945 by the victorious Free French.

Law, Andrew Bonar (1858-1923) Canadian-born Scottish Conservative statesman. He became a Conservative MP in 1900, party leader in 1911, and leader of the House (1916-21). Poor health forced his retirement in 1921, but he shortly after became prime minister (1922-23).

Lawrence, D[avid] H[erbert] (1885-1930) English novelist, poet and short-story writer. His novels, e.g. *Sons and Lovers* (1913), *The Rainbow* (1915) and *Lady Chatterley's Lover* (1928), caused much controversy for their frank treatment of sex, the latter book not being published in its full four-letter form until 1960.

Lawrence, Ernest Orlando (1901-58) American physicist. He was awarded the 1939 Nobel prize for physics for his important contributions to modern physics, including the invention of the cyclotron in 1929.

Lawrence, Gertrude [Gertrud Alexandra Dagmar Lawrence-Klasen] (1898-1952) English actress, noted for her long-standing professional relationship with Noel COWARD, many of whose plays, e.g *Private Lives* (1931) had parts written especially for her. Her films include *The Glass Menagerie* (1950).

Lawrence, T[homas] E[dward] (1888-1935) Welsh-born Anglo-Irish soldier and author, known as "Lawrence of Arabia." In World War I, he helped the Arab revolt against the Turks and was instrumental in the conquest of Palestine (1918). He supported Arab independence in the 1920s, and wrote *The Seven Pillars of Wisdom* (1926), a highly controversial memoir.

Lawson, Nigel *see* **Major, John**.

Leach, Bernard Howell (1887-1979) English potter (born in Hong Kong), who revolutionized the production of pottery by creating reasonably priced, attractively designed studio pottery for use in everyday life. His *A Potter's Book* (1940), describing his philosophy and production methods, remains the standard pottery reference work.

Leadbelly [Huddie Ledbetter] (1888-1949) American blues singer. Discovered in a Louisiana prison in 1933, where he was imprisoned for attempted murder, Leadbelly later recorded several songs that soon became recognized as folk/blues classics, e.g. "Rock Island Line" and "Goodnight, Irene."

Leakey, Louis Seymour Bazett (1903-72) Kenyan-born British archaeologist, and **Mary Douglas Leakey** (1913-) English archaeologist. Married in 1936, the Leakeys made several important discoveries about humanity's origins in East Africa. His books include *Olduvai Gorge* (1952); hers include *Disclosing the Past* (1984). Their son, **Richard Erskine Frere Leakey**

(1944-), is also a prominent (Kenyan) archaeologist; his works include *Origins* (1977).

Lean, Sir David (1908-91) English film director. His highly acclaimed films include *Brief Encounter* (1945), *Great Expectations* (1946), and the epics *Bridge on the River Kwai* (1957), *Lawrence of Arabia* (1962) and *Dr Zhivago* (1970). After 14 years absence from film-making, Lean made *A Passage to India* (1984), which received distinctly unfavourable reviews for its patronising and insensitive adaptation of the FORSTER novel.

Leavis, F[rank] R[aymond] (1895-1978) English literary critic. With his wife, **Queenie Dorothy Leavis** (1906-81), he made a major impact on literary criticism from the 1930s on, through such works as *New Bearings in English Poetry* (1932) and *The Great Tradition* (1948). The Leavises attacked the modern age of mass culture and advertising, which they saw as destructive of the true "organic" culture of old England, and advocated the close, "practical" study of a severely restricted group of authors, including Henry JAMES and CONRAD.

Le Carré, John [David John Moore Cornwell] (1931-) English novelist. His novels are sombre anti-romantic narratives of Cold War espionage, and usually have as their chief protagonist a disillusioned, cynical spy. Typical examples are *The Spy Who Came in From the Cold* (1963) and *Smiley's People* (1980).

Le Corbusier [Charles Edouard Jeanneret] (1887-1965) Swiss-born French architect and town planner. One of the most influential (and most praised and reviled) architects and planners of the century, his work is characterized by use of reinforced concrete and modular, standardized units of construction (based upon the proportions of the human figure), with the house

famously defined as a "machine for living in." His books
include *Towards a New Architecture* (1923).

Lederberg, Joshua (1925-) American geneticist. He shared
the 1958 Nobel prize for physiology or medicine (with George
Beadle and Edward Tatum) for his bacterial research. He
demonstrated the sexual reproduction of bacteria, and discovered the process by which genes are transmitted.

Le Duc Tho *see* **Kissinger, Henry**.

Lee Kuan Yew (1923-) Singaporean politician. The son of
wealthy Chinese parents, he became Singapore's first prime
minister (1959-), establishing a strict regime noted for its
economic achievements and Cromwellian authoritarianism.

Léger, Fernand (1881-1955) French painter. One of the leading Cubist painters, he was much influenced by industrial
imagery and machinery, and has been described as more "tu-
bist" (for his love of cylindrical forms) than Cubist.

Lehar, Franz (1870-1948) Hungarian composer and conductor, noted for his operettas, e.g. *The Merry Widow* (1905) and
The Land of Smiles (1929).

Leigh, Vivien [Vivien Mary Hartley] (1913-67) Indian-born
English stage and film actress. She became an international star
with *Gone With the Wind* (1939), in which she co-starred with
Clark Gable and for which she won an Oscar. Her other films
include *A Streetcar Named Desire* (1951), which also won her
an Oscar. She had a tempestuous marriage (1940-61) with
Laurence Olivier.

Lenin, Vladimir Ilyich [Vladimir Ilyich Ulyanov] (1870-
1924) Russian revolutionary leader and Marxist philosopher. A
dedicated Marxist with a striking gift for single-minded, vitri-

olic polemicism, he became leader of the Bolshevik ("Majority") wing of the Russian Social Democratic Party in 1903. He settled in Switzerland after the failure of the 1905 Revolution, and re-entered Russia with German connivance (in a "sealed" train) in March 1917, after the deposition of Tsar NICHOLAS II. He led the Bolshevik October Revolution, which overthrew KERENSKI's government, and led the Bolsheviks to victory in the Civil War (1918-21). The failure of his economic policy after the war led to the institution of the New Economic Policy of 1921, which fostered limited private enterprise. He was a brilliant demagogue, fully the equal of HITLER, with a comparable repertoire of dehumanizing words and phrases to apply to his enemies (although he was often less coherent than Hitler, e.g. his order to "execute and deport" the prostitutes of Nizhny Novgorod). He survived an assassination attempt in 1918, but suffered increasing ill health. After his death his embalmed corpse was placed in a mausoleum in Red Square for veneration. He left a final "Testament," which condemned STALIN as untrustworthy and gave guarded praise to TROTSKY. His works include *What is to be Done?* (1902) and *Imperialism: the Highest Stage of Capitalism* (1916). *See also* GORBACHEV.

Lennon, John (1940-80) English rock guitarist, singer and songwriter. With Paul MCCARTNEY, George HARRISON and Ringo STARR, he formed the Beatles, the most popular rock group ever. The success of the band was based on the songwriting partnership of Lennon/McCartney, whose songs, e.g. "Please Please Me" and "She Loves You," achieved phenomenal popularity. The group split in 1969, a contributory factor being Lennon's growing partnership with **Yoko Ono** (1933-), who became his second wife. His subsequent albums included, notably, *Imagine* (1971), the title song of which became the anthem of the declining hippy generation. Lennon was assassinated in New York.

Le Pen, Jean-Marie (1928-) French politician. He founded the right-wing National Front in 1972, a party identified by most observers as crypto-fascist with its crude anti-immigrant policies. He stood unsuccessfully for the presidency in 1988.

Lessing, Doris [May] (1919-) Iranian-born English novelist and short-story writer, brought up in Rhodesia. Her novels include the Children of Violence quintet, beginning with *Martha Quest* (1952) and ending with *The Five-Gated City* (1969), and the seminal feminist novel *The Golden Notebook* (1962). Her other works include science fiction novels, e.g. *Briefing for a Descent into Hell* (1971), and a stunning analysis of self-deception and political fanaticism, *The Good Terrorist* (1985).

Lewis, C[live] S[taples] (1898-1963) English novelist and critic. His works include studies of medieval literature, e.g. *The Allegory of Love* (1936), works of Christian apologetics, e.g. *The Problem of Pain* (1940), and science fiction novels, e.g. *Out of the Silent Planet* (1938). He is best remembered for his enchanting Narnia stories for children, e.g. *The Lion, the Witch and the Wardrobe* (1950).

Lewis, [Harry] Sinclair (1885-1951) American novelist. His work is particularly noted for its satirical view of small-town American life, his best-known novels being *Main Street* (1920), *Babbitt* (1922), and *Elmer Gantry* (1927). Lewis was the first American to win the Nobel prize for literature, in 1930.

Lewis, Norman (1914-) English novelist and travel writer. His two travel books include two modern classics, *A Dragon Apparent* (1952), on South-East Asia, and *Golden Earth* (1952), on Burma. His novels include *A Small War Made to Order*

(1966), a study of the Bay of Pigs invasion of Cuba, and *The Sicilian Specialist* (1975), a thinly fictionalized account of President KENNEDY's assassination. A staunch champion of tribal peoples, he exposed the genocidal campaign that has been waged against Brazilian Indians.

Lewis, [Percy] Wyndham (1882-1957) English painter, novelist and critic. His best-known fictional work is the novel *Apes of God* (1930), a withering satire on his contemporaries. He was also a leading member of the Vorticist group of artists. He was described by AUDEN AS "that lonely old volcano of the right."

Libby, Willard Frank (1908-80) American chemist. He was awarded the 1960 Nobel prize for chemistry for his role in developing the Carbon-14 radioactive method of dating.

Lichtenstein, Roy (1923-) American painter and sculptor. He became the leading Pop Art painter of the 1960s with his deadpan, highly coloured reproductions of sections of advertisements and cartoon strips, e.g. *Whaam* (1963).

Liddell, Eric Henry (1902-45) Scottish athlete, nicknamed the "Flying Scot." Liddell's refusal to compromise with his sabbatarian principles by running on a Sunday during the 1924 Paris Olympics, followed by his unexpected victory in the 400-metres race, caught the public imagination. Liddell's principled stance is the subject of the award-winning film *Chariots of Fire* (1981). He became a missionary and died in a Japanese prisoner-of-war camp in China.

Liddell Hart, Sir Basil Henry (1895-1970) English soldier and military historian, noted for his persistent advocacy of mechanized warfare and the development of air power after World War I. His many works on military strategy, including

Strategy—the Indirect Approach (1929), were highly influential upon modern military thinkers (including ROMMEL).

Liebknecht, Karl *see* **Luxembourg, Rosa.**

Ligeti, György Sándor (1923-) Hungarian composer. He fled to Vienna in 1956, where he soon became established as one of Europe's leading avant-garde composers (with STOCKHAUSEN's encouragement). His works include the large orchestral work *Apparitions* (1958-9) and the *Poème Symphonique* (1962) for a hundred metronomes.

Lindbergh, Charles Augustus (1902-74) American aviator. He became the first man to fly the Atlantic solo and nonstop with his 1927 New York to Paris flight in the monoplane *Spirit of St Louis*, described in his book, *Spirit of St Louis* (1953). The kidnap and murder of his infant son (1932) made world headlines.

Lipchitz, Jacques (1891-1973) Lithuanian-born sculptor, of Polish-Jewish parentage, resident in France from 1909 and in the US from 1941. He produced Cubist sculptures from 1916 and created mobile and "transparent sculptures" in the mid-1920s. His later work is often violent and dynamic, symbolic of modern totalitarianism.

Lipmann, Fritz *see* **Krebs, Sir Hans Adolf**.

Littlewood, Joan (1914-) English theatre director. Her theatre company, Theatre Workshop, was formed in 1945 and became one of the major left-wing theatre companies in the British theatre. Littlewood's productions include BRECHT's *Mother Courage* (1955), BEHAN's *The Quare Fella* (1956) and *Oh, What a Lovely War!* (1963), the latter, a bitter musical on World War I, being made into a highly successful film by Richard ATTENBOROUGH (1969).

Lloyd, Clive Hubert (1944-) Guyanian-born West Indian cricketer. A very fine batsman and fielder, he captained the West Indies team (1974-78, 1979-85). He retired in 1985, having been on the losing side only twice in 18 tests.

Lloyd, Harold (1893-1971) American film comedian. He made hundreds of short silent films, in which he played a bemused, bespectacled everyday young man getting into difficult situations, often involving scarifying stunts on high buildings, e.g. *Safety Last* (1923), which includes the famous sequence of him dangling from a clock face.

Lloyd George, David, 1st Earl of Dwyfor (1863-1945) Welsh Liberal statesman. As chancellor of the exchequer (1908-15) he introduced far-reaching reforms in British society, notably the introduction of old age pensions (1908), the National Insurance Act (1911), and the "people's budget" of 1909, the rejection of which by the Lords led to a constitutional crisis and the Parliament Act of 1911. Formerly a pacifist, he became minister of munitions (1915-16) and prime minister (1916-22) of coalition governments. Widely regarded as a brilliant politician, Lloyd George was also widely distrusted. He survived numerous scandals, e.g the Marconi share scandal of 1912, and was a notorious seller of honours to the highest bidder.

Lloyd Webber, Andrew (1948-) English composer. With the librettist **Tim Rice** (1944-), he composed several highly successful musicals, notably *Joseph and the Amazing Technicolour Dreamcoat* (1968), *Jesus Christ Superstar* (1970) and *Evita* (1978). Other successes were *Cats* (1982), adapted from T. S. ELIOT's *Old Possum's Book of Practical Cats*, *Starlight Express* (1984) and *Phantom of the Opera* (1986).

Lonsdale, Dame Kathleen (1903-71) Irish physicist, noted for innovative work in X-ray crystallography. A devout Quaker, she was imprisoned for a month after the outbreak of World War II for refusing to register (even though she would in fact have been exempted) for war work. She became the first woman member to be elected a fellow of the Royal Society (1945).

Lorca, Federigo García (1899-1936) Spanish poet and dramatist. His dramatic masterpiece is his trilogy of tragedies on the plight of oppressed Spanish women, *Blood Wedding* (1939), *Yarma* (1934) and *The House of Bernarda Alba* (1936). He was killed by Fascist forces near the beginning of the Spanish Civil War.

Loren, Sophia [Sophia Scicoloni] (1934-) Italian actress. A strikingly beautiful woman, she starred in films as diverse as the comedy *The Millionairess* (1960) and the grim war drama *Two Women* (1961).

Lorenz, Konrad [Zacharias] (1903-89) Austrian ethologist and zoologist. He shared the 1973 Nobel prize for physiology or medicine (with Niko TINBERGEN and Karl von FRISCH) for his work on animal behaviour. Regarded as the father of ethology, he is best known for his discovery of the "imprinting" of behaviour on young geese and for his (often controversial) works expounding his theories of human and animal behaviour, notably *KIng Solomon's Ring* (1949) and *On Aggression* (1963).

Lorre, Peter [Laszlo Lowenstein] (1904-64) Hungarian stage and film actor. His first major film performance, as the pathetic child murderer, in LANG's *M* (1931) established him as a star. His other films include *Casablanca* (1942) and *The Maltese Falcon* (1941), and CORMAN's horror comedy *The Raven* (1963).

Losey, Joseph (1909-84) American film director, resident in Britain from 1952. Losey's American films include the thriller

The Prowler (1951). He moved to Britain after being blacklisted during the McCARTHY era. His British films include *The Servant* (1963) and *Accident* (1967), both scripted by PINTER and starring BOGARDE, *The Go-Between* (1971) and *Don Giovanni* (1979).

Louis, Joe [Joseph Louis Barrow] (1914-18) American boxer, nicknamed the "Brown Bomber." He was world heavyweight champion for a record 12 years, defeating 25 challengers, and the second black champion (after Jack JOHNSON).

Lowell, Robert [Traill Spence], Jr (1917-77) American poet. His verse is intensely personal and marked by occasionally difficult private symbolism. Notable volumes include *Land of Unlikeness* (1944), *Life Studies* (1959) and *Near the Ocean*.

Lowei, Otto *see* Dale, Sir Henry Hallett

Lowry, L[aurence] S[tephen] (1887-1976) English painter. His paintings, which depict thin, dark "matchstick" figures against a background of Northern Industrial life, became very popular in the mid-1960s. Lowry's highly distinctive work, quite unlike that of any other artist, was largely ignored by both critics and public for most of his life.

Lowry, [Clarence] Malcolm (1909-57) English novelist and poet. His novels, e.g. *Ultramarine* (1933) and *Under the Volcano* (1947), often feature thinly veiled accounts of incidents from his own adventurous life.

Lukacs, Georg (1885-1971) Hungarian philosopher. He wrote two important volumes on literary criticism, *Soul and Form* (1910) and *The Theory of the Novel* (1916), before widening his interests to take account of politics after joining the Communist Party in 1918. His study of Marxism, *History and Class Consciousness* (1923), was denounced by the Soviet Communist party, and later by himself. He was minister of culture in NAGY's short-lived government (1956).

Lumière, Auguste Marie Louis Nicholas (1862-1954) and **Louis Jean Lumière** (1864-1948) French chemists and cinematographers. They invented the first operational cine camera and projector and a colour photography process. They also produced the first newsreels and probably the first movie, *La Sortie des usines* (1895).

Lumumba, Patrice (1925-61) Congolese statesman. He became first prime minister of the the former Belgian Congo in 1960, was deposed later in the year by MOBUTO and assassinated the following year. *See also* TSHOMBE.

Luthuli, Chief Albert John (1898-1967) South African nationalist. He became president of the African National Congress (1952-60), and was awarded the 1961 Nobel Peace Prize for his advocacy of nonviolent resistance to apartheid. He was "banned" by the South African government in 1959, and forbidden to leave Natal for the rest of his life. He was elected rector of Glasgow University in 1962.

Lutoslawski, Wiltold (1913-) Polish composer and teacher. He has written extensively, including chamber, piano and vocal music, but is best known for his orchestral works, e.g. *Concerto for Orchestra* (1954) and a *Cello Concerto* (1970).

Lutyens, Sir Edwin Landseer (1869-1944) English architect. His buildings, often highly picturesque, include neoclassical mansions and "Arts and Crafts" residences, the Viceroy's House in New Delhi and Liverpool's Roman Catholic Cathedral.

Luxembourg, Rosa (1871-1919) Polish-born German revolutionary and socialist theorist. She settled in Berlin in 1898, where she became a member of the Social Democratic Party. With **Karl Liebknecht** (1871-1919) she founded the revolutionary Spartacus League on the outbreak of World War I, and was imprisoned in 1915 for pacifism, She co-founded the German Communist Party after her release in 1918, and was killed with Liebknecht after the failure of the Spartacist-led revolt of 1919.

Lysenko, Trofim Denisovich (1898-1976) Russian geneticist and agronomist. His doctrinal approach to genetics, which rejected accepted Mendelian principles and advocated Lamarck's theory of inheritance through acquired characteristics, found favour with STALIN and did severe damage to the development of Soviet biology and agronomy. His influence gradually waned after Stalin's death.

M

MacArthur, Douglas (1880-1964) American general. Appointed commander of the US Far East forces in 1941, the Japanese forced him to withdraw from the Philippines in 1942, when MacArthur pledged "I shall return." He was appointed supreme Allied commander in the southwest Pacific in 1942, and gradually rolled back the Japanese forces, accepting their surrender in 1945. He also commanded the UN forces at the beginning of the Korean War (1950-51), being dismissed his command by TRUMAN.

Macaulay, Dame [Emilie] Rose (1881-1958) English novelist. Her works include social satires such as *Dangerous Ages* (1921) and later, more spiritual works reflecting her growing Anglican faith, notably *The Towers of Trebizond* (1956).

McCarthy, Joseph R[aymond] (1908-57) American politician He became a Republican senator in 1946 and embarked upon a populist crusade against supposed communist sympathizers in public life (1950-54) under the TRUMAN administration. McCarthy's wide and increasingly bizarre accusations against innocent people came to an end shortly after being accused, during a televised hearing, of having no shame.

McCarthy, Mary [Therese] (1912-89) American novelist, short-story writer and critic. Her most famous novel is *The Group* (1963), which created some controversy due to its open, matter-of-fact treatment of upper-middle-class female sexuality.

McCartney, Paul (1942-) English rock guitarist, singer and songwriter. He was a member of the Beatles (1961-70) with John LENNON, George HARRISON and Ringo STARR. With Lennon, he formed one of the most successful songwriting partnerships of the century. Among the songs credited solely to McCartney is the enormously popular ballad "Yesterday," one of the most recorded songs of the century. After the band's break-up, McCartney formed the group Wings with his wife, **Linda Eastman McCartney.**

McCullers, Carson [Smith] (1917-67) American novelist and short-story writer. Her works, many of which were filmed, usually centre on loners and misfits, and include *The Heart is a Lonely Hunter* (1940), *Reflections in a Golden Eye* (1941) and the short-story collection, *The Ballad of the Sad Café* (1951).

MacDiarmid, Hugh [Christopher Murray Grieve] (1892-1978) Scottish poet and critic. He was expelled from the Scottish Nationalist Party in the 1930s for Communist sympathies, and expelled shortly after from the Communist Party for Nationalist sympathies. His masterpiece is *A Drunk Man Looks at the Thistle* (1926), an allegory of awakening Scottish consciousness that influenced many Scottish writers. More broadly influential was his *First Hymn to Lenin* (1931), the first great leftist poem of the decade.

Macdonald, George (1824-1905) Scottish novelist and poet, remembered chiefly for his children's stories, e.g. *At the Back of the North Wind* (1871), and for two adult fantasy novels, *Phantastes* (1858) and *Lilith* (1895). His work has had a marked influence on modern fantasy writers, e.g. C. S. LEWIS.

MacDonald, [James] Ramsay (1866-1937) Scottish statesman. He became the first British Labour prime minister (1924,

1929-31) and was prime minister of the (mostly Conservative) coalition government of 1931-35, which the bulk of the Labour party opposed.

McEnroe, John [Patrick Jr] (1959-) American tennis player. He became Wimbledon singles champion (1981, 1983) and doubles champion (1979, 1981, 1983, 1984), becoming notorious in the process by his loud and foul-mouthed disagreements with umpires.

McGill, Donald [Fraser Gould] (1875-1962) English comic postcard artist, renowned for his slightly risqué seaside greeting cards ("I can't see my little Willie"), often featuring gargantuan wives and feeble little men. ORWELL's essay, "The Art of Donald McGill" (1944), examines the appeal of his work.

McIndoe, Sir Archibald [Hector] (1900-1960) New Zealand plastic surgeon. He became one of the world's leading plastic surgeons through his ingenious and caring rebuilding of the faces of badly burned RAF crews at his East Grinstead hospital during World War II.

Mackenzie, Sir [Edward Montague] Compton (1883-1972) English novelist. His best-known novels are *Sinister Street* (1914), a semi-autobiographical account of a privileged young man's life at Oxford University and in the London slums, and his series of very popular comic novels set in the Scottish Western Isles, particularly *Whisky Galore* (1947) and *Rockets Galore* (1957). He also wrote two novels on homosexual relationships, *Extraordinary Women* (1928) and *Thin Ice* (1956).

Mackintosh, Charles Rennie (1868-1928) Scottish architect and artist. He designed some of the finest art nouveau buildings, most of which are in Glasgow, notably the Glasgow School of Art (1897-1909) and the Cranston Willow tearooms.

Maclean, Donald *see* **Burgess, Guy**.

MacLeod, George [Baron MacLeod of Fuinary] (1895-1991) Scottish clergyman. Awarded the Military Cross and Croix de Guerre in World War I, he became a pacifist and Church of Scotland minister among the poor in Edinburgh and Glasgow in the 1920s and 30s. Regarded as the leading Scottish churchman of modern times, he founded the Iona Community, restoring the old cathedral and establishing the Community as an international and ecumenical place of worship.

Mac Liammóir, Micheál (1899-1978) Irish actor, writer and painter. Regarded as one of the finest Irish actors and raconteurs of his generation, with a mesmerizing stage presence, his one-man shows included *The Importance of Being Oscar* (1960), a tribute to Oscar Wilde.

McLuhan, [Herbert] Marshall (1911-80) Canadian critic and educator. His studies of mass culture and communication include *The Gutenberg Galaxy* (1962) and influential *The Medium is the Message (1967).*

Macmillan, Sir [Maurice] Harold, 1st Earl of Stockton (1894-1986) English Conservative statesman. He became prime minister (1957-63) in succession to EDEN. Christened "Supermac" by the cartoonist VICKY, he won the General Election of 1959 on the slogan "You've never had it so good" and gained much international respect for his "wind of change" speech in South Africa in 1958. His later years as premier were darkened by the PROFUMO scandal, and his manoeuvres against Rab BUTLER cost the latter the Tory leadership, which went to DOUGLAS-HOME. At the end of his life, he made a notably cutting speech in the House of Lords against THATCHER's privatization policies, "selling the family silver."

MacMillan, Sir Kenneth (1929-) Scottish choreographer. He became the Royal Ballet's principal choreographer in 1977. He had been associated with the company, and its predecessor, the Sadler's Wells Ballet, since the early 1950s. He was also director of the Royal Ballet (1970-77) in succession to ASHTON.

MacNeice, [Frederick] Louis (1907-63) Irish poet and scholar. He was one of the leading AUDEN generation of poets, and his collections include *Letters from Iceland* (1937, written with Auden) and *Autumn Journal* (1938).

Maeterlinck, [Count] Maurice (1862-1949) Belgian poet, writer and playwright. Trained as a lawyer, he turned to writing poetry under the influence of the Symbolist poets. His masterpiece is *Pelléas et Mélisande* (1892), the basis for the opera by DEBUSSY (1902). He was awarded the Nobel prize in literature in 1911.

Magritte, René (1898-1967) Belgian painter. He became a major surrealist painter in Paris in the 1930s, devising a style dubbed "magic realism" for its incongruous, dreamlike juxtaposition of carefully detailed everyday objects in dreamlike situations, e.g. men in bowler hats raining from the sky.

Mahler, Gustav (1860-1911) Austrian composer and conductor. Of Jewish birth, he became a Roman Catholic but remained subject to anti-semitic gibes while conductor of the Vienna State Opera (1897-1907). Regarded as both the last of the great Romantic composers of the 19th century and the first great composer of the modern era, his works include nine symphonies, song cycles, and the great symphonic song cycle, *The Song of the Earth* (1908).

Mailer, Norman (1923-) American novelist and essayist. His first novel, *The Naked and the Dead* (1948), based on his experiences in World War II, was highly successful. Subsequent works include the semi-autobiographical *An American Dream* (1966) and nonfiction works such as *The Executioner's Song* (1977), a gruesome "factional" study of a murderer.

Major, John (1943-   ) English Conservative politician. He became an MP in 1979 and was appointed a junior minister by THATCHER in 1981. His rise in the late 1980s was spectacular: he replaced **Sir Geoffrey Howe** (1926-   ) as foreign secretary in 1989, and later that year replaced **Nigel Lawson** (1932-   )as chancellor. After Thatcher's resignation in late 1990, Major was selected by his colleagues, to most people's surprise, as Tory leader and prime minister. The son of a trapeze artist, his stated aim is to create a "classless society" with consumer rights defined under a "citizen's charter."

Makarios III [Mikhail Khristodolou Mouskos] (1913-77) Cypriot archbishop and statesman. Archbishop of the Orthodox Church in Cyprus, he became first president of Cyprus (1959-77) after independence, with a brief hiatus in 1974 when he was removed from office after a coup by Greek Cypriot extremists forced him to flee to London. He opposed partition, but was powerless to prevent the proclamation of a Turkish state in the north after Turkey's invasion of 1974.

Malan, Daniel F[rançois] (1874-1959) South African politician. He became prime minister (1948-54). A fervent believer in a racially divided, hierarchical society dominated by whites, he was responsible for the apartheid legislation that separated South Africa's population into white, coloured and black.

Malcolm X [Malcolm Little] (1925-65) American black separatist leader. He abandoned his "slave" surname of Little in the early 1950s, by which time he had become a convert to Elijah

Muhammad's Nation of Islam while in jail for burglary. An advocate of violent response to racism, he was murdered by fellow black Muslims in a feud.

Malenkov, Georgi Maksimilianovich (1901-88) Soviet politician. He became *de facto* prime minister of the USSR after Stalin's death (whose private secretary he had been in the 1920s). He was deposed by Khruschev, and dispatched to manage a hydroelectric power plant.

Malraux, André (1901-76) French novelist, art historian and politician. He took part in revolutionary movements in China and southeast Asia (1924-7), fought for the republican cause in the Spanish Civil War (1936-9) and was a leader of the resistance movement in France during World War II. He served as minister of information in de Gaulle's government (1945-6) and as minister of cultural affairs (1959-69). His active life had a great influence on his novels, which include *La Condition humaine* (1933).

Mandela, Nelson [Rolihlahla] (1918-) South African lawyer and nationalist leader. Leader of the banned African National Congress, he was imprisoned in 1964 for life by the South African government. He became an extremely potent symbol of black resistance to the apartheid regime, and his eventual release in 1990 (engineered by de Klerk) was greeted with international joy, after which he increased his already formidable reputation by his dignified and cautious approach to reform. His second wife, **Winnie Mandela**, who had earlier made a notorious speech giving approval to the "necklacing" of black collaborators, was convicted in 1991 of complicity in the murder of a young black activist, with few observers expecting her to go to prison.

Mandelstam, Osip (1891-1938) Russian poet. The collections published in his lifetime include *Stone* (1913), *Tristia* (1925) and *Poems* (1928). He was denounced for reading a satirical poem about Stalin, and he and his wife, **Nadezhda Mandelstam** (1899-1980) were sent into exile in Siberia, where he died. Nadezhda's two books describing her husband's life and work, *Hope Against Hope* (1971) and *Hope Abandoned* (1974) affirm the resilience of the human spirit.

Manley, Michael [Norman] (1923-) Jamaican statesman. He became leader of the socialist People's National Party in 1969, and prime minister (1972-80). He lost two subsequent elections, but won the 1989 election with a much less radical policy programme. He is regarded as a spokesman for the Third World.

Mann, Thomas (1875-1955) German novelist and critic, primarily concerned with the role of the artist and the purpose of artistic creation in modern society. His works include *Death in Venice* (1912), *The Magic Mountain* (1930), and *The Confessions of the Confidence Trickster Felix Krull* (1954), a comedy. He was awarded the Nobel prize for literature in 1929 and fled Nazi Germany in 1933.

Mao Tse-tung *or* **Mao Ze Dong** (1893-1976) Chinese Communist statesman and Marxist philosopher. An adherent to SUN YAT-SEN's nationalist policies, he converted to Marxism and was one of the founders of the Chinese Communist Party (1922), and pursued a policy of limited cooperation with CHIANG KAI-SHEK's Kuomingtang until 1927. Mao then established a Soviet-style republic in Kiangsi province (1931-34), until forced by the Kuomingtang into the "Long March" of himself and his followers to northern China (1935-36). Following the Japanese occupation (1937-45), during which

Nationalists and Communists collaborated against the Japanese, the Communists won the resumed civil war and Mao established his People's Republic (1949). Mao's dictatorship became the most murderous in all history; as many as fifty million people may have died in his "Great Leap Forward" of collectivization (1958-62), and millions more died in purges, as he sought to break traditional patterns of Chinese family life. In 1966, he launched his "Cultural Revolution" (1966-69), during which his fanatical young Red Guards were given complete freedom to terrorize the population, in their campaign against "Confucianism" and "bourgeois democracy." The state worship of Mao reached depths remarkable even for the 20th century, with his works, e.g. the notorious *Little Red Book*, being regarded as holy writ. *See also* CHIANG CH'ING.

Marc, Franz (1880-1916) German painter. With KANDINSKY, he founded the *Blaue Reiter* group of expressionist artists. A devoutly religious man, most of his paintings were of animals portrayed in vivid colours, often merging into their backgrounds.

Marceau, Marcel (1923-) French mime artist. Regarded as the world's leading mime artist, his white-faced Bip character has become known world-wide. His films include *Silent Movie* (1976), in which Marceau's is the only speaking part.

Marciano, Rocky [Rocco Francis Marchegiano] (1923-69) American boxer. He became world heavyweight champion (1952-56), and never lost a professional fight.

Marconi, Guglielmo, Marchese (1874-1937) Italian physicist and electrical engineer. He shared the 1909 Nobel prize for physics for his development of wireless telegraphy. He sent signals across the English Channel in 1898, and across the

Atlantic in 1901, and later developed short-wave radio transmissions.

Marcos, Ferdinand E[dralin] (1917-89) Filipino politician. He was president of the Philippines (1965-86). An autocratic ruler, he declared martial law in 1972, after which he ruled by oppressive and idiosyncratic decree. He was deposed in 1986 after the popular unrest that brought AQUINO to power, and lived in exile in Hawaii with his wife, **Imelda**, who, after his death, returned to the Philippines and was sued by the Philippines government for corruption.

Marcuse, Herbert (1898-1979) German-born American philosopher. He became prominent in the 1960s as a theorist of the New Left, popular with student activists for his conveniently balanced condemnation of both capitalist and Soviet society. His works include *Eros and Civilisation* (1955) and *Soviet Marxism* (1958).

Markiewicz, [Constance Georgine] Countess (1868-1927) Irish nationalist. A member of the Anglo-Irish ruling class, she joined Sinn Fein in 1908 and was sentenced to death for her part in the 1916 Easter Rising, being reprieved in the amnesty of 1917. She became the first woman to be elected to the British Parliament in 1918, when she won a Dublin seat for Sinn Fein, but refused to take her seat.

Markova, Dame Alicia [Lilian Alicia Marks] (1910-) English ballerina. She became a member of DIAGHILEV's Ballet Russe (1924-29) and then of the Vic-Wells Ballet, where she became prima ballerina (1933-35).

Marks, Simon, 1st Baron Marks of Broughton (1888-1964) English businessman. He inherited the Marks and Spencer chain of shops, and, with Israel (later Lord) Seiff, built the chain into one of the most respected retail empires in the world, with a reputation for customer and staff care.

Marley, Bob [Robert Nesta Marley] (1945-81) Jamaican singer and songwriter. With his group, the Wailers, he became the world's leading reggae singer. A devout Rastafarian, and large-scale consumer of marijuana, he died from brain cancer. His songs include the haunting ballad "No Woman, No Cry."

Marshall, Alfred (1842-1924) English economist. His works, e.g. *Principles of Economics* (1890) and *Industry and Trade* (1919), have been of great influence on modern economics. He devised concepts such as "elasticity," "consumer surplus" and "time analysis."

Marshall, George C[atlett] (1880-1959) American general and statesman. He was chief of staff of the US army during World War II, and, as US secretary of state, oversaw the economic reconstruction of postwar Europe, through the Marshall Aid Plan, for which he was awarded the 1953 Nobel Peace Prize.

Marx Brothers An American comedy group of brothers (of German parents), consisting of **Arthur Marx (Harpo)** (1893-1964), **Milton (Gummo) (1894-1977), Herbert Marx (Zeppo)** (1901-79), **Julius Marx (Groucho)** (1895-1977) and **Leonard Marx (Chico)** (1891-1961). Their films, without Gummo, include *Monkey Business* (1932), *Duck Soup* (1933) and *A Night at the Opera* (1937). The anarchic humour of the Marx Brothers' films was enormously popular with both critics and public, with Groucho in particular enjoying a cult status among intellectuals. Groucho wrote several books, including *Groucho and Me* (1959) and a study of US income tax laws.

Masaryk, Tomás [Garrigue] (1850-1937) Czech statesman who founded (with BENES) the modern state of Czechoslovakia in 1918, and became the country's first president (1918-35). His works include *Russia and Europe* (1913). His son, **Jan [Garrigue] Masaryk** (1886-1948), was also a Czech statesman. He became foreign minister of the Czech government in exile in 1941. He returned to Czechoslovakia (with Benes). The circumstances of his death are unknown; he was found dead beneath the open window of his office. It is generally assumed that either he killed himself in grief at the Communist takeover of his country, or he was murdered by the Communists. His biography was written by Karel CAPEK.

Mascagni, Pietro (1863-1945) Italian composer. His works include a perennial favourite in opera houses around the world, the one-act *Cavalleria Rusticana* (1890).

Masefield, John [Edward] (1878-1967) English poet, whose best-known poem, from *Salt-Water Ballads* (1902) is "I must go down to the sea again." Many later poems, e.g. *The Everlasting Mercy* (1911) caused scandal with their frank treatment of rural themes. He was appointed poet laureate in 1930.

Mason, James (1909-84) English stage and film actor. His films include *A Star is Born* (1954), *Georgy Girl* (1966) and his last film, *The Shooting Party* (1984).

Mastroianni, Marcello (1924-) Italian actor. His films include VISCONTI's *White Nights* (1957) and FELLINI's *La Dolce Vita* (1960).

Mata Hari [Margarethe Geertruida Zelle] (1876-1917) Dutch spy. A dancer in Paris with many lovers, she became a German spy and was shot for treason.

Matisse, Henri (1869-1954) French painter and sculptor. In the period before World War I he became the leading painter of the group mockingly dubbed *Fauves* ("wild beasts"), so called for their love of bright colours and primitive form. A superb draughtsman, he also designed ballet sets for DIAGHILEV.

Matthews, Sir Stanley (1915-) English footballer. Regarded as one of the greatest wingers of all time (the "Wizard of Dribble"), he won 54 international caps in a career that spanned 22 years.

Maugham, W[illiam] Somerset (1874-1965) English novelist and dramatist. Trained as a doctor, he used his experiences working in the London slums for his first novel, *Liza of Lambeth* (1897). His best-known novels are *Of Human Bondage* (1915) and *The Moon and Sixpence* (1919), the latter based on the life of the painter Paul Gauguin. He was a British secret agent during World War I and his experiences form the basis of his spy novel, *Ashenden* (1928).

Maxwell, [Ian] Robert [Ropbert Hoch] (1923-91) Czech-born British newspaper proprietor, publisher and politician. He served with distinction in World War II, winning the Military Cross. He founded the Pergamon Press, specializing (very lucratively) in academic journals. He was a Labour MP (1964-70) and bought the Mirror Group of newspapers. In the late 1980s, he produced an extraordinary and much derided series of laudatory biographies of Communist dictators such as HONECKER and CEAUSESCU, just in time for their downfall. His mysterious death by drowning in the Canary Islands was followed by revelations of his mishandling of his companies' assets, particularly the pension funds.

Mayer, Louis B[urt] [Eliezer Mayer] (1885-1957) Russian-born American film producer. He joined with GOLDWYN to form Metro-Goldwyn-Mayer in 1924, and became one of the most powerful of the Hollywood moguls, producing such films as

Ben Hur (1926), and fostering the "star system." ("The reason so many people showed up at his funeral was because they wanted to make sure he was dead"—Goldwyn.)

Mead, Margaret (1901-78) American anthropologist. Her works, which include *Coming of Age in Samoa* (1928) and *Growing up in New Guinea* (1930), argue that cultural conditioning shapes personality, rather than heredity. The validity of much of her research is still debated.

Medawar, Sir Peter Brian (1915-87) Brazilian-born British zoologist. He shared the 1960 Nobel prize for physiology or medicine with the Australian virologist **Sir Frank Macfarlane Burnet** (1899-1985) for his work on immunological tolerance.

Meinhoff, Ulrike (1934-76) German terrorist. With **Andreas Baader** (1943-77) and others, she founded the "Red Army Faction" in 1970, an ultra-leftist terrorist organization dedicated to using violence to bring about the collapse of West German "capitalist tyranny." She and Baader died in prison, apparently having committed suicide.

Meir, Golda (1898-1978) Russian-born Israeli stateswoman, She emigrated to Palestine from the US, where she grew up (1921), and was active in the fight for a Jewish state. She was minister of labour (1949-56) and of foreign affairs (1956-66) before becoming Israel's first female prime minister (1969-74).

Meitner, Lise (1878-1968) Austrian-born Swedish physicist. She and Otto HAHN discovered the radioactive element protactinium (1918). With her nephew Otto FRISCH and others, she discovered the process of nuclear fission in the late 1930s.

Melba, Dame Nellie [Helen Porter Mitchell] (1861-1931) Australian soprano. Renowned for her light, pure voice, she became one of the world's leading prima donnas in the late

1880s. ESCOFFIER named an ice cream dish, "peach melba", after her.

Mendès-France, Pierre (1907-82) French statesman. He was appointed minister of the national economy by DE GAULLE in 1945, but resigned and joined the opposition the following year. He became prime minister (1954-55), and negotiated the peace treaty that ended the Vietnamese war.

Mengistu, Mariam Haile (1937-) Ethiopian dictator. He participated in the 1974 coup that toppled HAILE SELASSIE, and came to power in the 1977 coup against his erstwhile allies. A Marxist-Leninist, he dealt with subsequent risks of coups by personally shooting any of his colleagues felt to be a danger, and established a relentlessly brutal dictatorship. In 1991, as secessionists closed in on Addis Ababa, he fled to Kenya.

Menotti, Gian Carlo (1911-) Italian-born American composer, who settled in the US in 1928. His operas, for which he also wrote the librettos, include *Amelia Goes to the Ball* (1937) and *Amahl and the Night Visitors* (1951).

Menuhin, Sir Yehudi (1916-) American-born British violinist. An infant prodigy, he performed Mendelssohn's violin concerto at the age of 7 with the San Fransisco Symphony Orchestra. He became one of the world's leading virtuosos and founded a school (in 1962) for musically gifted children.

Menzies, Sir Robert Gordon (1894-1978) Australian Liberal statesman. He was appointed a privy counsellor in 1937, and was nicknamed "Pig-iron Bob" in 1938 after backing the Australian government's decision to sell pig iron to Japan during the Sino-Japanese war. He became prime minister (1939-41, 1949-66) and a respected arbiter in international affairs, e.g. during the Suez crisis.

Mercouri, Melina (1925-) Greek actress and politician. Her best-known film is *Never on Sunday* (1960). She became an MP in 1974 after the fall of the military junta, which she had bravely criticized and which had forced her into exile, and was appointed minister for culture and science in 1981.

Messerschmitt, Willy [Wilhelm Messerschmitt] (1898-1978) German aircraft designer and manufacturer. His planes include two notable fighters, the ME-109, a version of which won the world speed record in 1939, and the first jet combat aircraft, the ME-262.

Messiaen, Olivier (1908-92) French composer and organist. His rhythmically complex works, often influenced by birdsong, include *Quartet for the End of Time* (1941, performed before fellow prisoners in a German POW camp) and the massive Hindu-influenced *Turangallia* symphony (1946).

Messmer, Otto (1894-1985) American cartoonist. His "Felix the Cat" first appeared in *Feline Follies* (1920) and became the first cartoon superstar. "Felix kept on walking" became an international catchphrase.

Mies van der Rohe, Ludwig (1886-1969) German-born American architect. His German pavilion for the 1929 International Exhibition in Barcelona was widely praised, as were his designs for glass skyscrapers. He was director of the Bauhaus (1930-33) and emigrated to the US in 1937. He designed the New York Seagram Tower.

Milhaud, Darius (1892-1974) French composer. A member of "Les Six," he was a highly prolific composer. His works, mostly polytonal and often influenced by jazz, include symphonies, operas, songs and string quartets.

Miller, Arthur (1915-) American dramatist. His tragedies include three classics of the American stage: *Death of a Salesman* (1949), *The Crucible* (1952), a comment on McCARTHYism in the US, and *A View from the Bridge* (1955), inspired by Greek drama. He was married to Marilyn MONROE (1955-61) for whom he wrote the screenplay for her last film, *The Misfits* (1961).

Miller, [Alton] Glenn (1904-44) American composer, bandleader and trombonist. His dance band became one of the most popular in the world, with tunes such as "Moonlight Serenade" and "In the Mood." The plane carrying Miller and his band to play for the troops disappeared over the English Channel in 1944.

Millett, Kate (1934-) American feminist. Her works, notably *Sexual Politics* (1969), are cornerstones of feminist fundamentalism, arguing that society is constructed for the benefit of "male patriarchy," which uses the family as a device for repressing women.

Milligan, Spike [Terence Allan Milligan] (1918-) Indian-born Anglo-Irish comedian. With Peter SELLERS, the Welsh comedian and singer **Harry Secombe** (1921-) and the Anglo-Peruvian comedian **Michael Bentine** (1921-), he co-wrote and performed in the radio comedy series *The Goon Show* (1951-59), which became a highly influential comedy series, with its manic wit and surreal invention. Milligan's books include the novel *Puckoon* (1963) and autobiographies, e.g. *Adolf Hitler, My Part in his Downfall* (1971).

Millikan, Robert Andrews (1868-1953) American physicist. He was awarded the 1923 Nobel prize for physics for his determination of the charge on the electron, and did significant research on cosmic rays.

Milne, A[lan] A[lexander] (1882-1956) English writer and dramatist. His children's books, e.g. *When We Were Very Young* (1924), *Winnie-the-Pooh* (1926) and *The House at Pooh Corner* (1928), are much loved classics of children's literature.

Minnelli, Liza *see* **Garland, Judy**.

Miró, Joan (1893-1983) Spanish painter. He settled in Paris in 1920, where he became influenced by Picasso, and exhibited with the Surrealists in 1925. His dreamlike work, depicting highly coloured and curvilinear forms, became increasingly abstract over the years, and was influential on the American Abstract Expressionist painters.

Mitchell, R[eginald] J[oseph] (1895-1937) English aircraft designer. He designed the Supermarine Spitfire (1934-36), dying just after its acceptance by the RAF. The Spitfire, arguably the most beautiful plane ever built, went into full production in 1938, and played a significant part in the Battle of Britain. Over 19,000 were produced during World War II.

Mitterrand, François [Maurice Marie] (1916-) French statesman. A member of the Resistance during World War II, he became leader of the Socialist Party in 1971 and the first socialist president of France (1981-). A shrewd politician, he skilfully marginalized his enemies on both the left and the right throughout the 1980s, reneging on such early policies as nationalization in the process.

Mobuto, Sese Seko Kuku Ngbendu Wa Za Banga [Joseph Désiré Mobuto] (1930-) Zairean dictator. A colleague of Lumumba's in the late 1950s, he assumed complete power over the Congo in 1965, changing the country's name to Zaire in 1971. His notoriously corrupt regime—Mobuto is worth 3 or £4 billion—was backed by the Western powers for its supposedly anti-communist virtues.

Modigliani, Amedeo (1844-1920) Italian painter and sculptor. His best-known works are his African-influenced sculptures of elongated figures.

Moholy-Nagy, László (1895-1946) Hungarian-born American painter, sculptor and photographer. He taught at the Bauhaus (1923-28) and worked in many different mediums, notably photography, in which field he won recognition as a leading avant-garde photographer.

Molotov, Vyacheslav Mikhailovich [Vyacheslav Mikhailovich Scriabin] (1890-1986) Russian statesman. He joined LENIN's Bolsheviks in 1905 and became one of the few leading Bolsheviks to survive STALIN's purges. He was commissar for foreign affairs (1939-49), negotiated the nonaggression pact with Nazi Germany and attended the founding conference of the UN in 1945. As minister for foreign affairs (1953-56), his reiterated *nyet* to diplomatic overtures became a byword.

Mondrian, Piet [Pieter Cornelis Mondriaan] (1872-1944) Dutch painter. He settled in Paris in 1909, where he was influenced by the Cubists and Fauvists, particularly MATISSE. He developed a style of painting based on grids of lines against strong colours, and co-founded the De Stijl group of Dutch artists.

Monk, Thelonius [Sphere] (1917-82) American jazz pianist and composer. He became a member of Dizzy GILLESPIE's band in 1946 and formed his own band in 1947, which later included many talented saxophonists, e.g. COLTRANE. His compositions include "Round Midnight."

Monod, Jacques-Lucien (1910-76) French biochemist. He shared the 1965 Nobel prize for physics with **François Jacob** (1920-) for their work on clusters of genes ("operons") round chromosomes.

Monroe, Marilyn [Norma Jean Baker *or* Mortenson] (1926-62) American film actress. She became the leading "dumb blonde" sex symbol in the movies with such films as *Gentleman Prefer Blondes* (1953). Her other films include *Bus Stop* (1956) and the classic comedy *Some Like It Hot* (1959). Her last film, *The Misfits* (1961), was written by her third husband, Arthur MILLER. Her death was apparently due to an overdose of sleeping pills.

Montessori, Maria (1870-1952) Italian educationalist. Her book *The Montessori Method* (1912), which set out her educational method of encouraging the child to learn at her or his own pace without restraint, was very influential on modern pedagogy. She was the first woman in Italy to be awarded a medical degree.

Montgomery of Alamein, Bernard Law, 1st Viscount (1887-1970) English soldier. In World War II he was given command of the 8th Army in Egypt in 1942, and won the Battle of Alamein later that year against ROMMEL's forces, a victory recognized by CHURCHILL as a turning point in the war. He later commanded the Allied land forces on D-Day, and accepted Germany's surrender on Luneeburg Heath.

Moore, G[eorge] E[dward] (1873-1958) English philosopher. A strong influence on his fellow student Bertrand RUSSELL, Moore became one of the leading philosophers of his day with the publication of his *Principia Ethica* (1903), an analysis of the non-analysable nature of good and of the value of friendship. He regarded philosophy's main concern as the analysis of everyday life.

Moore, Henry [Spencer] (1898-1986) English sculptor. His monumental sculptures, e.g. *The Madonna and Child* (1943) at

St Matthew's Church, Northampton, often semi-abstract in style but always (after a flirtation with Surrealism) based on organic form, resulted in him becoming the best known of modern sculptors, usually perceived as "the man who makes statues and puts holes in them."

Morgan, Thomas Hunt (1866-1945) American geneticist and biologist. He was awarded the 1933 Nobel prize for physiology or medicine for his research into chromosomes and heredity.

Moro, Aldo (1916-78) Italian Christian democrat statesman. He was prime minister (1963-68, 1974-76) and brought the Communist Party into close cooperation with his centre-left coalition shortly before his abduction and murder by the Red Brigade.

Morris, Desmond [John] (1928-) English zoologist. His studies of animal and human behaviour, *The Naked Ape* (1967) and *The Human Zoo* (1968) popularized versions of the theories of behaviourists such as LORENZ and TINBERGEN, were bestsellers in the late 1960s and 70s.

Morrison, Herbert Stanley, Baron Morrison of Lambeth (1888-1965) English Labour politician. He became home secretary (1940-45) in CHURCHILL's World War II cabinet and is credited with having written much of the manifesto that took Labour to power after the war when he became leader of the House of Commons (1945-51).

Jim Morrison (1943-71) American rock singer and songwriter. His band, The Doors, with sombre doom-laden songs such as "The End," became a huge cult after his death (from alcohol and drug abuse).

Morton, Jelly Roll [Ferdinand Joseph Lemott] (1885-1941) American jazz pianist, composer and bandleader. Regarded as one of the founders of New Orleans jazz, his band, the Red Hot Peppers, became one of the most popular jazz bands of the mid-20s, between the ragtime and swing eras.

Moseley, Henry Gwyn-Jeffries (1887-1915) English physicist. His research in radioactivity using X-rays led to the discovery of what he called the "atomic numbers" of the elements.

Mosley, Sir Oswald [Ernald] (1896-1980) English Fascist leader. First elected to Parliament as a Conservative (1918-22), he became an Independent (1922-24), then a Labour MP (1924, 1929-31), and finally founder and leader of the British Union of Fascists (1932-36). The thuggery and demagoguery of his movement failed to attract much support beyond hoodlums and newspaper tycoons, and he was interned during World War II.

Mossbauer, Rudolf Ludwig (1929-) German physicist. He shared the 1961 Nobel prize for physics with the American physicist **Robert Hofstadter** (1915-) for his discovery of the "Mossbauer effect," involving gamma radiation in crystals.

Mountbatten, Louis [Francis Victor Albert Nicholas], [1st Earl Mountbatten of Burma] (1900-79) British naval commander and statesman. The great-grandson of Queen Victoria and uncle of Prince PHILIP, he served with distinction in the Royal Navy during World War II, becoming Supreme Allied Commander in South-East Asia (1943-45). He was appointed viceroy of India (1947), and oversaw the transfer of power to the independent governments of India and Pakistan. Regarded as a strong influence on Prince CHARLES, he was murdered by an IRA bomb while sailing off Ireland.

Mugabe, Robert [Gabriel] (1924-) Zimbabwean statesman. He was imprisoned for ten years (1964-74) for his opposition to white rule in Rhodesia (as Zimbabwe then was), being released under Ian Smith's amnesty of 1974. He became leader of the Zimbabwe African National Union and became prime minister (1980-) following the end of white minority rule. A Roman Catholic and a Marxist, Mugabe merged his ruling party with the Zimbabwe African People's Union in 1988 to form a one-party state.

Mujibur Rahman, Sheik (1920-75) Bangladeshi politician. He became the first prime minister of Bangladesh (1972-75) following the bloody civil war and secession from Pakistan in 1972, and was subsequently elected president (1975). He assumed dictatorial powers and was assassinated during a military coup.

Muldoon, Sir Robert [David] (1921-) New Zealand statesman. He became National Party prime minister (1975-84), and has held several important international posts, notably with the International Monetary Fund and the World Bank.

Mulliken, Robert Sanderson (1896-1986) American chemist and physicist. He was awarded the 1986 Nobel prize for chemistry for his work on molecular structure and on chemical bonding.

Munch, Edvard (1863-1944) Norwegian painter. An Expressionist, his works, e.g. *The Scream*, are noted for their strong use of primary colours and emotions.

Munthe, Axel [Martin Frederik] (1857-1949) Swedish physicist and psychiatrist. His autobiographical book, *The Story of San Michele* (1929), describing his experiences while practising medicine, became a world bestseller.

Murdoch, [Keith] Rupert (1931-) Australian-born American newspaper tycoon. He inherited an Australian newspaper group from his father and subsequently expanded into Britain, where he turned the *Sun* into Britain's bestselling "sex and sleaze" tabloid. He later bought *The Times* and *The Sunday Times* and the publisher Collins, and established the satellite television network, Sky Television in 1989. The immense losses from the latter enterprise were alleviated by tapping into the reserves of other parts of his empire. His expansion into the US market from the late 1970s necessitated his acquisition of US citizenship in 1985.

Musgrave, Thea (1928-) Scottish composer. Her early works were often on Scottish themes, e.g. the chamber opera *The Abbott of Drimock* (1955). Later compositions, often in serial form, include choral works and concertos.

Mussolini, Benito [Amilcare Andrea] (1883-1945) Italian dictator. Originally a socialist, he founded his fascist "Blackshirt" party in 1919, and was elected to parliament in 1921, establishing himself as dictator ("Il Duce") in 1922 following a march on Rome. He formed the Axis with HITLER in 1937 and declared war on the Allies in 1940. He was deposed in 1943 and rescued by German paratroops, but was later executed by partisans.

Muzorewa, Bishop Abel *see* **Smith, Ian**.

Myrdal, [Karl] Gunnar (1898-1987) Swedish economist. He shared the 1974 Nobel prize for economics with HAYEK, largely for his work on the application of economic theory to the economies of the Third World.

Nabokov, Vladimir (1899-1977) Russian-born American novelist, who wrote in both Russian and English. His most famous novel is *Lolita* (1955), but *Pale Fire* (1962) better demonstrates his gift for narrative and sharp, ironic wit.

Nader, Ralph (1934-) American lawyer and consumer protectionist. His book, *Unsafe at Any Speed* (1965), which described the woeful standards of car construction, became a best-seller and resulted in government legislation on car safety regulations. Nader and his followers ("Nader's Raiders") publicized many such cases of consumer abuse in the late 1960s and 70s.

Nagy, Imre (1896-1958) Hungarian statesman. He fought with the Bolsheviks during the Russian civil war and held various ministerial posts in the postwar communist Hungarian government. He was appointed prime minister (1953-55), and was forced to resign after attempting to liberalize communist policies. He became premier again in 1956, and was replaced by KÁDÁR after the Soviet invasion of that year. Two years later, he was murdered by Russian troops. His body was reburied in Budapest in 1989, with full state honours.

Namier, Sir Lewis Bernstein (1888-1960) Polish-born British historian. A specialist in 18th-century history, his technique of analysing the minutiae of the period's characters, events and institutions was enthusiastically followed by his students, resulting in what was called the "Namier school" of history. His works include *The Structure of Politics at the Accession of George III* (1929).

Nansen, Fridtjof (1861-1930) Norwegian explorer, scientist and statesman. He traversed Greenland (1888-89) and almost reached the North Pole in 1895, achieving a record latitude. He subsequently organized oceanographic expeditions, and was appointed commissioner for refugees (1920-22) by the League of Nations. He was awarded the 1922 Nobel Peace Prize for his humanitarian work.

Nash, Paul (1889-1946) English painter. He was an official war artist in both World Wars. He began his career as a landscape painter and flirted briefly with surrealism in the late 1930s. His paintings, which often have a visionary and occasionally abstract quality, include *Battle of Britain* and *Totes Meer*.

Nasser, Gamal Abdel (1918-70) Egyptian soldier and statesman. He took a leading part in the coup that deposed **King Farouk** (1920-65) in 1952, and became prime minister in 1954. He became president (1956-70) and precipitated the Suez Crisis by nationalizing the Suez Canal (1956). The US refusal to endorse Britain and France's invasion of Egypt resulted in Nasser acquiring enormous prestige in the Third World. His rule was also marked by the construction of enormously wasteful civic projects, such as the construction of the Aswan Dam, and by two lost wars against Israel.

Navratilova, Martina (1956-) Czech-born American tennis player. Regarded as the leading female tennis player of her day, she defected to the US in 1975, becoming a citizen in 1981, and was world champion twice, 1980 and 1984.

Needham, Joseph (1900-) English biochemist and historian. His works include several studies of the philosophy of science, e.g. *The Sceptical Biologist* (1929), and a huge survey of Chinese science, *Science and Civilisation in China* (1954-84).

Nehru, Jawaharlal (1889-1964) Indian nationalist leader and statesman. The son of the nationalist lawyer, **Motilal Nehru** ("Pandit" Nehru) (1861-1931), he joined the Indian National Congress in 1919 and was imprisoned many times in the 1930s and 40s for his nationalist views. He became the first prime minister of India (1947-64) following independence and the partition of the subcontinent into India and Pakistan. His daughter Indira GANDHI became prime minister in 1966.

Neill, A[lexander] S[utherland] (1883-1973) Scottish educationalist. He established his school at Summerhill in 1927 in order to demonstrate the success of his progressive and anti-authoritarian educational ideas. He wrote many books, e.g. *A Dominie's Log* (1916) promoting his methods.

Nernst, Walther Hermann (1864-1941) German physical chemist. He was awarded the 1920 Nobel prize for chemistry for his proposal of the heat theorem, which was formulated as the third law of thermodynamics.

Neruda, Pablo [Ricardo Neftali Reyes] (1904-73) Chilean poet and diplomat, noted for his highly political verse and for highly personal, cryptic lyrics. He was awarded the Nobel prize for literature in 1971.

Nervi, Pier Luigi (1891-1949) Italian architect and engineer. An exponent of the virtues of reinforced concrete, his designs include the Pirelli skyscraper (1958) in Milan and San Francisco cathedral (1970).

Newman, Paul (1925-) American film actor. His films include

Hud (1963), *Cool Hand Luke* (1967), *Butch Cassidy and the Sundance Kid* (1969) and *The Color of Money* (1986), the last earning him an Oscar. A political activist of the moderate left, he has also raised considerable sums of money for charity through sales of his own-name salad dressing.

Nicholas II (1868-1918) Russian tsar (1895-1917). A weak ruler, alternating between bursts of liberalization and repression, his authority was seriously weakened by Russia's defeat in the war with Japan (1904-05). He was deposed by the Bolsheviks in 1917, who later murdered him and his German-born wife, **Feodorovna Alexandra** (1872-1918) and their children.

Nicholson, Ben (1894-1982) English painter. Influenced both by Cubism and Wyndham LEWIS's Vorticism in his early career, he became one of Britain's leading abstract artists in the 1950s, receiving many honours from home and abroad.

Nicholson, Jack (1937-) American film actor. One of CORMAN's many protégés, he made many films before becoming a star with *Easy Rider* (1969). His later, often manic performances include *One Flew Over the Cuckoo's Nest* (1975), for which he won an Oscar, and *The Shining* (1980). He also won an Oscar for *Terms of Endearment* (1983).

Nicklaus, Jack [William] (1940-) American golfer. One of the greatest golfers of all time, he won more major tournaments than any other player in history, including the British Open (1966, 1970, 1978) and the US Open (1967, 1972, 1980).

Niebuhr, Helmut Richard (1894-1962) American theologian. His highly influential works on Protestant theology, which call for a radical re-examination of the Christian's role in society, include *Radical Monotheism and Western Culture* (1960). His brother, **Reinhold Niebuhr** (1892-1971), was also a very influential Protestant theologian, whose works include *Moral Man and Immoral Society* (1932).

Nielsen, Carl [August] (1865-1931) Danish composer. The first prominent polytonal Danish composer, his works include six symphonies, two operas and concertos.

Niemeyer, Oscar (1907-) Brazilian architect. Influenced by LE CORBUSIER, he designed many extravagantly modernist public buildings in Brazil, notably for the new capital, Brasilia, which were hailed as triumphs of modern architecture and planning. Many of his buildings are now in a state of terminal decay, due to a typically 20th-century failure to match building material and design to climate and environment.

Niemöller, Martin (1892-1984) German Lutheran pastor. A submarine commander in World War I, he was ordained in 1924 and became an outspoken opponent of HITLER and Nazi ideology. He was imprisoned in concentration camps (1937-45), surviving the war despite an order from Hitler at its close for his execution. He became president of the World Council of Churches (1961-68) and a prominent pacifist.

Nijinsky, Vaslav (1890-1950) Russian ballet dancer and choreographer. He became a protégé of DIAGHILEV, and is regarded as one of the greatest ballet dancers of all time. He choreographed STRAVINSKY's *Rite of Spring* (1913).

Niven, David [James David Graham Nevins] (1910-83) Scottish film actor. He arrived in Hollywood in 1935, where he was classed as "Anglo-Saxon Type No. 2008." After a variety of small parts, he appeared with his close friend, Errol FLYNN, in *The Charge of the Light Brigade* (1936). He returned to Britain after war was declared, and gave distinguished service in the army. He returned to Hollywood after the war, where he re-established himself as the model urbane Englishman. He published two highly entertaining volumes of autobiography, *The Moon's a Balloon* (1971) and *Bring on the Empty Horses* (1975) and, oddly, was never honoured by any British government.

Nixon, Richard Milhous (1913-) American Republican politician. He very narrowly failed to defeat KENNEDY in the 1960 presidential election, and became the 37th president of the US in 1969. He became the first president to resign from office, in 1974, following the "Watergate" scandal (and was pardoned by Gerald FORD in 1974). A hate figure of the Left in the early 1970s, his reputation has since undergone considerable reassessment, with more stress being given to his ending of the Vietnam war and rapprochement with China, than to the sleazy aspects of his period in office.

Nkrumah, Kwame (1909-72) Ghanaian statesman. He became the first president of Ghana (1957-66) after independence. His rule became increasingly dictatorial and corrupt, and he was deposed while visiting China.

Nolan, Sir Sidney [Robert] (1917-) Australian painter. His paintings draw heavily upon Australian history and folklore, e.g. his series of works based on the figure of the bushranger Ned Kelly.

Novello, Ivor [Ivor Novello Davies] (1893-1951) Welsh songwriter, composer and actor. His songs include "Keep the Home Fires Burning," which was hugely popular with British soldiers during World War I, and "We'll Gather Lilacs." His musicals include *Careless Rapture* (1936) and *The Dancing Years* (1939).

Nuffield, William Richard Morris, 1st Viscount (1877-1963) English car manufacturer and philanthropist. He began his business as a bicycle repair man in the early 1890s, and began building cars in the early 20th century. The first Morris car came out in 1913, and he developed a Henry FORD-like system of mass production of cars, notably the Morris Oxford and the Morris Minor. He gave away a large part of his very large fortune to charitable foundations.

Nureyev, Rudolf (1939-) Russian ballet dancer and choreographer (he defected in 1961 and became an Austrian citizen in 1982). Regarded as the successor to NIJINSKY, he formed a partnership with FONTEYN at the Royal Ballet in London in 1962, and has performed throughout the world. He has also appeared in several films, notably KEN RUSSEL's camp *Valentino* (1977).

Nyerere, Julius [Kambarage] (*c*.1922-) Tanzanian statesman. He became president (1962-85) and negotiated the union of Tanganyika and Zanzibar (1964), which formed Tanzania. Widely regarded as Africa's leading statesman and notably austere in his personal life, he was brought up a Roman Catholic and became attracted to Marxism, which he combined with what he claimed were African values to produce his version of African socialism, which was based on the removal of around nine million peasants—by force—from their ancestral lands into collectives (*ujemaa*, "self-reliance," villages), where they were expected to produce food for the state. The project crashed. Nyerere gave up the presidency in 1985, but retained leadership of his party. His invasion of Uganda in 1978 brought AMIN's dictatorship to an end.

O

Obote, [Apollo] Milton (1924-) Ugandan politician. He became Uganda's first prime minister (1962-66) after independence, and became president (1966-71) after deposing King Mutesa II. Obote was in turn deposed by AMIN, and became president again (1980-85) after Amin's overthrow. He was deposed again in 1985, and was given political asylum in Zambia.

O'Brien, Conor Cruise (1917-) Irish statesman, critic, historian and dramatist. He was HAMMARSKJÖLD's UN representative in Katanga during the Congo crisis of 1961, about which he wrote the play *Murderous Angels* (1968). A strong opponent of the IRA, he has been described as the "ORWELL of the Right." His other works include a collection of political and literary essays, *Passion and Cunning* (1988).

O'Casey, Sean (1880-1964) Irish dramatist. His three early plays, *The Shadow of a Gunman* (1923), *Juno and the Paycock* (1924) and *The Plough and the Stars* (1926) reflect the patriotism that followed the Easter Rising of 1916. Later plays, e.g. *The Silver Tassie* (1928), were less controversial.

Ochoa, Severo *see* **Kornberg, Arthur**.

Odets, Clifford (1903-63) American dramatist. A committed socialist, his masterpiece is *Waiting for Lefty* (1935), a play about a taxi drivers' strike.

Oistrakh, David Feodorovitch (1908-74) Russian violinist. A widely admired virtuoso, he made several international tours in the 1950s and 60s. His son, **Igor Davidovitch Oistrakh** (1931-), has also acquired an international reputation as a violinist.

Oldenburg, Claes [Thure] (1929-) Swedish-born American sculptor. He became one of the leading pop art sculptors in the early 1960s, with his "giant objects," representations of food-stuffs such as hamburgers, and his "soft sculptures," e.g. the *Soft Typewriter*.

Olivier, Laurence [Kerr], [Baron Olivier of Brighton] (1907-89) English stage and film actor and director. Regarded as the leading British actor of the modern era, he played all the major Shakespeare roles and became an international film star with *Wuthering Heights* (1939) and *Rebecca* (1939). He produced, directed and starred in films of *Henry V* (1945) and *Hamlet* (1948), and in the 1950s showed his astonishing versatility in roles such as the fading music hall comedian Archie Rice in OSBORNE's *The Entertainer* (1957). He became director of the National Theatre (1962-73). His second wife (of three) was Vivien LEIGH.

O'Neill, Eugene [Gladstone] (1888-1953) American drama-tist. His early plays, e.g. *Beyond the Horizon* (1920) and *Desire Under the Elms* (1924) established him as one of America's finest dramatists. His greatest plays are *Mourning Becomes Electra* (1931), a tragedy based on Aeschylus's *Oresteia* trilogy, and *Long Day's Journey into Night* (1940-41), a study of family breakdown. He was awarded the Nobel prize for litera-ture in 1936.

Ono, Yoko *see* **Lennon, John.**

Oppenheimer, J[ulius] Robert (1904-67) American nuclear physicist. He directed the Los Alamos atom bomb project (1943-45). He resigned from the project after the dropping of the bombs on Hiroshima and Nagasaki, and argued for cooperation with the USSR on the control of nuclear weapons. Long regarded as a security risk for his left-wing sympathies, his security clearance was revoked after his refusal to work on the hydrogen bomb.

Orff, Carl (1895-1982) German composer. His best-known work is the popular *Carmina Burana* (1937), a "secular oratorio" based on medieval poems. His other works include the opera *Antigone* (1949).

Ortega, Daniel (1945-) Nicaraguan politician. One of the leaders of the Sandinista resistance movement that overthrew Somoza's dictatorship in 1979, he became president of Nicaragua (1985-90). A charismatic figure who pursued socialist policies, Ortega became a notable hate figure for the REAGAN administration, which gave backing to the right-wing "Contra" forces in their guerrilla war against the Sandinistas. Ortega was succeeded as president by Violetta Chamorro, whose centrist party won the 1989 election.

Ortega y Gasset, José (1883-1955) Spanish philosopher. His best-known work is *The Revolt of the Masses* (1929), which argued that democracy in the modern era could easily lead to tyrannies of either the left or right. An opponent of FRANCO, he left Spain when Franco came to power, returning in 1946.

Orwell, George [Eric Arthur Blair] (1903-50) Indian-born English novelist and essayist. An upper-middle class socialist, his first published work was Down and Out in Paris and London (1933), a description of his often gruesome experiences as a tramp. His other great nonfiction works are *The Road to Wigan Pier* (1937), a study of poverty in northern England, and *Homage to Catalonia* (1939), an account of his experiences with the Republican forces in the Spanish Civil War. His two greatest novels have become classics: *Animal Farm* (1945), a grim allegory of the history of the Soviet Union, and *Nineteen Eighty-Four* (1949), an even grimmer picture of a totalitarian world.

Osborne, John (1929-) English dramatist. His first play, *Look Back in Anger* (1956), gave its name to the "Angry Young Men," a group of young playwrights who replaced the drawing-room comedies of 1950s British theatre with realistic dramas of working-class life. The best known of his later plays are *The Entertainer* (1957), depicting Osborne's view of post-Imperial Britain, and *Luther* (1961), a psychological study of Martin Luther.

Oswald, Lee Harvey (1939-63) American alleged assassin of President KENNEDY. He was arrested shortly after Kennedy's murder in Dallas in 1963, and was himself shot dead before he could come to trial by **Jack Ruby** (1911-64), a shady nightclub owner. Oswald repeatedly denied killing Kennedy, whose assassination has spawned many conspiracy theories, the likeliest of which seems to be that an unholy alliance of US Intelligence agents and right-wing Cubans used Oswald as a scapegoat.

Owen, David [Anthony Llewellyn] (1938-) English politician. Trained as a doctor, he was a Labour MP from 1966, becoming foreign secretary (1977-79) in CALLAGHAN's cabinet. He resigned from the Labour Party in 1981 to found the Social Democratic Party with JENKINS and others. He refused to accept the merger of the SDP with the Liberal Party in 1987, but dissolved the SDP in 1990 and announced his own intention of quitting politics in 1991.

Owens, Jesse [James Cleveland Owens] (1913-80) American athlete. One of the finest athletes of his generation, he won four gold medals (for the 100 metres, 200 metres, long jump and 4 x 100 metres relay) in the dramatic setting of the 1936 Berlin Olympics. The great public annoyance this gave HITLER, who was visibly upset on film at this black man defeating his "Aryan" supermen, was much enjoyed worldwide.

P

Padarewski, Ignacy Jan (1860-1941) Polish pianist, composer and statesman. Widely regarded as the greatest pianist of his day, he served as prime minister for ten months in 1919. He became president of the Polish government in exile in 1940.

Pahlavi, Mohammed Reza (1919-80) shah of Iran. He succeeded his father in 1941 and gradually established a dictatorship, funded by oil wealth and guarded by his increasingly brutal "Savak" secret police. He introduced some social reforms, notably with regard to women's position in society, but was forced to flee his country in 1979 as the fundamentalists led by KHOMEINI undermined his rule. He died in Egypt.

Paisley, Ian [Richard Kyle] (1926-) Northern Ireland Protestant clergyman and Unionist politician. He formed his Free Presbyterian Church in 1951, and was elected to parliament for North Antrim in 1970. A highly vocal opponent of Irish nationalism and Roman Catholicism, he is nonetheless regarded as a fair and impartial constituency MP.

Pankhurst, Emmeline (1858-1928) English suffragette and feminist. She and her daughter **Dame Christabel Harriette Pankhurst** (1880-1958) founded the Women's Social and Political Union in 1903, a campaigning organization for women's suffrage. With other suffragettes, Emmeline was frequently imprisoned then released under the "Cat and Mouse" act, a government device to avoid the publicity gained by the suffragette hunger strikes. She abandoned her campaign on the outbreak of World War I, and joined the Conservative Party in 1926. Her daughter **Sylvia Pankhurst** (1882-1960) was also a suffragette as well as a pacifist.

Papandreou, Andreas George (1919-   ) Greek socialist politician. He lived in exile during the military dictatorship, returning to Greece in 1974. He became Greece's first socialist prime minister (1981-89), the last years of his administration being clouded by his public affair with a much younger woman and financial scandals.

Pareto, Vilfredo (1848-1923) Italian economist and sociologist. A highly influential economist, his work is regarded as anticipatory of both Fascist and modern welfare economics. His best-known work is *Mind and Society* (1916).

Parker, Charlie *or* **Bird** [Charles Christopher Parker] (1920-55) American jazz alto saxophonist. He became the leading exponent of "bop" jazz in the 1940s, and worked closely with Dizzy GILLESPIE. His life ended prematurely through drug and alcohol abuse.

Parker, Dorothy [Rothschild] (1893-1967) American journalist, poet and short-story writer, noted for her dry wit and sharply ironic epigrams and satires, many of which were first published in *New Yorker* magazine.

Parsons, Talcott (1902-79) American sociologist. His writings formed the basis for the functionalist school of sociology. His works include *The Structure of Social Action* (1937) and *Social Structure and Personality* (1964).

Pasolini, Pier Paolo (1922-75) Italian film director, poet, novelist and critic. His films include *The Gospel According to*

St Matthew (1964), a plain and much praised film version of the Gospel using amateur actors, and the bleakly decadent *Saló or the 120 Days of Sodom* (1975), the latter being described by one critic as a "terminal film in every sense." A Marxist in politics, he was an ardent consumer of casual homosexual sex, his last pick-up resulting in his murder.

Pasternak, Boris [Leonidovich] (1890-1960) Russian poet and novelist. A highly original and passionate lyric poet, his position under a regime that demanded safe verse praising its achievements forced him to turn to translation for a living; his translations of Shakespeare's plays are still highly valued. His great novel *Dr Zhivago* was first published in Italy in 1958. He was awarded the Nobel prize for literature but was forced to decline it by the Soviet authorities.

Patton, George S[mith] (1885-1945) American general, nicknamed "Old Blood and Guts." A brilliant tank commander, he used his armoured divisions in the cavalry tradition, cutting enemy lines with great speed and daring. In World War II he commanded the Allied invasion of North Africa (1942-43), captured Sicily and Palermo (1943) and led the 3rd US army across France and Germany to the Czech border (1944-45). The film *Patton* (1970) gives a fair picture of the man.

Paul VI [Giovanni Battista Montini] (1897-1978) Italian pope. He was elected pope (1963-78) in succession to JOHN XXIII, and continued the trend towards reforms instituted by his predecessor and the Second Vatican Council. His encyclical *Humanae Vitae* (1968), however, reaffirmed the total opposition of the Church towards abortion and "artificial" methods of contraception.

Pauli, Wolfgang (1900-58) Austrian-born American physicist. He was awarded the 1945 Nobel prize for physics for his discovery of the "exclusion principle" in 1924, and postulated the existence of the neutrino (later established by FERMI).

Pauling, Linus Carl (1901-) American chemist. He was awarded the 1954 Nobel prize for physics for his research into chemical bonding and molecular structure, and the 1962 Nobel Peace Prize for his criticisms of nuclear testing and deterrence. He has published widely in many scientific fields. His book *Vitamin C and the Common Cold* (1970) recommends large daily doses of Vitamin C to build protection against colds.

Pavarotti, Luciano (1935-) Italian tenor. Regarded as one of the most powerful tenor singers of the modern era, and probably the heaviest, he became a leading opera singer and very popular concert performer in the late 1960s. His recording of "Nessun Dorma," from PUCCINI's opera *Turandot*, became a massive hit after being used as the theme for the 1990 World Cup broadcasts.

Pavlov, Ivan Petrovich (1849-1936) Russian physiologist. He was awarded the 1904 Nobel prize for physiology or medicine for his work on the physiology of digestion, and conducted experiments on the conditioning of reflexes, e.g. his conditioning of dogs to salivate in response to metronomes.

Pavlova, Anna (1882-1931) Russian ballerina. FOKINE choreographed *The Dying Swan* for her. She also worked with DIAGHILEV, and became one of the most famous ballerinas in the world.

Pears, Sir Peter (1910-86) English tenor. He formed a lifelong personal and professional partnership with Benjamin BRITTEN, whose tenor opera roles, e.g. *Peter Grimes* (1945), were written for Pears, as were several song cycles. He co-founded the Aldeburgh Festival (1948) with Britten.

Pearse, Patrick *or* **Padraic [Henry]** (1879-1916) Irish revolutionary. A prominent spokesman for the Gaelic cultural revival, he joined the Irish Revolutionary Brotherhood in 1915 and was executed for his part in the 1916 Easter Rising.

Pearson, Lester B[owles] (1897-1972) Canadian Liberal statesman. He became prime minister (1963-68) and was awarded the 1957 Nobel Peace Prize for his role as mediator during the Suez Crisis.

Peary, Robert Edwin (1856-1920) American naval commander and Arctic explorer. He is credited with being the first man to reach the North Pole (1909).

Peierls, Sir Rudolf Ernst (1907-) German-born British physicist. With Otto FRISCH, he demonstrated the feasibility of an atom bomb during World War II. He joined the Los Alamos project in 1943.

Pelé [Edson Arantes do Nascimento] (1940-) Brazilian footballer. An inside forward, he is universally recognized as one of the most skilful and entertaining soccer players of all time. He scored over a thousand goals in his professional career.

Perón, Juan Domingo (1895-1974) Argentinian dictator. Influenced by MUSSOLINI and (to a lesser extent) HITLER, Perón became president (1946-55) through a shrewd mixture of social reform and demagogic appeals to the poor. He was deposed by the army in 1955, and lived in exile in Spain, and was re-elected president (1973-74) on his return. His success was based to a large extent on his first wife, **Eva Perón** (1919-52), an ex-actress nicknamed "Evita," who was an even more skilful player of the populist card and is still venerated in Argentina. His second wife, **Isabel Perón** (1931-), a dancer, was vice-president to her husband (1973-74) and president (1974-76) until ousted by a military coup.

Perry, Fred[erick John] (1909-) English-born American tennis and table-tennis player. He became the world champion table-tennis player in 1929, and became one of the most successful lawn tennis players of the 1930s, winning every major tournament.

Perutz, Max Ferdinand *see* **Kendrew, Sir John Cowdery**.

Pétain, Henri Philippe Omer (1856-1951) French soldier and statesman. He was appointed marshal of France in 1918 in recognition of his generalship during World War I, particularly his stubborn defence ("They Shall Not Pass") of Verdun (1916). He became head of the collaborationist Vichy government (1940-44) and was sentenced to death for treason at the end of World War II (later commuted to life imprisonment).

Peterson, Oscar [Emmanuel] (1925-) Canadian jazz pianist and composer. A virtuoso pianist in the mode of his friend Art TATUM, his Oscar Peterson Trio became one of the best-known small jazz groups of the 1950s.

Petit, Roland (1924-) French dancer and choreographer. His innovative work, blending realism with exuberant fantasy, has been highly influential on contemporary dance. His works include a *Carmen* (1949) and dance sequences in several US films, e.g. *Daddy Longlegs* (1955, starring Fred ASTAIRE).

Philby, Kim [Harold Adrian Russell Philby] (1911-88) English journalist and secret-service double agent. The most prominent of the Cambridge School of Treason, he became a Soviet agent in 1933. He was recruited to the British Secret Service in 1940, and became head of anti-communist espionage (1944-46). He fled to the USSR in 1963 and published *My Silent War* in 1968.

Philip, Prince, [Duke of Edinburgh] (1921-   ) Greek-born British naval officer and prince consort. The nephew of MOUNT-BATTEN, he married the then Princes ELIZABETH in 1947.

Piaf, Edith [Edith Giovanna Gassion] (1915-63) French singer and songwriter. Nicknamed "Little Sparrow" for her small size and frail appearance, her songs, nostalgic and romantic, include the well-known "Non, je ne regrette rien." She died of drug and alcohol abuse.

Piaget, Jean (1896-1980) Swiss psychologist. His studies of children's intelligence and perception, notably his research on cognitive functions and development, were highly influential on modern educationalists. His works include *The Child's Conception of the World* (1926).

Picasso, Pablo (1881-1973) Spanish painter and sculptor. Regarded as the most influential artist of the modern era, he moved to Paris in 1901, where, with BRAQUE, he was the founder of Cubism. His "blue period" (1901-04) works include *The Blue Room* (1901); Cubist works include *Les Demoiselles d'Avignon* (1906-07). He designed costumes and scenery for DIAGHILEV from 1917, exhibited with the surrealists in the mid-1920s, and created his strongest and perhaps best-known image *Guernica* (1937) in response to the fascist bombing of that Basque town during the Spanish Civil War.

Pickford, Mary [Gladys Mary Smith] (1893-1979) Canadian-born American film star. She was dubbed "The World's Sweetheart" after the enormous success of such silent films as *Rebecca of Sunnybrook Farm* (1917), and co-founded the United Artists film studio (1919) with Charlie CHAPLIN and D. W. GRIFFITH. Her second husband (1920-35) was Douglas FAIRBANKS.

Piggott, Lester [Keith] (1935-) English jockey. Regarded as one of the finest flat-racing jockeys of modern times, he won the Derby nine times. He was jailed (1987-8) for tax evasion.

Pilsudski, Józef Klemens (1867-1935) Polish soldier and statesman. He became provisional president (1918-21) and, as marshal of Poland (1919-21), held the Bolshevik army's advance into Polish territory in 1920. He became prime minister (1926-28, 1930).

Pinochet [Ugarte], Augusto (1915-) Chilean general and dictator. He led the 1973 coup that deposed ALLENDE and became president (1974-90). He ruthlessly suppressed dissent and instituted monetarist economic polities. In 1988, he asked for a public mandate in a pebiscite and was firmly defeated. Pinochet retired from the presidency in 1990, while retaining his military command.

Pinter, Harold (1930-) English dramatist, known for his halting, menacing dialogue and sinister pauses in such plays as *The Birthday Party* (1958) and *The Caretaker* (1960). He has also written several screenplays.

Piper, John (1903-) English artist. His works include a highly acclaimed series of paintings of war-damaged buildings during his period as an official war artist during World War II and the designs for Coventry Cathedral's stained glass. His books include *British Romantic Artists* (1942) and *Buildings and Prospects* (1949).

Pirandello, Luigi (1867-1936) Italian dramatist and novelist. His two best-known plays are *Six Characters in Search of an Author* (1921) and *Henry IV* (1922), both of which question theatrical conventions. He was awarded the Nobel prize for literature in 1934.

Pius XII [Eugenio Pacelli] (1876-1958) Italian pope. He preserved the neutrality of the Church during World War II, in which he maintained diplomatic relations with both Axis and Allies. He pursued a strong anti-communist policy after the war.

Planck, Max [Karl Ernst Ludwig] (1858-1947) German physicist. He formulated the quantum theory and was awarded the 1918 Nobel prize for physics.

Plath, Sylvia (1932-63) American poet and novelist. She published only two books in her lifetime: *Colossus* (1960), a collection of poems, and a semi-autobiographical novel, *The Bell Jar*. She was married to Ted HUGHES, and committed suicide.

Pollock, [Paul] Jackson (1912-56) American painter. He became the leading exponent of action painting, a development of Abstract Expressionism, in the late 1940s. Pollock's action paintings consisted of pinned-down canvases covered in paint randomly scattered all over them.

Pol Pot *or* **Saloth Sar** [Kompong Thom] (1929-) Cambodian Communist politician. He led the Communist Khmer Rouge forces that overthrew the Cambodian government in 1976, after which he became prime minister. His pro-Chinese government then instituted a fearful MAOist dictatorship, which cost the lives of up to three million people. The Khmer Rouge regime was overthrown by the Russian-backed Vietnamese invasion of 1979, but subsequently fought a guerrilla campaign against the Vietnamese puppet regime, with some success. Most governments in the world gave reluctant recognition to the Khmer Rouge as the legitimate government of Cambodia. Pol Pot's official "retirement" in 1985 is generally regarded as an attempt at sanitizing the Khmer Rouge image.

Pompidou, Georges [Jean Raymond] (1911-74) French statesman. He joined DE GAULLE's staff in 1944 and became Gaullist prime minister (1962-68). He was dismissed in 1968 by De Gaulle following the May student riots in Paris. After De Gaulle resigned, Pompidou was elected president (1969-74).

Popper, Sir Karl [Raimund] (1902-) Austrian-born British philosopher. His book *The Logic of Scientific Discovery* (1934) proposed "falsifiability" as the criterion by which to judge whether or not a particular proposition can be said to be scientific or not, and described psychoanalysis and Marxism as examples of non-falsifiable "pseudosciences." His books, *The Open Society and its Enemies* (1945) and *The Poverty of Historicism* (1957), examine the totalitarian implications of political thought from Plato to Marx.

Porter, Cole [Albert] (1891-1964) American songwriter and composer. His highly popular songs, much admired for their wit and lyricism, include "Let's Do It," "Begin the Beguine" and "Night and Day."

Poulenc, Francis (1899-1963) French composer. A member of Les Six, he is particularly noted for his his settings of verses from poets such as Apollinaire (*see* DELAUNAY). Other works include chamber music and sacred choral pieces.

Pound, Ezra [Weston Loomis] (1885-1972) American poet and critic. Notable poetry volumes include *Quia Pauper Amaris* (1919) and the unfinished *Cantos* (1925-70). A generous supporter of younger writers, e.g. T. S. ELIOT, HEMINGWAY, he lived in Italy from 1925 and broadcast propaganda against the Allies during World War II. He was committed to a US mental asylum after the war until 1958, when he returned to Italy.

Powell, [John] Enoch (1912-) English Conservative politician. A professor of Greek at Sydney University when he was 25, he rose from private to brigadier in the course of World War II and was elected to parliament in 1950. An outspoken opponent of immigration into Britain and of the Common Market, he refused to stand for the Conservatives in 1974, advising his supporters to vote Labour, a gesture which some observers credit with giving Labour victory. He was an Ulster Unionist MP (1974-87).

Powell, Michael (1905-80) English film producer and director. With the screenwriter **Emeric Pressburger** (1902-88), he made several films that have subsequently been hailed as important works, e.g. *The Life and Death of Colonel Blimp* (1943), *I Know Where I'm Going* (1945) and *The Red Shoes* (1948).

Presley, Elvis [Aaron] (1935-77) American rock singer. He became one of the most popular (and controversial) singers in the world in the mid-1950s, with his interpretation of songs such as "Blue Suede Shoes" and "Hound Dog." Condemned by some for the blatant sexual charge in his performances, he became universally recognized as a great popular singer, and an outstanding interpreter of ballads. He died of drug and alcohol abuse, compounded by obesity. He starred in the critically acclaimed western *Flaming Star* (1960).

Pressburger, Emeric *see* **Powell, Michael.**

Priestley, J[ohn] B[oynton] (1894-1984) English novelist and dramatist. His huge output includes the novel *The Good Companions* (1929) and the plays, *Time and the Conways* (1937) and *An Inspector Calls* (1947). During World War II he made morale-raising broadcasts, which made him one of the best-known literary figures of the time.

Profumo, John Dennis (1915-) English Conservative politician. He was an MP (1940-63) and secretary of state for war (1960-63), but resigned after admitting misleading the House of Commons about his affair with **Christine Keeler** (1942-), who was also sexually involved with a Russian diplomat. He became involved with charitable work, for which he was awarded a CBE (1976)

Prokofiev, Sergei Sergeyevich (1891-1953) Russian composer and pianist. He left Russia in 1918 and returned in 1936 (he died on the same day as STALIN). His works include seven symphonies, the ballets *Romeo and Juliet* (1935) and *Cinderella* (1944), piano and violin concertos, and the well-known orchestral "fairy tale," *Peter and the Wolf* (1936).

Puccini, Giacomo (1858-1924) Italian composer. His operas, e.g. *La Bohème* (1896), *Tosca* (1900) and *Madam Butterfly* (1904), are regarded as the last great lyrical and dramatic works in the tradition of Italian opera.

Qaddafi, Moammar al- *see* **Gaddafi, Moammar al-**.

Quant, Mary (1934-) English fashion designer. Her most famous design was the miniskirt, which became the symbol of "swinging sixties" London.

Quayle, Sir [John] Anthony (1913-89) English actor and director. He worked with the Shakespeare Memorial Theatre (1948-56, now the Royal Shakespeare Company), helping to establish its international standing. He appeared in several films, e.g. *Woman in a Dressing Gown* (1957) and *The Guns of Navarone*(1961), but was principally a stage actor, founding his own classical touring company, Compass (1982).

Quale, [J.] Dan[forth] (1947-) American Republican politician. Elected a congressman for Indiana (1977) and senator (1981), BUSH selected him as his presidential running mate (1988) and he was elected vice-president of the US (1989).

Quine, Willard van Orman (1908-) American philosopher and logician. Noted for his criticisms of empiricism, his works include *Set Theory and its Logic* (1963) and *Word and Object* (1961).

Quisling, Vidkun (1887-1945) Norwegian fascist leader. He was installed as prime minister (1942-45) by the Nazis, and was executed for treason after the war. His name is now used to define any person who aids an occupying power to establish its rule.

R

Rachmaninov, Sergei (1873-1943) Russian composer and pianist. Influenced by Tchaikovsky, his music was very much in the 19th-century romantic tradition. His works include three symphonies, four piano concertos, the *Rhapsody on a Theme by Paganini* (1934) and many songs.

Radhakrishnan, Sir Sarvepalli (1888-1975) Indian philosopher and statesman. His works, which stress the similarities between Western and Hindu culture, include *The Hindu View of Life* (1926) and *An Idealist View of Life* (1932).

Raman, Sir Chandrasekhara Venkata (1888-1970) Indian physicist. He was awarded the 1930 Nobel prize for physics for his discovery of the Raman effect during his researches into the diffusion of light.

Ramanujan, Srinivasa (1887-1920) Indian mathematician. A self-taught prodigy with considerable intuitive powers, he sent a large number of theorems to Godfrey HARDY, who arranged for him to study at Cambridge University. He became the first Indian to be elected a Fellow of the Royal Society (1919).

Rambert, Dame Marie [Cyvia Rambam] (1888-1982) Polish-born British ballet dancer, teacher and producer. After working with DIAGHILEV and NIJINSKY, she settled in Britain in 1917. She formed the Ballet Club in 1931, which, renamed the Ballet Rambert in 1935, became the most influential ballet company in Britain.

Ramphal, Sir Shridath Surrendranath, "Sonny" (1928-) Guyanan statesman. As secretary-general of the Commonwealth (1975-89), he took an active and influential role in world affairs.

Ramsey, Sir Alf[red] (1922-) English footballer and manager of the England national team that won the World Cup in 1966.

Ranjitsinhji [Vibhaji], Prince [Kumar Shri] (1872-1933) Indian maharajah and cricketer, nicknamed the "Black Prince" of cricket, he batted for Sussex (with C. B. FRY) and England. After service in World War I commanding Indian troops, he became maharajah of Nawanagar in 1918, and was noted for his progressive rule.

Rasputin, Grigori Yefimovich (1871-1916) Russian monk. Notably licentious when young, he became a monk and, claiming to have healing powers, became a cult figure among the Russian aristocracy, and a member of the royal household in 1907. He achieved considerable influence over the Tsarina Alexandra (*see* NICHOLAS II), and was assassinated in 1916.

Rattigan, Sir Terence [Mervyn] (1911-77) English dramatist. Many of his plays, e.g. the melodramas of middle-class hypocrisy and crisis, *The Browning Version* (1948) and *The Deep Blue Sea* (1952) have become firm favourites. He also wrote *Ross* (1960), a psychological study of T. E. LAWRENCE.

Ravel, [Joseph] Maurice (1875-1937) French composer. Influenced by FAURÉ and DEBUSSY, he became one of the leading impressionist composers of his time. His works include the overture *Schéhérazade* (1899), the small orchestral piece *Bolero* (1928) and several works for piano and for the ballet.

Ravi Shankar (1920-) Indian sitar player and composer. Regarded as one of India's greatest modern musicians, he became world-famous after teaching George HARRISON to play the sitar in the 1970s, and made several very popular international tours. Another pupil was Philip GLASS. He wrote and performed the music scores for Satyajit RAY's Apu trilogy of films.

Ray, Man (1890-1976) American photographer and painter. A founder (with DUCHAMP) of New York Dadaism, he moved to Paris in 1921 where he became a leading exponent of surrealist photography.

Ray, Satyajit (1921-92) Indian film director. His films, popular in art houses the world over, include the Apu trilogy of life in rural India, i.e. *Pather Panchali* (1955), *Aparajito* (1956) and *Apu Sansar* (1959), and *The Chess Players* (1977).

Reagan, Ronald [Wilson] (1911-) American film actor, Republican statesman and 40th president of the US (1980-89). He appeared in around fifty films, including *Bedtime for Bonzo* (1951), which co-starred a chimpanzee, and (his last) the fine thriller *The Killers* (1964). He was president of the Screen Actors Guild (1947-52, 1959-60). His second wife, the actress **Nancy Davis** (1923-), whom he married in 1952, is often credited with transforming the liberal trade unionist into a conservative. Reagan became governor of California in 1967, and defeated CARTER in the 1980 presidential election. He pursued strong monetarist deflationary economic policies, revoked as much liberal social legislation as he could, and adopted a doctrinaire anti-communist foreign policy, which reached its limits in his crusade against Nicaragua's Sandinista government.

Redgrave, Sir Michael [Scudamore] (1908-85) English stage and film actor. One of the finest actors of his generation, with a distinctively intellectual approach to his craft, his stage roles included *Hamlet* (1949-50) and *Uncle Vanya* (1963). His films include *The Lady Vanishes* (1938), *The Browning Version* (1951) and *The Go-Between* (1971). His daughter, **Vanessa Redgrave** (1937-), became a highly successful stage and film actress, winning an Oscar for *Julia* (1977). She is also noted for her political activism and was a leading campaigner for the Workers' Revolutionary Party.

Reed, Sir Carol (1906-76) English film director. His films include *The Third Man* (1949), written by Graham GREENE and starring Orson WELLES, a bleak thriller set in postwar Vienna that is one of the most highly praised films ever made. Other films include the spy comedy (from a Greene novel) *Our Man in Havana* (1959).

Reinhardt, Django [Jean Baptiste Reinhardt] (1910-53) Belgian guitarist. A French-speaking gipsy, he formed the Quintette de Hot Club de Paris with GRAPPELLI, which became the most highly regarded jazz group in Europe.

Reith, John Charles Walsham, [1st Baron Reith of Stonehaven] (1889-1971) Scottish engineer, who was appointed first manager of the British Broadcasting Company (later Corporation) in 1922. Renowned for his high moral purpose, and criticized by some for his autocracy, he did much to shape the BBC into an institution of great influence. The annual BBC Reith Lecture was instituted in 1947 in his honour.

Renoir, Jean (1894-1979) French film director. The son of the impressionist painter **Pierre Auguste Renoir** (1841-1919), his films, often described as "humanist" for their compassion and sense of humanity's unity, include two classics of the cinema, *La Grande Illusion* (1937) and *La Régle du jeu* (1939).

He fled the German occupation of France to the US in 1941, where he became a naturalized American.

Resnais, Alain (1922-) French film director. One of the best known of the French "New Wave" directors, his films include the romance *Hiroshima mon amour* (1959) and the experimental, 'surrealist' *Last Year in Marienbad* (1961), the latter attracting praise and derision in about equal amounts.

Reynolds, Albert (1933-) Irish politician. Elected in 1977 as a Fianna Fáil member, he held several posts under HAUGHEY but was sacked by him (1991). He eventually succeeded as Taoiseach (1992) and was faced almost immediately by a constitutional crisis concerning abortion.

Rhine, Joseph Banks (1895-1980) American psychologist. He founded parapsychology, the study of ESP and related mental phenomena, such as telekinesis. His claim that his experiments in thought transference produced results better than could have been obtained by chance, has not been accepted by scientists. His works include *New Frontiers of the Mind* (1937).

Ribbentrop, Joachim von (1893-1946) German Nazi diplomat. He served HITLER as foreign minister (1938-45), signing the German-Soviet treaty with MOLOTOV, and was convicted and hanged for war crimes at Nuremberg.

Rice, Tim *see* **Lloyd Webber, Andrew**.

Richard, Cliff [Harry Roger Webb] (1940-) Indian-born English pop singer and film actor. His first hit record, with his backing group the Drifters (renamed the Shadows) was "Move It" in 1958, since when he has become an institution in British popular music. His films include the musicals *The Young Ones* (1961) and *Summer Holiday* (1962), and the satirical *Expresso Bongo* (1959).

Richard, Keith *see* **Jagger, Mick**.

Richards, Sir Gordon (1904-) English jockey. He rode 4,870 winners and was champion jockey 26 times. He won 14 Classic races (the Derby once).

Richards, Viv (1952-) Antiguan-born West Indian cricketer. He was captain of the West Indies (1985-91), and was regarded as one of the best batsmen and fielders in modern cricket. He retired in 1991.

Richardson, Sir Ralph [David] (1902-83) English stage and film actor. Ranked with GIELGUD and OLIVIER as among the finest British actors of the 20th century, Richardson became a leading actor in the 1930s, equally at home with the classics and modern roles. Notable film roles include Buckingham in Olivier's film of *Richard III* (1955), the head of the secret service in *Our Man in Havana* (1960) and God in *Time Bandits* (1981). (The critic Kenneth TYNAN had long before observed that Richardson was the actor best suited to play God.)

Richthofen, Manfred, Baron von (1882-1918) German fighter pilot, nicknamed the "Red Baron." He commanded the 11th Chasing Squadron ("Richthofen's Flying Circus") in World War I, and was credited with shooting down 80 allied aircraft. He was killed in action, probably by ground fire.

Rilke, Rainer Maria (1875-1926) Prague-born Austrian poet. His lyrical, mystical poems, in e.g. *Duino Elegies* (1922) and *Sonnets to Orpheus* (1923), are regarded as amongst the finest religious verse of the 20th century.

Rivera, Diego (1886-1957) Mexican painter. He is especially noted for his murals, which combine traditional Mexican and Indian themes with Marxist-Leninist didacticism. His mural for the Rockefeller Center (later replicated in Mexico) was destroyed because it included a portrait of LENIN.

Robeson, Paul [Le Roy] (1898-1976) American bass singer and actor. He qualified as a lawyer before becoming a highly popular stage actor in the 1920s. Notable performances include *Showboat* (1927) and *Othello* (1940). His warm, sensitive recordings of spirituals and folk songs were also very popular. A noted advocate of civil rights for blacks, he came under strident attack in the US for supposed Communist sympathies and spent much of his life from the early 1960s in seclusion.

Robinson, Joan Violet (1903-83) English economist. She became one of the leading theorists of the "Cambridge School" of economists, and developed, following KEYNES, macroeconomic theories of growth and distribution. Her works include *Introduction to Modern Economics* (1973).

Robinson, John [Arthur Thomas] (1919-83) English Anglican prelate and theologian. His best-selling book, *Honest to God* (1963), inspired by the thinking of (predominantly German) theologians, created much public controversy with its portrayal of God as an inner presence rather than an external "father in the sky."

Robinson, Mary (1944-) Irish barrister, politician and president (1990-) of the Republic of Ireland. Notably liberal in her policies, she won wide support from parties opposed to her conservative Fianna Fáil opponent.

Robinson, Sir Robert (1886-1975) English chemist. He was awarded the 1947 Nobel prize for chemistry for his work on plant extracts. He also made significant contributions to the study of plant pigments.

Robinson, Sugar Ray [Walker Smith] (1920-89) American boxer. A highly skilled boxer, he was world welterweight champion (1946-51) and world middleweight champion five times from 1951 to 1960.

Robson, Dame Flora (1902-84) English stage and film actress. She was especially noted for her historical roles, e.g. as

Queen Elizabeth in the highly patriotic film *Fire over England* (1937).

Rodgers, Richard [Charles] (1902-79) American composer. With the librettist Lorenz HART, he created musicals such as *The Boys from Syracuse* (1938) and *Pal Joey* (1940). After Hart died, Rodgers collaborated with HAMMERSTEIN on several more successful musicals, e.g. *Oklahoma* (1943) and *The Sound of Music* (1959).

Rogers, Ginger *see* **Astaire, Fred**.

Rogers, Richard (1933-) Italian-born English architect. His designs include the Lloyds building (1979) in London, a steel and glass confection that typifies the controversial nature of his frontiersmanship approach to architectural technology.

Rogers, Will[iam Penn Adair] (1879-1935) American humorist and actor, nicknamed the "cowboy philosopher." A highly skilled rodeo performer, he came to exemplify, for many Americans, the common man in rhetorical arms against injustice and governmental stupidity. He appeared in several John FORD movies, most notably *Judge Priest* (1934).

Rolls, Charles Stewart (1877-1910) English motor car manufacturer and aviator. He joined Henry ROYCE in car manufacture in 1906, and made the first nonstop double flight across the English Channel in 1910, shortly before his death in a plane crash.

Romero y Galdames, Oscar Arnulfo (1917-80) Salvadorean Roman Catholic prelate. Appointed archbishop in 1977 he was a conservative both in theology and politics, and became an outspoken opponent of the murderous campaigns of the El Salvador government's semi-official death squads, for which he was assassinated.

Rommel, Erwin (1891-1944) German soldier. After distinguished service in World War I, he became a Nazi supporter in the 1920s. During World War II, he commanded the Afrika Korps in North Africa, earning the nickname the "Desert Fox" for his brilliant tactics, but was defeated at El Alamein by MONTGOMERY's troops. He committed suicide after the discovery of his complicity in the July assassination attempt on HITLER (*see* STAUFFENBERG).

Roosevelt, Franklin D[elano] (1882-1945) American Democratic statesman. He became 32nd president of the US (1933-45) after defeating HOOVER in 1933, and, in order to deal with the crisis of economic collapse, instituted far-reaching "New Deal" reforms in US society, e.g. his massive Public Works Administration programme of public spending and establishment of basic social security measures. He was a popular and highly effective leader during World War II, dying shortly after the Yalta summit meeting with CHURCHILL and STALIN. His wife, **[Anna] Eleanor Roosevelt** (1884-1962), was an active and popular First Lady, supporting her husband during his illness with polio and writing several books, e.g. *It's Up to the Women* (1933) and *The Moral Basis of Democracy* (1940). After his death she worked with the UN as US representative to the General Assembly (1946-52) and as chairman of the Human Rights Commission (1947-51).

Roosevelt, Theodore (1858-1919) American Republican statesman. A notably bellicose figure who organized a corps of irregular soldiers, dubbed "Roosevelt's Rough Riders," during the Spanish-American War (1898), he became 26th president of the US (1901-09) after President McKinley's assassination. He legislated against big business monopolies, intervened forcefully during the Panama civil war to protect the construction of the Panama Canal, and won the 1906 Nobel Peace Prize for mediating the end of the Russo-Japanese war. He split the Republican presidential vote in 1912 by standing as a Progressive (letting Woodrow WILSON in).

Rostropovich, Mstislav (1927-) Russian cellist. One of the outstanding cellists of modern times, he has also given many recitals as a pianist, often accompanying his wife, the singer **Galina Vishnevskaya** (1926-), in song recitals. He made public his support of SOLZHENITSYN in 1970, and left the USSR in 1975.

Rothko, Mark [Marcus Rothkovitch] (1903-70) Russian-born American painter. Having passed through Expressionism and Surrealism, in the late 1940s he adopted the Abstract Expressionist style of painting for which he became famous, creating large canvases with almost luminous rectangles of colour.

Rothschild, [Nathaniel Mayer] Victor, 3rd Baron (1910-90) English zoologist and banker. A member of the European-wide Rothschild dynasty of bankers and intellectuals, he succeeded to his father's title in 1937. After distinguished service in British Intelligence during World War II, he became a prominent scientist and also served on various government committees. He was in charge of the government's central policy review staff (1971-74). His works include *A Classification of Living Animals* (1961).

Rous, Francis Peyton (1879-1970) American pathologist. With the Canadian-born surgeon **Charles Brenton Huggins** (1901-), he shared the 1966 Nobel prize for physiology or medicine for his innovative cancer research. Much of his work, e.g. his discovery of the Rous Sarcoma Virus, had been done over fifty years previously.

Roussel, Albert (1869-1937) French composer. His early works were influenced by Impressionist and 18th-century composers. His later works, e.g. the choral piece *Evocations* (1912), show the influence of oriental music.

Royce, Sir [Frederick] Henry (1863-1933) English engineer. In partnership with Charles ROLLS, he founded the car firm Rolls-Royce in 1906. The Rolls-Royce marque, e.g. the Silver Ghost (1907), became a modern symbol of wealth and of first-rate engineering design.

Rubbra, [Charles] Edmund (1901-86) English composer. A traditionalist composer, Rubbra found much of his inspiration in English lyric poetry, and in his religious beliefs (originally an Anglican, he converted to Roman Catholicism in 1948). His works include 11 symphonies.

Rubinstein, Artur (1888-1982) Polish-born American pianist. An outstanding concert pianist, he was particularly noted for his Chopin recitals. He became a US citizen in 1946.

Ruby, Jack *see* **Oswald, Lee Harvey.**

Rushdie, Salman (1947-) Indian-born British novelist. His first major success was *Midnight's Children* (1981), a fantasy on post-independence India. After the publication of *Satanic Verses* (1988), Ayatollah KHOMEINI of Iran pronounced a death sentence for blasphemy on Rushdie, who has had to go into hiding.

Rusk, [David] Dean (1909-) US secretary of state (1961-69). Notable for being a firm Cold Warrior and a strong supporter of the Vietnam War, which he saw as a crusade against communism, he served under KENNEDY and JOHNSON.

Russell, Bertrand [Arthur William] 3rd Earl Russell (1872-1970) British philosopher, mathematician and political reformer.

He studied mathematics at Cambridge under WHITEHEAD, and published his *Principles of Mathematics* in 1903. With Whitehead, he wrote *Principia Mathematica* (1910-13). His other works include *Problems of Philosophy* (1912) and *A History of Western Philosophy* (1945). Russell became the best-known philosopher of his time, making notable contributions to mathematical and philosophical theory, e.g. in set theory and, with the help of his student, WITTGENSTEIN, logical positivism. He was a pacifist during World War I and a noted campaigner against nuclear weapons. He was awarded the 1950 Nobel prize for literature.

Russell, Ken (1927-) English film director. He is especially noted for his film biographies of musicians, which began with a film for television on ELGAR (1962) and (on DELIUS), *A Song of Summer* (1968), and progressed through increasingly bizarre works such as (on Tchaikovsky) *The Music Lovers* (1970) to the lunatic *Lisztomania* (1975).

Ruth, Babe [George Herman Ruth] (1895-1948) American baseball player. Regarded as the finest all-rounder in the history of baseball, as pitcher with the Boston Red Sox (1914-19) and batter for New York Yankees (1920-34), his total of 714 home runs was unsurpassed until 1974. He finished his career as coach for the Brooklyn Dodgers.

Rutherford, Ernest [1st Baron Rutherford of Nelson] (1871-1937) New Zealand physicist. He was awarded the 1908 Nobel prize for chemistry for his work in the radioactive transformation of atoms. In 1911, he deduced the existence of the atom's structure, and was the first scientist to split the atom.

Rutherford, Dame Margaret (1892-1972) English actress. Notable for her engaging portrayal of eccentrics, she portrayed

Agatha CHRISTIE's Miss Marple in several films in the 1960s.

Ryder, Sue *see* **Cheshire, Sir Leonard.**

Ryle, Gilbert (1900-76) English philosopher. He became one of the leading "linguistic" philosophers of his generation, asserting that philosophy's function is to disentangle the misconceptions caused by linguistic conception. His works include *The Concept of Mind* (1949) and *Plato's Progress* (1966).

Ryle, Sir Martin (1918-84) English astronomer. He was awarded the 1974 Nobel prize for physics for his work in the field of radio astronomy, which, in the 1960s, led to the conclusion that the universe is not in a "steady state." He was astronomer royal (1972-82).

S

Sabin, Albert Bruce (1906-) Polish-born American microbiologist. He developed the Sabin polio vaccine in the mid-1950s, which, due to its effectiveness and oral administration, supplanted the SALK vaccine.

Sadat, [Mohammed] Anwar El (1918-81) Egyptian statesman. He succeeded NASSER as president in 1970. After the 1973 war with Israel, he signed a peace treaty with BEGIN, for which they were awarded the 1978 Nobel Peace Prize. He was assassinated by Islamic fundamentalist soldiers during a military parade.

Sakharov, Andrei Dimitrievich (1921-89) Russian physicist and dissident. Regarded as one of the greatest nuclear physicists, he developed the Russian hydrogen bomb in the 1950s. He subsequently campaigned for international control of nuclear weapons and for civil rights in the Soviet Union, and was awarded the 1975 Nobel Peace Prize. He was sent into internal exile in 1980, and released on GORBACHEV's intervention in 1986. He was elected to the Congress of People's Deputies in 1989.

Salam, Abdus *see* **Weinberg, Steven.**

Salazar, António de Oliveira (1889-1970) Portuguese dictator. A former professor of economics, he was prime minister (1932-68), during which time he gradually assumed dictatorial powers. He retired in 1968.

Salk, Jonas Edward (1914-) American physician and micro-biologist. He developed the Salk vaccine (by inoculation) against polio (later supplanted by the SABIN vaccine).

Saloth Sar *see* **Pol Pot**.

Sanger, Frederick (1918-) English biochemist. He was awarded two Nobel prizes for chemistry (1958, 1980), the first for his work on protein structure and the sequence of amino acids, the second for his work on the structure of nucleic acids.

Santayana, George (1863-1952) Spanish-born American philosopher, critic and poet. His works include *The Life of Reason* (1905-06) and *Realms of Being* (1927-40).

Sapir, Edward *see* **Whorf, Benjamin Lee**.

Sartre, Jean-Paul (1905-80) French philosopher, novelist and dramatist. His attempts at reconciling existentialist philosophy with Marxism are now of historical interest only. His novels, however, e.g. *Nausea* (1938), are highly readable. Several of his plays, e.g. *The Flies* (1943) and *Huis clos* (1944, in English *No Exit*) are frequently performed.

Satie, Erik [Alfred Leslie] (1866-1925) French composer (his mother was a Scottish composer). Satie's cool, simple, classically inspired compositions, e.g. "Three Pieces in the form of a pear" (1903, for two pianos), often had very odd titles, and were influential on DEBUSSY and RAVEL. COCTEAU helped bring his work to a wider public, and collaborated with him on a ballet commissioned by DIAGHILEV, *Parade* (1917), for which PICASSO designed the sets.

Sato Eisaku (1901-75) Japanese Liberal-Democrat prime minister (1964-72). He was awarded the 1974 Nobel Peace Prize for his opposition to the nuclear arms race.

Saussure, Ferdinand de (1857-1913) Swiss linguist. Regarded as one of the founders of modern linguistics, he established the "structuralist" approach to language as a social phenomenon, focusing on the arbitrary relationship between the word as "linguistic sign" and the thing it signifies. His works include *Course in General Linguistics* (1916).

Savage, Michael Joseph (1872-1940) Australian-born New Zealand Labour politician. He became the first Labour prime minister of New Zealand (1935-40).

Schlesinger, John [Richard] (1926-) English film director. His films include *Billy Liar* (1963), *Midnight Cowboy* (1969) and *Sunday, Bloody Sunday* (1971).

Schlick, Moritz (1882-1936) German philosopher. One of the founders of the "Vienna Circle" logical positivist school, his works include *Problems of Ethics* (1930). He was murdered by one of his students.

Schmidt, Helmut (1918-) West German Social Democrat statesman and chancellor. A former leader in the Hitler Youth, he won the Iron Cross during the war. He succeeded Willy BRANDT as chancellor (1974-82) and fostered relations with East Germany, resigning from politics in 1983.

Schnabel, Artur (1882-1951) Austrian pianist and composer. Noted in particular for his interpretations of Beethoven, Schubert and Mozart, he settled in the US from 1939, after the Nazi seizure of Austria.

Schoenberg, Arnold [Franz Walter] (1874-1951) Austrian composer (US citizen from 1941). His early works, e.g. the huge choral/orchestral *Gurrelieder* (1900), are lush chromatic compositions in the late romantic tradition. He then began composing atonal works, such as the second string quartet

(1908), and eventually developed his serial or "twelve-tone method" style of composition in such works as *Suite for Piano* (1924). He settled in the US in 1933, where he recovered his Jewish faith, an experience mirrored in his powerfully moving *Kol Nidre* (1938).

Schrödinger, Erwin (1887-1961) Austrian physicist. He shared the 1933 Nobel prize for physics (with DIRAC) for his formulation of his wave equation, which was the starting point for the study of wave mechanics in quantum theory. He fled from Germany to Britain in 1933, when the Nazis came to power.

Schumacher, Ernst (1911-77) German-born British economist. His book, *Small is Beautiful* (1973), became a founding text of the conservationist movement, with its critique of Western industrialism and advocacy of local, small-enterprise development.

Schuschnigg, Kurt von (1897-1977) Austrian statesman. A staunch opponent of HITLER, he succeeded DOLLFUSS as Christian Socialist chancellor in 1934, and was imprisoned by the Nazis (1938-45).

Schweitzer, Albert (1875-1965) Alsatian medical missionary, theologian, musician and philosopher. In 1913, he founded a missionary hospital at Lambaréné, Gabon, which attracted worldwide interest for Schweitzer's avowed aim of helping Africa in the spirit of "atonement" rather than benevolence. He was awarded the 1952 Nobel Peace Prize. His works include *The Quest of the Historical Jesus* (1906) and *On the Edge of the Primeval Forest* (1922).

Scorsese, Martin (1942-) American film director. Born into a poor Italian-American family in New York, his original intention was to become a priest. His films include *Taxi Driver*

(1976), *Raging Bull* (1980) and *Goodfellas* (1990), these three films starring the actor most associated with Scorsese's work, Robert DE NIRO.

Scott, C[harles] P[restwich] (1846-1932) English journalist. He became editor of *The Manchester Guardian* in 1872, which he transformed into one of the most respected newspapers in the world. Although his politics were Liberal (he was a Liberal MP, 1895-1906) his insistence on journalistic integrity ("Comment is free, facts are sacred") became proverbial. He was a strong opponent of the Boer War and supported women's suffrage.

Scott, Sir Peter [Markham] (1909-89) English naturalist and artist. The son of Robert SCOTT, his support and publicity for the conservation lobby was notably influential, particularly through his television documentaries and many books. He founded the Severn Wild Fowl Trust in 1948. His books include an autobiography, *The Eye of the Wind* (1961).

Scott, Robert Falcon (1868-1912) English explorer. He led two Antarctic expeditions (1901-04, 1910-12). He died with four companions on his last expedition, having reached the South Pole a month after AMUNDSEN. He was the father of Sir Peter SCOTT.

Scriabin, Alexander Nikolayevich (1872-1915) Russian composer and pianist. His compositions often involved extra-musical effects, e.g. *Prometheus* (1909), a piece for piano accompanied by coloured light projected on a screen. He envisaged all the arts coming together in one great apocalyptic future performance (by himself).

Seaga, Edward (1930-) American-born Jamaican politician. He became prime minister (1980-89) when his Labour Party defeated MANLEY'S National Party in the 1980 general election, and lost power to Manley's party in 1989.

Searle, Ronald [William Fordham] (1920-) English cartoon-ist and writer. Recognized at the outset of his career as a prodigious talent by Max BEERBOHM, he is known primarily as the creator of the monstrous St Trinian's schoolgirls, who feature in several of his works, e.g. *Back to the Slaughterhouse* (1951). Regarded, particularly in the US and France, as one of the finest graphic artists of the 20th century, he still lacks official recognition in Britain. His haunting book *To the Kwai— and Back: War Drawings 1939-45* (1986), a record of his experiences as a Japanese prisoner of war, also received scant notice.

Secombe, Harry *see* **Milligan, Spike**.

Segovia, Andrés [Marquis of Salobreña] (1894-1987) Span-ish guitarist. An internationally recognized virtuoso, he initiated a revival of interest in the classical guitar, with composers such as FALLA writing works for him.

Sellers, Peter (1925-80) English actor and comedian. One of the founders of the Goon Show (*see* Spike MILLIGAN), he became an international star with KUBRICK's black nuclear comedy *Dr Strangelove* (1963), in which he played three parts. He achieved further popularity as Inspector Clouseau in such films as *The Pink Panther* (1963).

Senghor, Léopold Sédar (1906-) Senegalese politician and poet. A classics teacher in Paris in the 1930s, he helped develop the concept of "negritude" with other black writers, which chiefly involved writing (in French) polemical works celebrating African culture. (His poems were extravagantly praised by Western Marxists, notably SARTRE.) He became the president of Senegal (1960-80), maintaining his power by a shrewd mixture of persecution (holding French support by labelling all his opponents as Marxists) and conciliation of the Muslim majority.

Sennett, Mack [Michael Sinnott] (1880-1960) Canadian-born American film director and producer. After working for D. W. GRIFFITH, he formed his Keystone Studio in 1912, where he produced the manic "Keystone Cop" comedies, which achieved international success. He also produced Charlie CHAPLIN's first films.

Serling, Rod (1924-75) American television dramatist. An ex-paratrooper, his TV plays include the much acclaimed *Requiem for a Heavyweight* (1956, broadcast live). He also created and introduced the innovative fantasy series *The Twilight Zone* (1959-64), episodes of which often had rather beguiling titles, e.g. "Deathshead Revisited."

Shackleton, Sir Ernest Henry (1874-1922) Anglo-Irish explorer. He served in Robert SCOTT's Antarctic expedition, being invalided home in 1903. He commanded two further expeditions (1908-09, 1914-16), with one of his teams discovering the south magnetic pole in 1909. He died in South Georgia preparing for a fourth expedition.

Shankar, Ravi *see* **Ravi Shankar.**

Shankly, Bill [William Shankly] (1913-81) Scottish footballer and manager. Regarded as one of the outstanding football managers of the century, he transformed Liverpool into one of the most successful clubs of modern times. A renowned football fanatic, he once notoriously observed that football was more important than life or death.

Shaw, George Bernard (1856-1950) Anglo-Irish dramatist and critic. He began his literary career as a drama, literary and music critic in the 1880s, and after a false start in novel-writing, began writing plays in the 1890s. The plays, e.g. *Man and Superman* (1903), *Major Barbara* (1905) and *Pygmalion* (1913) have been very successful thanks to Shaw's mastery of witty dialogue. He was awarded the Nobel prize for literature in 1925.

Sherrington, Sir Charles Scott (1857-1952) English physiologist. He shared the 1932 Nobel prize for physiology or medicine for his research into reflex action. His works include *The Integrative Action of the Nervous System* (1906).

Shevardnadze, Eduard Ambrosievich (1928-) Soviet politician. Appointed by GORBACHEV as foreign minister in 1985, he attracted much notice in the West with his formulation of the "SINATRA Doctrine," i.e. each country should peacefully construct its foreign policy on a "My Way" basis. He resigned in 1990, warning of the threat of a reactionary coup. During the attempted coup of 19 August 1991, he joined YELTSIN in defying the coup leaders from the Russian parliament building in Moscow.

Shockley, William Bradford (1910-89) American physicist. He shared, with BARDEEN and the Chinese-born American physicist **Walter Brattain** (1902-87), the 1956 Nobel prize for physics for his development of the junction transistor. Shockley was also a highly controversial proponent of the view that heredity determines intelligence.

Shostakovich, Dimitri Dimitriyevich (1906-75) Russian composer. Many of his works, notably the opera *A Lady Macbeth of Mtensk* (1930), were severely attacked by Soviet cultural apparatchiks for their disregard of the canons of socialist realism. His works include 15 symphonies, 15 string quartets and song cycles.

Sibelius, Jean (1865-1957) Finnish composer. His works

reflect his strong Finnish nationalism, e.g. the tone poem *Finlandia*, and often draw on the Finnish traditional epic, *Kalevala*. He also composed seven symphonies and a violin concerto.

Sickert, Walter [Richard] (1860-1942) German-born British painter (of Dutch/Danish parentage). After studying in Paris, he became a strong influence on many British artists, most notably on the artists forming the Camden Town Group. His subject matter was usually London low (or bohemian) life.

Sihanouk, Prince Norodom (1922-) Cambodian statesman, formerly (elected) king of Cambodia (1941-55). He abdicated (in favour of his father) to become prime minister (1955-60) after independence from France in 1955, becoming head of state in 1960. He was deposed by a military coup in 1970 and fled to China, forming an alliance with POL POT's Khmer Rouge, who seized Cambodia in 1975. He again became head of state in 1975 and was deposed by Pol Pot the following year. After the Vietnamese invasion of 1979, Sihanouk formed a government in exile, in an uneasy alliance with the Khmer Rouge.

Sikorski, Wladyslaw (1881-1943) Polish general and statesman. In 1940, he became premier of the Polish government in exile and commander in chief of the Free Polish armed forces. The Soviet Union ceased to recognize his government after the 1943 revelation that the Russians had been responsible for massacring thousands of Polish officers in the Katyn forest. Sikorski died in a plane crash.

Sikorsky, Igor Ivan (1889-1972) Russian-born American aeronautical engineer. He built (in 1913) the first four-engined aircraft, and emigrated to the US in 1918, where he established the Sikorsky Aero Engineering Company (1926). He built the first successful helicopter in 1939, the VS-300, which suffered from teething troubles (the first model was incapable of flying forwards).

Simpson, Wallis *see* **Windsor, Duke of.**

Sinatra, Frank [Francis Albert Sinatra] (1915-) American singer and film actor. He became a highly popular "crooner" of romantic songs in the 1940s, and won an Oscar for his part in *From Here to Eternity* (1952). One of the highest paid entertainers of all time, he is regarded as one of the finest modern popular singers, with a finely tuned jazz-like sense of phrasing.

Singer, Isaac Bashevis (1904-91) Polish-born American Yiddish writer. Much of his fiction deals with the now vanished world of Polish Judaism, e.g. *The Magician of Lublin* (1960). He was awarded the Nobel prize for literature in 1978.

Skinner, B[urrhus] F[rederic] (1904-) American psychologist. Influenced by John B. WATSON, he developed various techniques of behavioural psychology to illustrate his theory of "learning laws." His "Skinner box," in which rats learned to pull particular levers in order to get food, is a famous example of his approach. His works include *Beyond Freedom and Dignity* (1971).

Smith, Bessie [Elizabeth Smith] (1895-1937) American blues singer, nicknamed the "Empress of the Blues." She became very popular with jazz audiences in the 1920s, and made several classic recordings with Louis ARMSTRONG. She died in a car crash.

Smith, Ian [Douglas] (1919-) Zimbabwean politician. He was prime minister of Rhodesia (1964-79), and declared UDI (unilateral declaration of independence) from Britain in 1965 in order to maintain white minority rule. Majority rule came in

1979, with **Bishop Abel Muzorewa** (1925-) serving as caretaker premier (1979-80). MUGABE's ZANU party won the 1980 election. Smith resigned his leadership of his party in 1987.

Smith, Stevie [Florence Margaret Smith] (1902-71) English poet and novelist. Her graceful, melancholic, and occasionally fiercely funny verse has been much admired, especially the collection *Not Waving but Drowning* (1957).

Smuts, Jan Christian (1870-1950) South African statesman and philosopher. He commanded Boer forces during the Boer War, and became prime minister (1919-24, 1939-48). Respected worldwide as a statesman of depth, the common epithet for him among his own people was "tricky," particularly when he joined with the Allies in World War II. He devised the philosophy of "holism," explained in his *Holism and Evolution* (1926).

Sobers, Gary [Sir Garfield St Auburn] (1936-) West Indian cricketer. Regarded as one of the finest all-rounders of all time, he scored more than 8,000 runs (26 centuries), also taking 235 wickets and 110 catches in Test cricket. He was knighted in 1975, when he retired.

Soddy, Frederick (1877-1956) English chemist. He was awarded the 1921 Nobel prize for chemistry for his discovery of isotopes during his research in radioactivity.

Solti, Sir Georg (1912-) Hungarian-born British conductor. A student under both BARTÓK and KODÁLY, he left Hungary for Switzerland in 1939 as anti-semitic repression intensified. His recording of Wagner's Ring cycle was particularly renowned.

Solzhenitsyn, Aleksandr Isayevich (1918-) Russian novelist and historian. His novella, *One Day in the Life of Ivan*

Denisovich (1962), was based on his experiences in a Soviet labour camp and was published in the USSR during a brief thaw in cultural restrictions. Subsequent works, e.g. the novel *The First Circle* and his study of the labour camp system, *The Gulag Archipelago*, had to be published abroad (1968, 1973-5). He was awarded the Nobel prize for literature in 1970, and was deported from the USSR in 1974. He settled in Vermont in the US but has announced his intention to return to Russia.

Sondheim, Stephen [Joshua] (1930-) American songwriter and composer. He studied with HAMMERSTEIN and wrote the lyrics for BERNSTEIN's *West Side Story* (1958), before writing the music and lyrics for several musicals, e.g. *A Funny Thing Happened on the Way to the Forum* (1962), *A Little Night Music* (1973) and *Into the Woods* (1986).

Sopwith, Sir Thomas [Octave Murdoch] (1888-1989) English aeronautical engineer. He founded the Sopwith Aviation Company in 1912, and designed and built the Sopwith Camel, one of the most successful fighter planes of World War I.

Spassky, Boris Vasilyevich (1937-) Russian chess player. He was world champion (1969-72), losing his title to Bobby FISCHER in a ludicrously over-publicized contest that was much more of a Cold War phenomenon than a chess match.

Spence, Sir Basil (1907-76) Indian-born Scottish architect. Famous for a few highly prestigious buildings, such as Coventry Cathedral (1951), and notorious for some disastrous council housing, such as his council flats in Glasgow, the merit of Spence's work is hotly contested. (He reputedly remarked to Glasgow housewives complaining about his work that he would not accept criticism from non-architects.)

Spencer, Lady Diana *see* **Charles, Prince.**

Spencer, Sir Stanley (1891-1959) English painter. An isolated figure in modern art, he is best known for his series of religious paintings, particularly *The Resurrection* (1923-27), which depicts the residents of his home village, Cookham, rising from their graves. He also produced portraits, landscapes, and, in his capacity as a war artist, his *Shipbuilding on the Clyde* series of panels.

Spengler, Oswald (1880-1936) German philosopher. His historicist study, *The Decline of the West* (1918-22), argued that civilizations rise and fall in inexorable cycles, and that Western civilization could thus be expected to decay according to the same immutable laws that destroyed previous civilizations.

Spielberg, Steven (1947-) American film director and producer. His first film (for TV), *Duel* (1971), won high praise for Spielberg's skilful manipulation of tension. His subsequent films include some of the most successful films ever made, e.g. *Jaws* (1975), *Close Encounters of the Third Kind* (1977), *E.T.* (1982) and *Raiders of the Lost Ark* (1981).

Spock, Dr [Benjamin McLane] (1903-) American pediatrician. His book *The Common Sense Book of Baby and Child Care* (1946) had a huge influence on many middle-class parents of the postwar generation, with its advocacy of a "permissive," non-authoritarian approach to the raising of infants (later works made tactical withdrawals from the more extreme positions taken in the earlier work). A passionate opponent of the Vietnam war, he helped form the People's Party, and was a candidate in the presidential election of 1972.

Stalin, Joseph [Josef Vissarionovich Dzhugashvili] (1879-1953) Soviet dictator. Born in Georgia, he was expelled in 1899 from an orthodox seminary in Tiflis for expounding Marxism.

He became an active revolutionary on behalf of the Social Democratic Party and was imprisoned several times, escaping with surprising ease each time. After the Bolshevik Revolution, he was appointed commissar for nationalities, and became general secretary of the Central Committee in 1922, a position he held until his death. Despite LENIN's so-called "Testament" listing his shortcomings, Stalin manoeuvred his way into absolute power, shrewdly playing BUKHARIN and his "rightist" allies against TROTSKY and other "leftists." He forcibly collectivized Soviet agriculture in the 1930s and developed the Soviet Union's industrial base, using (and killing) many millions of "Gulag" prisoners as slave labour. His purges of the 1930s destroyed most of the surviving old Bolsheviks, such as BUKHARIN, as well as the army leadership. He signed a peace treaty with HITLER IN 1939, and seized Poland's eastern territories after Hitler's September invasion. Hitler's invasion of the Soviet Union in 1941 was spectacularly successful in the first year, with large sections of the population welcoming the Germans as liberators, but forceful resistance from the Red Army, notably in the defence of Leningrad, the battle of Stalingrad, and in massive infantry and tank battles, led directly to the defeat of Hitler's regime and the occupation of eastern Europe by Stalin's forces. After Stalin's death, KHRUSCHEV came to power and denounced Stalin's brutality and "personality cult" in a secret—but leaked—speech.

Stanislavsky, Konstantin (1863-1938) Russian director and actor, who was co-founder of the Moscow Art Theatre in 1897. The influence of his theory of acting, requiring an actor to immerse himself in the "inner life" of the character he is playing and so convey to the audience the hidden reality behind the words, has been immense. His theory is contained in such works as *An Actor Prepares* (1929) and *Building a Character* (1950).

Starr, Ringo [Richard Starkey] (1940-) English rock drummer and singer. He was the Beatles' drummer (1962-70), and occasionally sang on their records, notably "Yellow Submarine."

Stauffenberg, Count Berthold von (1907-44) German soldier. He was one of the chief conspirators in the 20 July 1944 assassination attempt on HITLER, shortly after which he was executed.

Steel, Sir David [Martin Scott] (1938-) Scottish Liberal politician. He became leader of the Liberal Party in 1976, following Jeremy THORPE's resignation. He led the Liberals during their partnership with David OWEN's SDP (1981-88), and resigned his leadership when the Liberals merged with the SDP to form the Liberal Democrats under ASHDOWN's leadership.

Steichen, Edward (1879-1973) Luxembourg-born American photographer. He was a founder of the Photo-Secession group with STIEGLITZ and others, and organized *The Family of Man* (1955) photography exhibition, which was highly influential in its portrayal of the unity of mankind.

Stein, Gertrude (1874-1946) American author, who settled in Paris in 1902. There she became a focal point for a group of writers and artists, including HEMINGWAY, Sherwood ANDERSON and PICASSO. Her own best-known work is her autobiography, *The Autobiography of Alice B. Toklas* (1933), eccentrically presented as if it were the work of her life-long companion.

Stein, Jock [John Stein] (1922-85) Scottish footballer and manager. He was manager of Glasgow Celtic (1965-78), during which period his club won nine consecutive league championships and became the first non-Latin club to win the European Cup in 1967 (finalists in 1968). He was manager of the Scotland team, and died during a match against Wales.

Steiner, Rudolf (1861-1925) Austrian philosopher. Influenced by theosophy, he formed his own movement of ''anthroposophy'' in 1912, dedicated to developing the innate human capacity for spiritual perception, through self-expressing activities such as art and dance. Many "Steiner schools" have been established throughout the world to teach children according to Steiner's principles.

Stevenson, Adlai E[wing] (1900-65) American Democrat politician. A noted liberal and intellectual, who was much respected abroad, he stood twice against EISENHOWER as the Democratic presidential candidate (1952, 1956). His campaign speeches were published as *Call to Greatness* (1954) and *What I Think* (1956).

Stewart, Jackie [John Young Stewart] (1939-) Scottish racing driver. He was world champion (1969, 1971, 1973), retiring in 1973 to pursue a highly successful career in business and as a sports commentator.

Stieglitz, Alfred (1864-1946) American photographer. He formed the Photo-Secession group with Edward STEICHEN, which became a highly influential force for establishing photography as an art form. He also founded the magazine *Camera Work* (1903-17).

Stockhausen, Karlheinz (1928-) German composer. Regarded as the leading exponent of twelve-tone, or serial, music, he also used electronic sounds in his work. His work includes *Gruppen* (1959), for three orchestras, and *Kontakte* (1960).

Stokowski, Leopold (1882-1977) British-born American conductor (of Polish-Irish descent). A noted showman and popularizer of classical music, he is best known for his collaboration with Walt DISNEY in conducting the music for *Fantasia* (1940) (in which he shakes hands with Mickey Mouse).

Stopes, Marie [Charlotte Carmichael] (1880-1958) Scottish scientist and birth-control pioneer. She was the youngest Doctor of Science in Britain (1905) and acquired an international reputation as a palaeobotanist. The breakdown of her marriage (annulled in 1917) led her to the study of sex education, in which field she soon became a world authority and household name. Her book *Married Love* (1918), a frank analysis of sex within marriage, became an international best-seller (banned for a while in the US). She established a birth control clinic in Holloway in London (1920), which gave free contraceptive advice to the poor.

Stoppard, Tom (1937-) Czech-born British dramatist. His plays, e.g. *Rosencrantz and Guildenstern are Dead* (1966), *The Real Inspector Hound* (1968) and *The Real Thing* (1982) have been very successful because of their sharp, witty wordplay and fast, cleverly plotted action.

Strauss, Richard (1864-1949) German composer and conductor. His works include a series of richly orchestrated tone poems, e.g. *Till Eulenspiegel* (1894-95) and *Also Sprach Zarathustra* (1895-96), operas, e.g. *Elektra* (1909) and *Der Rosenkavalier* (1911), and the *Four Last Songs* (1948). He collaborated with ZWEIG on *The Silent Woman* (1935), which was banned by the Nazis after four performances.

Stravinsky, Igor Feodorovich (1882-1971) Russian composer. He composed ballet scores for DIAGHILEV, e.g. *Petrushka*

(1911) and *The Rite of Spring* (1913), the first performance of the latter being regarded as a milestone in modernist music. He later composed several austerely neoclassical works, such as the opera-oratorio *Oedipus Rex* (1927), which also displayed the influence of SCHOENBERG's serial techniques. Other works include the Symphony in C Major (1940), and the opera *The Rake's Progress* (1951), on which AUDEN collaborated.

Suharto, Thojib N J (1921-) Indonesian general and statesman. He launched a brutal campaign of repression against communists and other dissidents in the mid-1960s, and assumed executive power in 1967 after president **Achmad Sukarno** (1901-70), the first president of Indonesia, resigned in his favour.

Sukarno, Achmad *see* **Suharto.**

Sun Yat-sen *or* **Sun Zhong Shan** (1866-1925) Chinese nationalist leader and statesman. Influenced by Marx and by Western democratic principles, he organized a revolutionary league based on the "Three People's Principles" of nationalism, democracy and reform. He played a leading role in the overthrow of the Manchu dynasty and became first president of the Republic of China in 1911-12, resigning to lead a revolt against General Yaun Shih-kai. With Soviet help, he regained power in 1923. After his death, the Kuomintang under CHIANG KAI-SHEK split from the Communists.

Sutherland, Graham [Vivian] (1903-80) English painter. He was an official war artist (1941-45) and subsequently became a portrait painter of note. His portrait of CHURCHILL (1955) was destroyed by Lady Churchill.

Sutherland, Dame Joan (1926-) Australian soprano. She became one of the world's leading bel canto operatic sopranos in the 1950s and 60s, and retired in 1990.

Suzman, Helen (1917-) South African politician. She became an MP for the liberal United (later Progressive, then Democratic) Party in 1953, retiring in 1989. She has been a long and consistent campaigner against apartheid.

Suzuki, Daisetsu Teitaro (1870-1966) Japanese Buddhist philosopher. His works on Zen Buddhism, such as *Studies in Zen* (1955), played a key role in popularizing the principles of Zen Buddhism in the West.

Szasz, Thomas Stephen (1920-) Hungarian-born American psychiatrist. He became noted in the early 1960s as a fierce critic of orthodox psychoanalysis, and argued that mental illness is in reality a myth fostered as an agent of repression in such works as *The Myth of Mental Illness* (1961). He argues that the only true mental illnesses are "diseases of the brain" and that much of what passes for mental illness should be classed as "problems of living." He also attacked LAING and the anti-psychiatry movement in *Schizophrenia: The Sacred Symbol of Psychiatry* (1979).

T

Taft, William Howard (1857-1930) American Republican statesman. He became the 27th president of the US (1909-13) in succession to Theodore ROOSEVELT. More conservative in his policies than Roosevelt, he alienated the reformist wing of the Republican Party. He was appointed chief justice of the Supreme Court (1921-30), and became a noted isolationist in the 1930s.

Tagore, Rabindranath (1861-1941) Indian poet and philosopher. Although known primarily as a poet, he also wrote plays, essays and novels and short stories. Regarded by many Bengalis as their greatest writer, he was awarded the 1913 Nobel prize for literature and became venerated as a sage in Western intellectual circles. He was knighted in 1915, but repudiated the title in 1919 as a protest against the Amritsar Massacre of 1919.

Tambo, Oliver (1917-) South African politician. He joined the African National Congress in 1944, and when the ANC was banned in 1960 left South Africa to set up an expatriate section. During MANDELA's imprisonment, he was the ANC's acting president (1967-77) and president (1977-91).

Tanaka, Kakuei (1918-) Japanese politician. He was the Liberal Democratic minister of finance (1962-64), minister of international trade (1971) and prime minister (1972-74). He established diplomatic relations with Communist China, but was forced to resign following charges of taking bribes from Lockheed, for which he was tried (1983) and imprisoned.

Tange, Kenzo (1913-) Japanese architect. Influenced by LE CORBUSIER and by traditional Japanese building styles, his buildings include the Hiroshima Peace Centre (1949-55) and St Mary's Cathedral in Tokyo (1965).

Tansley, Sir Arthur George (1871-1955) English botanist. One of the pioneers of the study of plant ecology, he was the first president (1913-15) of the British Ecological Society. His works include *Practical Plant Ecology* (1923) and *The British Islands and Their Vegetation* (1939).

Tarkovsky, Andrei (1932-86) Russian film director, with a distinctive elegaic and often enigmatic style. The simplest of his seven feature films is his first, *Ivan's Childhood* (1962), his films steadily becoming more complex and allegorical, e.g. *Andrei Rublev* (1966), his two remarkable science fiction essays, *Solaris* (1972) and *Stalker* (1979), and his two films made in exile from the USSR, *Nostalgia* (1983) and *The Sacrifice* (1986). Tarkosky also directed a production of *Boris Godunov* for the Royal Opera, which was taken to Moscow in 1990.

Tati, Jacques [Jacques Tatischeff] (1908-82) French actor and film director. An ex-rugby player, he became an international comedy star with his Monsieur Hulot creation, an engagingly incompetent character hopelessly at odds with the modern world. Five Hulot films were made, including *Mr Hulot's Holiday* (1953) and *Mon Oncle* (1958).

Tatum, Art[hur] (1910-56) American jazz pianist. Blind in one eye and partially sighted in the other, he was largely self-taught on the piano and became an acclaimed virtuoso of jazz piano music in the "swing" mode.

Tatum, Edward Lawrie (1909-75) American biochemist. With the American geneticist **George Wells Beadle** (1903-89), he demonstrated that biochemical reactions in cells are controlled by particular genes. With LEDERBERG, he discovered the phenomenon of genetic recombination in bacteria. All three shared the 1958 Nobel prize for physiology or medicine.

Tavener, John Kenneth (1944-   ) English composer. He studied under Lennox BERKELEY, and became noted particularly for his religious compositions, e.g. the cantata *Cain and Abel* (1965) and the opera *Therese* (1973-76).

Taylor, A[lan] J[ohn] P[ercivale] (1906-90) English historian. Often a controversial figure (he argued that World War II was produced by accident as much as by HITLER's design), he was admired by his peers for his research and insight into modern European history, and became the historian best known to the British public through his (often unscripted) live lectures to television audiences. His works include *The Origins of the Second World War* (1961) and *The Trouble Makers* (1957).

Taylor, Elizabeth (1932-) English-born (of American parents) American stage and film actress. Her films as a child include *National Velvet* (1944)—*see also* Shirley WILLIAMS—and *Little Women* (1949). Regarded as one of the most beautiful film stars of her generation, her films include *Cat on a Hot Tin Roof* (1958), *Butterfield 8* (1960) and *Who's Afraid of Virginia Woolf?* (1966), the last two earning her Oscars. The latter film also co-starred her 5th husband, Richard BURTON, whom she married twice.

Teilhard de Chardin, Pierre (1881-1955) French Jesuit theologian, philosopher and palaeontologist. He developed a theory of evolution, described in *The Phenomenon of Man* (1955) and other works, which he claimed was compatible with Roman Catholic teaching. All creation, in his view, is evolving progressively towards what he called the "Omega Point" of unity in God. The Church refused to let his books be published in his lifetime.

Te Kanawa, Dame Kiri (1944-) New Zealand soprano. She is regarded as one of the world's leading operatic sopranos, and is particularly noted for Mozart and Italian opera roles.

Teller, Edward (1908-) Hungarian-born American physicist. He studied in Germany and under BOHR at Copenhagen, leaving Germany in 1933 after HITLER's rise to power. He settled in the US in 1935, where he became one of the leading figures in the development of nuclear weapons at Los Alamos. He was dubbed the "father of the hydrogen bomb" (tested 1952), and was almost unique among his colleagues for having few moral qualms about his work.

Temple, Shirley (1928-) American film actress and Republican politician. She became the world's leading child film star with films such as *Dimples* (1936) and *Wee Willie Winkie* (1937). She later developed a career in politics under her married name of Shirley Temple Black, her posts including Ambassador to Ghana (1974-76).

Teng Hsiao-p'ing *see* **Deng Xiao Ping**.

Tenzing Norgay *see* **Hillary, Edmund**.

Terry, Dame Ellen Alice (1847-1928) English actress. Her remarkably long stage career began in 1856 at the age of nine in a Shakespeare production by Charles Kean, and ended in

1925. She formed a long partnership in Shakespearian roles with Sir Henry Irving, and had a close friendship (and long correspondence) with SHAW, who wrote many roles for her, e.g. Lady Cicely in *Captain Brassbound's Conversion* (1905).

Thant, U (1909-74) Burmese diplomat. He succeeded HAM-MARSKJÖLD as secretary general of the United Nations (1961-72), and was widely admired for his role as a tactful mediator, most notably during the Cuban missile crisis.

Thatcher, Margaret Hilda (1925-) English Conservative stateswoman. She was much influenced by her father, Albert Roberts, a grocer who was twice Conservative mayor of Grantham. She worked as a research chemist after graduating from Oxford, then became a barrister specializing in taxation law. She became MP for Finchley in 1959 and, as secretary of state for education and science (1970-74), became a hate figure for many when she ended provision of free school milk. She defeated HEATH in the Tory leadership campaign of 1975, becoming the first woman to lead a major British political party. As prime minister (1979-1990), she launched an ideological crusade (dubbed "Thatcherism") against what she perceived as the entrenchment of socialism in British, the principal elements of her attack being free-market policies and the privatization of nationalized industries. Her period of office was marked by rising unemployment and by the Falklands War of 1982, the success of which many believed to be the decisive factor in the Conservative's huge election victory of 1983 over FOOT's Labour party. Her relationship with the next Labour leader, KINNOCK, was notably confrontational, and she gave strong support to REAGAN's forceful anti-communist foreign policy. Her policies were widely disliked by her political opponents and by moderate Tories, the latter forming small resistance groups around figures such as Heath and **Michael Heseltine** (1933-), and (in the House of Lords) MACMILLAN (who made a speech denouncing privatization as "selling the family silver"). Abroad, she was condemned by Soviet spokesmen as the "Iron Lady," a tag she adopted with great joy, and was reviled by many Third World leaders. Her reception abroad, however, was often very warm. For many women, particularly in Africa, where she was rapturously received, she became a powerful role model. She welcomed GORBACHEV as a "man we can do business with," and was acclaimed by figures such as HAVEL for her part in bringing the Cold War to an end. Increasing dissension within her cabinet, over such issues as the highly controversial Community Charge (or Poll Tax) and the disarray of the Health Service, led to her resignation in 1990 and the election of MAJOR as prime minister.

Theresa of Calcutta, Mother [Agnes Gonxha Bojaxhiu] (1910-) Yugoslavian-born (of Albanian parentage) Roman Catholic nun and missionary. She became a member of the Sisters of Loretto and trained in medicine in Paris, founding her own Order of the Missionaries of Charity in 1950. Venerated by many people as a living saint, her work in Calcutta with orphans and with the dying led to her being awarded the 1979 Nobel Peace Prize. Her order now has over 200 branch houses worldwide.

Thomas, Dylan [Marlais] (1914-53) Welsh poet with a hard-drinking, boisterous reputation. His poems are exuberant, often florid and occasionally obscure. His best-known single work is *Under Milk Wood* (1954), a radio drama in poetic prose.

Thomson, D[avid] C[ouper] (1861-1954) Scottish newspaper proprietor. His Dundee-based group included *The Sunday*

Post, a straight-laced paper with virtual saturation circulation in Scotland, and many children's comics, particularly the *Dandy* (1937) and *Beano* (1938). Thomson was a notably conservative and paternalistic figure who refused to recognize trade unions. *See also* Dudley WATKINS.

Thomson, Sir George Paget (1892-1975) English physicist. He shared the 1937 Nobel prize for physics with the American physicist **Clinton Joseph Davisson** (1881-1958) for their (independent) discovery of the diffraction of electrons by crystals. His works include *Theory and Practice of Electron Diffraction* (1939).

Thomson, Sir Joseph John (1856-1940) English physicist. He was awarded the 1906 Nobel prize for physics for his discovery (1906) of the electron, one of the most significant discoveries in physics. Seven of his assistants and pupils (e.g. RUTHERFORD) went on to win Nobel prizes, and many others became professors.

Thomson, Roy [Herbert] [1st Baron Thomson of Fleet] (1894-1976) Canadian-born British newspaper proprietor. He began buying radio stations and newspapers in Canada in the 1930s, subsequently expanding into the US and Britain. He bought *The Times* (1966) and *Sunday Times* (1959).

Thorndike, Dame Sybil (1882-1976) English actress. Notable for her long acting career, from 1904 to the late 60s, she created many roles, including SHAW's *Saint Joan* (1924).

Thorpe, [John] Jeremy (1929-) English Liberal politician. Leader of the Liberal Party (1967-76), he resigned after being accused of conspiring to murder a male model, Norman Scott, who claimed to have been Thorpe's lover. Thorpe was acquitted.

Thurber, James [Grover] (1894-1961) American humorist, cartoonist and essayist, much of whose work first appeared in *New Yorker* magazine, including his most famous story, "The Secret Life of Walter Mitty."

Tillich, Paul [Johannes] (1886-1965) German-born American theologian and philosopher. He served as a Lutheran military chaplain in World War I, and became a brave critic of the Nazis, who barred him from teaching in 1933. He emigrated to the US, becoming a citizen in 1940. His highly influential theological work addresses the problems of matching traditional forms of Christian belief with an increasingly secular, and doubting, modern society. His works include *The Courage To Be* (1952) and *Systematic Theology* (1951-63).

Tinbergen, Jan (1903-) Dutch economist (brother of Niko TINBERGEN). He shared the 1969 Nobel prize for economics with the Norwegian economist **Ragnar Frisch** (1895-1973) for their work in the field of econometrics. His works include *Econometrics* (1941).

Tinbergen, Niko[laas] (1907-88) Dutch ethologist (brother of Jan TINBERGEN). He shared the 1973 Nobel prize for physiology or medicine (with LORENZ and von FRISCH) for his ground-breaking studies of animal behaviour, which established ethology as a science. His works include *The Herring Gull's World* (1953) and *Animal Behaviour* (1965).

Tippett, Sir Michael (1905-) English composer. A pacifist, he was jailed for three months during World War II as a conscientious objector. His works include several operas, e.g. *The Midsummer Marriage* (1955) and *The Knot Garden* (1970), the oratorio *A Child of our Time* (1941), symphonies, song cycles and chamber music. His books include *Moving into Aquarius*

(1959, revised 1974).

Tito, Marshal [Josip Broz] (1892-1980) Yugoslav statesman. He fought with the Bolsheviks during the Russian civil war and became secretary general of the Yugoslav Communist Party in 1937. In 1941, after the German invasion of Yugoslavia, he organized a partisan force to fight the occupiers, and succeeded in diverting British aid from other guerrilla forces to his own. After the war, he established a Communist government and broke with STALIN, but maintained a repressive regime. He succeeded in preserving a fragile Yugoslav unity, but 11 years after his death the break-up of the Yugoslav state began with Slovenia, then Croatia, declaring independence from the Serbian-dominated state in 1991.

Todd, Alexander Robertus, Baron Todd of Trumpington (1907-) Scottish biochemist. He was awarded the 1957 Nobel prize for chemistry for his research into the chemical structure of nucleotides.

Togliatti, Palmiro (1893-1964) Italian Communist politician. He helped found the Italian Communist Party (with GRAMSCI and others) and became party secretary (1926-64). He lived in exile in the Soviet Union during MUSSOLINI's rule, where a city on the Volga was named after him. He returned to Italy in 1944, and helped build the Italian communist party into the largest in Western Europe.

Tojo, Hideki (1884-1948) Japanese soldier. He became minister of war (1940-44) and prime minister (1941-44). He resigned in 1944 after losses in the Pacific theatre of war, and was executed as a war criminal.

Tolkien, J[ohn] R[onald] R[euel] (1892-1973) South African-born British fantasy writer and scholar. Probably the most influential (and best-selling) fantasy writer, the works on which his fame rests are *The Hobbit* (1937) and the three-volume *Lord of the Rings* (1954-5)

Tolstoy, Count Leo [Nikolayevich] (1828-1910) Russian novelist, dramatist, short-story writer and philosopher. His autobiographical trilogy, *Childhood* (1852), *Boyhood* (1854) and *Youth* (1857), is one of the most remarkable ever published by a young man. His spiritual self-questioning resulted in some of the world's greatest works of fiction, notably *War and Peace* (1863-9), a panoramic epic of the Napoleonic invasion of Russia, and *Anna Karenina* (1875-77), a tragic tale of adulterous love, which raises profound questions about personal and social morality.

Tortelier, Paul (1914-91) French cellist, conductor and composer. He performed with BEECHAM in 1947, after which he toured worldwide as a soloist. A renowned teacher of the cello, his pupils included Jacqueline DU PRÉ.

Torvill, Jayne (1957-) and **Dean, Christopher** (1958-) English ice-dance skaters. They became world champions (1981-83), European champions (1981-82, 1984) and Olympic champions (1984). Their Olympic win was achieved with an unprecedented top score of 6.0 from all nine judges. Their best-known routine used RAVEL's *Bolero* as the score.

Toscanini, Arturo (1867-1957) Italian conductor. Regarded as one of the most authoritarian conductors of all time, he was renowned for his fanatical devotion to authenticity and disdain for showy interpretation of the score, and for his remarkable musical memory.

Toynbee, Arnold [Joseph] (1889-1975) English historian. His major work is *A Study of History* (1934-61), which compares civilizations past and present in terms of a rhythmic process of growth and decay. An abridgement of his work published in 1947 became a best-seller, with Toynbee acquiring the reputation of a prophet in the US, although fellow historians were often sharply critical of his methodology.

Tracy, Spencer (1900-1967) American film actor. He won two Oscars in a row, for *Captains Courageous* (1937) and *Boy's Town* (1938). He had a long personal and professional relationship with Katharine HEPBURN.

Trevelyan, George Macaulay (1876-1962) English historian. His highly readable works include *History of England* (1926) and *English Social History* (1944) and several biographies, e.g. *Grey of Falloden* (1937).

Trotsky, Leon [Lev Davidovich Bronstein] (1879-1940) Russian revolutionary. Arrested at the age of 19 for political agitation, he was exiled to Siberia, escaping to join LENIN in London in 1902. An advocate of "permanent revolution," he believed that socialism could not be built in one country alone, and supported the Mensheviks against Lenin's Bolsheviks. He returned to Russia in 1917, where he joined the Bolsheviks and was largely responsible for creating and directing the victorious Red Army during the civil war. His influence in the party declined after Lenin's death in 1924, and he was forced into exile by STALIN in 1929. He settled in Mexico in 1937, where he was assassinated by a Russian agent. A ruthless, charismatic figure, Trotsky's influence as a focal point for Leninist dissent against Stalinism was large. Initially critical of Lenin's iron grip on the party leadership as undemocratic, he recanted this view after the Bolshevik revolution, arguing, with a fair measure of casuistry, that any resemblances between Stalin's dictatorship and Lenin's (and his own use of terror) were merely superficial.

Trudeau, Pierre [Elliott] (1919-) Canadian Liberal politician. He became an MP in 1965 and, succeeding PEARSON, prime minister (1968-79, 1980-84). A member of a wealthy Montreal family, he was a strong opponent of the Quebec separatist movement. He retired from politics in 1985.

Trueman, Freddy [Frederick Sewards Trueman] (1931-) English cricketer. A notable fast bowler, he played for Yorkshire for 19 years (1949-68) and played in 67 Tests, taking a record 307 wickets in one match. He was also a batsman, scoring over 9,000 runs (making three centuries). On retirement, he became a popular commentator.

Truffaut, François (1932-84) French film director, critic and actor. One of the *Cahiers du Cinema* group of film critics, his first film, the semi-autobiographical *The Four Hundred Blows* (1959), was widely praised. His other films include *Jules et Jim* (1961) and *The Last Metro* (1980). He has acted in several films, e.g. SPIELBERG's *Close Encounters of the Third Kind* (1977) and in his own charming *Day for Night ("La Nuit Américaine"* 1973), in which Graham GREENE had a small uncredited walk-on role.

Truman, Harry S. (1884-1972) American Democratic statesman. He became 33rd president of the US (1945-52) after Franklin D. ROOSEVELT's death, and authorized the dropping of the atom bombs on Hiroshima and Nagasaki. He initiated the change in US foreign policy towards the Soviet Union expressed as the "Truman doctrine," a policy of containment of communism and aid towards groups or nations resisting communism, and approved the MARSHALL Plan of aid for Britain and Western Europe.

Tshombe, Moise Kapenda (1919-69) Congolese politician.

He declared Katanga's independence from the Congo (now Zaire) in 1960, but was forced to concede defeat in 1963. Exiled in Spain, he returned in 1964 to become Congolese premier, and was ousted by MOBUTO in 1965. He went back to Spain, was kidnapped and taken to Algeria in 1967, where he died under arrest.

Turing, Alan Mathison (1912-54) English mathematician. Regarded as one of the most important computer theoreticians, he developed the concept of an idealized computer called the "Universal Automaton" (later called the "Turing Machine") in his paper "On Computable Numbers" (1937). The computer, he posited, would be able to modify its own program through a sequence on paper tape of 1s and 0s. Turing also took part in the vitally important code-breaking project at Bletchley Park in World War II, which deciphered the German "Enigma" codes. He committed suicide after being charged with a homosexual offence.

Tynan, Kenneth [Peacock] (1927-80) English theatre critic. As critic for *The Observer* (1954-63), he was noted for his sharp wit, often directed at stage censorship, and for his vigorous promotion of the new "kitchen sink" drama of the mid-1950s (e.g. OSBORNE'S plays) and "socially useful" plays, such as BRECHT'S. He is now principally remembered for his revue *Oh Calcutta* (1969).

U

Ulbricht, Walter (1893-1973) East German Communist politician. He left Germany for the Soviet Union in 1933, returning in 1945 in the wake of the Red Army. As general secretary of the East German Socialist Unity [i.e. Communist] Party (1946-71), he supervised the sovietization of East German society, crushed the Berlin workers' rebellion of 1953 and built the Berlin Wall in 1961.

Urey, Harold Clayton (1893-1981) American chemist. He was awarded the 1934 Nobel prize for chemistry for his isolation of the heavy hydrogen isotope, deuterium. He worked on the production of heavy water during World War II.

Ustinov, Sir Peter [Alexander] (1921-) British actor, director, dramatist and raconteur (of Russian-French parentage). His plays include *The Love of Four Oranges* (1951) and *Romanoff and Juliet* (1956). Other works include an autobiography, *Dear Me* (1977). He is best known as an engaging raconteur in one-man shows and on television.

Utrillo, Maurice (1883-1955) French painter. Noted particularly for his street scenes of Paris, his "White Period" paintings of 1908-14 are particularly sought after.

V

Valentino, Rudolph [Rodolfo Guglielmi di Valentina d'Antonguolla] (1895-1926) Italian-born American film actor. He became the leading screen personification of the romantic hero in such films as *The Four Horsemen of the Apocalypse* (1921) and *The Son of the Sheik* (1926). He died of peritonitis, his funeral attended by hordes of hysterical women.

Van Allen, James Alfred (1914-) American physicist. He discovered, through detectors on the US satellite *Explorer I*, the Van Allen radiation belts outside the Earth's atmosphere.

Van der Post, Sir Laurens [Jan] (1906-) South African novelist, travel writer and mystic. His works are strongly influenced by JUNG and display a strong sympathy for the "primitive" peoples of the world. His novels include *The Seed and the Sower* (1963), based on his experiences a a prisoner of war of the Japanese in World War II and filmed as *Merry Christmas, Mr Lawrence* (1982). His travel books include two African classics, *Venture to the Interior* (1952) and *The Lost World of the Kalahari* (1958).

Varèse, Edgard (1883-1965) French-born American composer and conductor. His (usually orchestral) compositions are noted for their combination of the extreme registers of instruments with taped and electronic sounds. His works include *Hyperprism* (1923) and *Ionisation* (1925).

Vaughan Williams, Ralph (1872-1958) English composer. Like HOLST, he was heavily influenced by traditional English music, particularly English folk song. His works include the choral *Sea Symphony* (1910), *Fantasia on a Theme by Thomas Tallis* (1910), operas, ballet music and song cycles.

Vavilov, Nikolai Ivanovich (1887-1943) Russian botanist and plant geneticist. He developed a "principle of diversity," which states that the original source of a cultivated plant will be found to lie within the area containing the greatest diversity of the plant. His theories were attacked by LYSENKO, resulting in Vavilov's imprisonment and death in a Soviet labour camp.

Veblen, Thorstein (1857-1929) American economist (of Norwegian parentage). Regarded as the founder of the school of institutional economics, he drew a famous distinction between the industrial process, which tends towards efficiency of production, and the demands of business, which may restrict output in the name of profit. His works include *The Theory of the Leisure Class* (1899) and *The Theory of Business Enterprise* (1904).

Verwoerd, Hendrik Frensch (1901-66) South African politician. Anti-British and pro-German, he opposed South Africa's entry into World War II, and became prime minister (1958-66). He fostered apartheid, banned the ANC (1960) and took South Africa out of the Commonwealth in 1961. He was assassinated by a deranged white man.

Vicky [Victor Weisz] (1913-66) German-born British cartoonist. He became one of the leading left-wing political cartoonists and caricaturists of his day, notably with the *Daily Mirror* and *Evening Standard*. His cartoon creations included "Supermac," his cruelly accurate parody of MACMILLAN.

Vidal, [Eugene Luther] Gore (1925-) American novelist, dramatist and critic. His American historical fiction provides an unofficial and waspishly entertaining alternative history of the US and its leaders, e.g. *Burr* (1973) and *1876* (1976). His work includes several important essay collections, e.g. *The Second American Revolution* (1982) and *Armageddon* (1987).

Villa, Pancho [Francisco Villa, originally Doroteo Arango] (*c.*1877-1923) Mexican revolutionary. A former bandit, his forces aided ZAPATA in the seizure of Mexico City (1914-15). Villa's forces sparked off the US invasion of 1916-17 by killing some US civilians.

Villa-Lobos, Heitor (1887-1959) Brazilian composer and conductor. When he was 18, he joined an expedition up the Amazon to collect folk music. He settled in Paris (1923-30), where his work, combining elements of traditional Brazilian music with the European classical tradition, became highly popular. He composed over 2,000 works, including 12 symphonies, 16 string quartets, five operas and symphonic tone poems.

Visconti, [di Modrone], Count Luchino (1906-76) Italian film director. An aristocrat, he became a Marxist in the 1930s. He began his career as a stage designer, then worked as an assistant to RENOIR. His films include *The Leopard* (1963), *The Damned* (1969) and *Death in Venice* (1971), the latter two starring BOGARDE.

Vishnevskaya, Galina *see* **Rostropovich, Mstislav**.

von Braun, Wernher (1912-77) German-born American rocket engineer. The technical director (1937-45) of the German rocket project at Peenemunde in World War II, he designed the V-1 and V-2 rocket bombs that were launched in random attacks against southern England in 1944. Captured by the US, he was put to work on US rocket research, including the development of the Saturn moon rockets.

von Neumann, John (1903-57) Hungarian-born American mathematician. He was one of the founders of the theory of games, i.e. the application of statistical logic to the choice of game strategies. He also made significant contributions to quantum theory and to computer research, and was a consultant on the development of the atom bomb.

Voroshilov, Klimenti Yefremovich (1881-1969) Soviet military leader and statesman. A Red Army commander in the civil war, he was commissar for defence (1925-40), in charge of the Red Army. He became president (1953-60) after his friend STALIN's death.

W

Waldheim, Kurt (1918-) Austrian diplomat. After service as a Nazi intelligence officer in World War II, he entered the Austrian diplomatic service and became secretary-general of the United Nations (1972-82) and president of Austria (1986-). Revelations about his role in the Nazi genocide machine in Yugoslavia during the war surfaced in the late 1980s. Waldheim's critics have pointed out that his repeated claim that he knew nothing of the Holocaust can only mean that he was the worst intelligence officer in the Nazi apparatus.

Walesa, Lech (1943-) Polish trade union leader and statesman. An electrician at the Gdansk Lenin Shipyard, he was dismissed several times for organizing strikes, and became the leader of the free trade union, Solidarity, in 1980, which forced substantial concessions from the Polish government. After the imposition of martial law in 1981, Solidarity was banned and Walesa imprisoned (1981-82). After his release, he was awarded the 1983 Nobel Peace Prize, in which year Pope JOHN PAUL II visited Poland. A skilled negotiator, Walesa succeeded in getting Solidarity re-legalized and, in 1989, in the first free elections in eastern Europe since the 1940s, a Solidarity government was formed with Walesa as president.

Waller, Fats [Thomas Wright Waller] (1904-43) American jazz pianist and composer. Renowned for his sense of humour, he became one of America's favourite entertainers and a much admired exponent of the "stride" school of the jazz piano. His many compositions include "Honeysuckle Rose" and "Ain't Misbehavin'."

Wallis, Sir Barnes [Neville] (1887-1979) English aeronautical engineer. He designed the R100 airship, the Wellington bomber and in World War II the "bouncing bombs" used in the famous "Dambuster" bombing raid on the Mohne and Eder dams (1943).

Walter, Bruno [Bruno Walter Schlesinger] (1876-1962) German-born American conductor. Noted for his concerts and recordings of the great German romantic composers, he is particularly associated with the works of his friend MAHLER. He held various important posts in German and Austrian music, e.g. with the Salzburg Festival, but, being Jewish, was forced to leave Germany in 1933 and Austria in 1938. In the US, he conducted both the Metropolitan Opera and the New York Philharmonic.

Walton, Sir Earnest *see* **Cockcroft, Sir John Douglas.**

Walton, Sir William [Turner] (1902-83) English composer. His works include a setting of Edith Sitwell's poem *Façade* (1921-22), a self-consciously off-the-wall piece for voice and instruments that failed to shock the English bourgeoisie as much as was hoped. His other works include the oratorio *Belshazaar's Feast* (1930-31), and several film scores, e.g. for OLIVIER's *Henry V* (1944).

Warburg, Otto Heinrich (1883-1970) German biochemist and cell physiologist. A member of a notably intellectual Jewish family, he was decorated while serving with the Prussian Horse Guards in World War I. His work on cell metabolism and respiration, with particular reference to cancer research, earned him two Nobel prizes for physiology or medicine (1931, 1944), but he was unable to accept the latter by HITLER's decree.

Ward, Dame Barbara Mary [Baroness Jackson of Lodsworth] (1914-81) English economist and conservationist. She became a highly influential advocate of conservation and fair distribution of the earth's resources during the 1960s. Her works include *The Rich Nations and the Poor Nations* (1962) and *Spaceship Earth* (1966).

Warhol, Andy [Andrew Warhola] (1930-87) American pop artist and film-maker (of Czech parentage). He became the prime exponent of pop art in the early 1960s, with deliberately mundane works such as his reproductions of Campbell's soup cans and his repetitive portraits of contemporary icons such as PRESLEY, MAO and Marilyn MONROE. His films include the three-hour *Sleep* (1963) and *Chelsea Girls* (1966). In 1968, he survived an assassination attempt by one of his "starlets." His books include *From A to B and Back Again* (1975).

Watkins, Dudley [Dexter] (1907-69) English cartoonist. He became the D. C. THOMSON organization's chief cartoonist in the 1930s (the first allowed to sign his name), creating such characters as Desperate Dan for the *Dandy* (1937) and Oor Wullie for the *Sunday Post* (1936). The strong surreal element in Watkins' work—Desperate Dan lives in a Wild West version of Dundee policed by British Bobbies—has been much commented on. Watkins was a deeply religious Protestant, very dapper in appearance.

Watson, James Dewey (1928-) American biologist. He and Francis CRICK discovered the "double helix" structure of DNA, for which they shared (with Maurice WILKINS) the 1962 Nobel prize for physiology or medicine. His works include *The Double Helix* (1968) and *The DNA Story* (1981).

Watson, John B[roadus] (1878-1958) American psychologist. He became the leading theorist and proponent of behaviourism with his view that a scientific approach to psychology can only be based on studies of behaviour under laboratory conditions. His works include *Behavior—An Introduction to Comparative Psychology* (1914). *See also* SKINNER.

Watson-Watt, Sir Robert Alexander (1892-1973) Scottish physicist. Asked by the Air Ministry in 1935 to develop a "death ray," he instead played a major role in the development of radar, thus equipping RAF pilots with a significant advantage at the onset of World War II.

Watts, Charlies *see* **Jagger, Mick.**

Waugh, Evelyn [Arthur St John] (1903-66) English novelist known for his brilliant satires, e.g. *Vile Bodies* (1930) on the brittle postwar world of upper-class England, *Scoop* (1938) on war reporting, and *The Loved One* (1948) on Californian burial practices. His work also had a deeper tone, resulting from his conversion to Catholicism in 1930. His best-known novel, *Brideshead Revisited* (1945), although still a satire displays a growing spiritual concern. His masterpiece is his *Sword of Honour* trilogy, i.e. *Men at Arms* (1952), *Officers and Gentlemen* (1955) and *Unconditional Surrender* (1961), based on his own experiences with the Communist partisans in Yugoslavia in World War II.

Wayne, John [Marion Michael Morrison] (1907-79) American film actor. The best-known member of the John FORD "family" of actors, Wayne's first major role was as the Ringo Kid in *Stagecoach* (1939). Other classic westerns he starred in are Ford's *The Searchers* (1956) and *She Wore a Yellow Ribbon* (1949) and HAWKS' *Red River* (1948). Despite never having served in the Forces, Wayne, very much a political right-winger, became identified in the public mind as the definitive tough and laconic man of action. He was, however, when directed by Ford and Hawks, capable of conveying rich and surprising depth, as well as being a screen actor of outstanding presence. He directed and starred in *The Green Berets* (1968), which is notorious for closing with the sun setting in the East, and was awarded an Oscar for *True Grit* (1969).

Webb, Beatrice [Potter] (1858-1943) and **Webb, Sidney James**, [Baron Passfield] (1859-1947) English social reformers and economists. Married in 1892, the Webbs were, with George Bernard SHAW and H. G. WELLS, the leading propagandists of Fabian socialism, Sidney Webb having been a founder of Fabianism in 1884. Their books together include *The History of Trade Unionism* (1894, which LENIN translated into Russian), and *Industrial Democracy* (1897). They co-founded the London School of Economics (1895), founded the *New Statesman* (1913) and produced hordes of pamphlets and articles. Their *Soviet Communism: a New Civilisation?* (1935), a gushing account of the wonderful achievements of STALIN, is one of the key bad books of modern political thought. Beatrice's autobiography, *My Apprenticeship* (1926), has been highly praised.

Weber, Max (1864-1920) German sociologist. Regarded as one of the founders of sociology, he devised the concept of "ideal types" of real situations for comparative purposes, and emphasized the role of religious values and charismatic personalities in changing society. His works include *The Protestant Ethic and the Spirit of Capitalism* (1930).

Webern, Anton von (1883-1945) Austrian composer. He studied under SCHOENBERG and became one of the leading exponents of his teacher's serial form of composition. His works include *Three Little Pieces* (1914), for cello and piano, and *Five Pieces for Orchestra* (1911-13).

Weil, Simone (1909-43) French philosopher. From an intellectual Jewish family, she chose to live as a farm and industrial labourer during the 1930s, and worked for the Republican forces during the Spanish Civil War. She later developed a strong interest in Roman Catholic mysticism. She left France in 1942 and worked for the French Resistance in London, where she starved herself to death in sympathy with the inmates of the Nazi camps. Her religious works, all posthumous, include *Waiting for God* (1951) and *Gravity and Grace* (1952).

Weill, Kurt (1900-1950) German composer, noted especially for his collaborations with BRECHT, e.g. *The Threepenny Opera* (1928). He fled from Germany in 1935, settling in the US.

Weinberg, Steven (1933-) American physicist. He devised a theory of the unity of the forces operating on elementary particles (now called the Weinberg-Salam theory) that was independently arrived at by the Pakistani physicist **Abdus Salam** (1926-), and later developed by the American physicist **Sheldon Glashow** (1932-). All three shared the 1979 Nobel prize for physics.

Weismuller, Johnny (1903-84) American swimmer and film star. He was the first man to swim 100 metres in less than a minute, 440 yards in under five minutes. He won five Olympic gold medals (1921-28) and achieved further fame starring as Tarzan in 19 films in the 1930s and 40s. He is credited with inventing the Tarzan "yodel."

Weizmann, Chaim [Azriel] (1874-1952) Russian-born chemist and Israeli statesman. A distinguished scientist, he became a British subject in 1910, developing a synthetic acetone that aided the production of explosives. He participated in the negotiations for a Jewish homeland that resulted in the Balfour Declaration (1917) and became first president of Israel (1949-52).

Welles, [George] Orson (1915-85) American stage and film director and actor. He achieved great notoriety with his radio production of WELLS's *War of the Worlds* in 1938, which sparked off mass panic in the US, many of his listeners becoming convinced that a Martian invasion was imminent. He co-wrote, produced and directed one of the greatest films of all time, *Citizen Kane* (1941), based on the life of Randolph HEARST. His other films include *The Magnificent Ambersons* (1942), *Macbeth* (1948) and *Othello* (1951). His other acting roles include, most notably, Harry Lime in REED's masterpiece, *The Third Man* (1949).

Wells, H[erbert] G[eorge] (1866-1946) English novelist and short-story writer. His science fiction works include several classics, e.g. *The Time Machine* (1895), *The War of the Worlds* (1898) and *The Shape of Things to Come* (1933). He was a propagandist with the Webbs and others for Fabian socialism, and his novels on contemporary themes generally address their subject matter from a "progressive" viewpoint, e.g. *Ann Veronica* (1909), and sometimes with a comic or satirical element, e.g. *Love and Mr Lewisham* (1900) and *The History of Mr Polly* (1910).

West, Mae (1892-1980) American vaudeville artist, dramatist and film actress. Several of her plays were banned for obscenity, notably *Sex* (1926), for which she was also briefly imprisoned. She became a major star, renowned for her sardonic wit and powerful sexuality, with such films as *She Done Him Wrong* (1933) and *My Little Chickadee* (1940). Her autobiography is *Goodness Had Nothing to Do With It* (1959).

Wheeler, Sir [Robert Eric] Mortimer (1890-1976) Scottish archaeologist. Noted for his excavations, especially in the Indus Valley, on Romano-British sites and at Maiden Castle, and for his innovative methodology, Wheeler, a flamboyant figure, became a household name in Britain in the 1950s through his many television appearances and popular articles. His works include *Archaeology and the Earth* (1954) and an autobiography, *Still Digging* (1955).

Whitehead, A[lfred] N[orth] (1861-1947) English mathematician and philosopher. With his pupil, Bertrand RUSSELL, he wrote *Principia Mathematica* (1910-13), a highly acclaimed work that was described as the most important contribution to the study of logic since Aristotle. His other works include *Science and the Modern World* (1925) and *Process and Reality* (1929), the latter being an attempt at defining a new philosophy of science.

Whitlam, [Edward] Gough (1916-) Australian Labor politician. He became prime minister (1972-75), and was dismissed by Sir John Kerr, the governor-general, for refusing to call a general election. Labor was defeated in the ensuing election, and Whitlam retired from parliament in 1978. His works include *The Italian Inspiration in English Literature* (1980).

Whittle, Sir Frank (1907-) English aeronautical engineer. He designed the first operational jet engine for aircraft. The first successful flight was made in a Gloster in 1941. Whittle's first patent had been taken out in 1930, and it was not until 1939 that the British government took a reluctant interest in the project.

Whorf, Benjamin Lee (1897-1941) American linguist. Influenced by the German-born American linguist **Edward Sapir** (1884-1939), he devised what became known as the Sapir-Whorf hypothesis, i.e. the assertion that "users of markedly different grammars…arrive at somewhat different views of the world." His theory derives from his comparison between the Hopi language and "standard average European" language.

Wiener, Norbert (1894-1964) American mathematician. Advised by his tutor, Bertrand RUSSELL, to study mathematics, he coined the term "cybernetics" for the feedback mechanism in electronics, the theory of which is expanded in works such as *Cybernetics* (1948). His other works include *The Human Use of Human Beings* (1950) and the autobiographies, *Ex-Prodigy* (1953) and *I am a Mathematician* (1956).

Wilder, Billy [Samuel Wilder] (1906-) Austrian-born American film director and screenwriter. He emigrated to the US in the 1930s, winning Oscars for *The Lost Weekend* (1945), *Sunset Boulevard* (1950) and *The Apartment* (1960). Other films include *Double Indemnity* (1944), *The Seven Year Itch* (1955) and *Some Like it Hot* (1959).

Wilkins, Maurice Hugh Frederick (1916-) New Zealand physicist and biologist. Originally a physicist, he turned to biophysics after working on atom bomb research. His and Rosalind FRANKLIN's research into DNA structure resulted in CRICK and WATSON's discovery of the "double helix" structure of DNA, for which Wilkins, Crick and Watson shared the 1962 Nobel prize for physics.

Williams, Shirley [Vivien Teresa Brittain] (1930-) English politician. The daughter of the feminist writer **Vera Brittain** (1893-1970), she lost the lead role in the film *National Velvet* (1944) to Elizabeth TAYLOR. She became a Labour MP in 1964, and formed the Social Democratic Party with JENKINS, OWEN and Rodgers in 1981, becoming the party's first elected MP (1981-83). She retired from politics to become a professor ar Harvard University.

Williamson, Malcolm (1931-) Australian-born British composer. Master of the Queen's Music since 1975, his works include several operas, e.g. *Our Man in Havana* (1963), and music for film and television and for children.

Wilson, Sir [James] Harold [Baron of Rievaulx] (1916-) English Labour statesman. He served in World War II as a civil servant and became an MP in 1945. He held various ministerial posts before succeeding GAITSKELL as Labour leader in 1963. He became prime minister (1964-70, 1974-76). Originally on the soft left of his party, he became a strong defender of US policy on Vietnam and imposed a statutory incomes policy to deal with the country's balance of payments crisis in the mid-1960s. He unexpectedly resigned in 1976, with CALLAGHAN succeeding him as prime minister.

Wilson, [Thomas] Woodrow (1856-1924) American Democratic statesman. He became 28th president of the US (1913-21). Re-elected in 1916 on a policy of neutrality, he declared war on Germany following the sinking of US vessels by U-boats. His "fourteen points" speech of January 1918 set out US conditions for ending the war, including the disbandment of the German, Austro-Hungarian and Ottoman empires and their replacement by national states, and imposed the armistice with Germany on Britain and France. His last months in office were much troubled by ill health.

Windsor, Duke of [formerly Edward VIII] (1894-1972) English monarch, (1936). He succeeded his father, GEORGE V, to the throne, and became highly popular with the British public for his apparent concern at the lot of the unemployed ("something must be done"). He abdicated to marry the American divorcée, **Wallis Simpson** (1896-1986), after BALDWIN had made plain his opposition to the notion of Mrs Simpson becoming queen. He married her in 1937, after which they lived in exile, the Duke becoming governor of the Bahamas during World War II.

Wingate, Orde [Charles] Major-General (1903-44) English soldier. An ardent Zionist, he became proficient in irregular tactics while aiding Jewish settlers in Palestine in the mid-1930s. In 1942 he organized the "Chindits," specially trained jungle troops who caused much disruption to the Japanese supply lines during the Burma campaign in World War II. Notably erratic in his behaviour—he attempted to commit suicide in 1941 and habitually received visitors while cleaning his body with a toothbrush—Wingate became a national hero. He died in a plane crash.

Wittgenstein, Ludwig [Josef Johann] (1889-1951) Austrian-born British philosopher. He studied under Bertrand RUSSELL (1912-13), who observed that he was soon learning as much from his pupil as he had taught him. On the outbreak of World War I, Wittgenstein returned to Austria to serve as an artillery officer, and was captured on the Italian front in 1918. While a POW, he wrote and sent to Russell his *Tractatus Logico-Philosophicus* (1921), a series of aphoristic propositions on the boundaries of language and philosophy in relation to the world. During the 1920s, influenced by TOLSTOY's asceticism, he gave his considerable inherited wealth away and worked as a schoolteacher. His posthumous *Philosophical Investigations* (1953) retracts the confident assertions of the *Tractatus*, focusing instead on the concept of language as a series of games in which "The meaning of the word is its use in language."

Wittig, Georg (1897-) German chemist. He made several important contributions to organic chemistry, e.g. the discovery of phosphorous ylides, and shared the 1979 Nobel prize for chemistry with the English-born American chemist **Herbert Brown** (1912-) for their work on boron compounds.

Wodehouse, P[elham] G[renville] (1881-1975) English novelist and short-story writer who became a US citizen in 1955. His most famous creations, in e.g. *The Inimitable Jeeves* (1923) and *Carry on Jeeves* (1925), are Bertie Wooster, a giddy young upper-middle-class man, and his butler Jeeves, a shrewd and immensely competent man. Wodehouse also wrote lyrics for musicals in collaboration with composers such as Jerome KERN and Irving BERLIN. Interned during World War II, he foolishly made some innocuous broadcasts from Germany, which led to his being branded a traitor. He was given an honorary knighthood.

Wood, Sir Henry [Joseph] (1869-1940) English conductor. He founded the London Promenade Concerts (the "Proms") in 1895, which he conducted until his death. He published an autobiography, *My Life of Music* (1938).

Woolf, [Adeline] Virginia (1882-1941) English novelist and critic. She married (1912) the novelist and social reformer **Leonard [Sidney] Woolf** (1880-1969), and their home became the centre of the so-called "Bloomsbury Group" of writers and artists. Her novels, e.g. *Jacob's Room* (1922), *To the Lighthouse* (1927) and *The Waves* (1931), are written in a fluid, poetic style, and are recognized as being among the most innovative of the 20th century. She suffered greatly from mental illness, and drowned herself.

Wright, Frank Lloyd (1869-1959) American architect. Regarded as one of the greatest modern architects, he sought to develop an architecture with traditionally American "organic" values of harmony between a building and its environment. His buildings include the Tokyo Imperial Hotel (1916-20) and the Guggenheim Museum of Art in New York (1959). His books include *Autobiography* (1932).

Wright, Orville (1871-1948) and **Wright, Wilbur** (1867-1912) American aviators and brothers. Cycle manufacturers, they designed and built the first heavier-than-air flying machine, a 12-horse power biplane, *Flyer I*, which flew for 120 feet in 1903. They formed an aircraft production company in 1909, in which year the US Signal Corps purchased one of their models.

Wyman, Bill *see* **Jagger, Mick**.

Yeats, W[illiam] B[utler] (1865-1939) Anglo-Irish poet and dramatist. His early works include several important collections of poems, e.g. *The Wanderings of Oisin* (1889), which reflect his concern with Irish myth and legend. His play, *Cathleen ni Houlihan* (1902) demonstrated his support of Irish patriotism, and he later feared it had sent men to their deaths against the British. Following Irish independence, he became a member of the Irish senate. He was awarded the Nobel prize for literature in 1923. His brother, **Jack Yeats** [John Butler Yeats] (1870-1957) was an illustrator, particularly of comic strips and children's books, before turning to painting and writing.

Yeltsin, Boris Nikolayevich (1931-) Russian politician. A member of the Communist party since 1960, he was brought into the Soviet Politburo by GORBACHEV in 1985, in which year he was appointed head of the Moscow party organization. His subsequent assault on the ingrained inefficiency and corruption of that body resulted in his demotion from the post and from the Politburo. In the free elections of 1989, he was elected to the Congress of People's Deputies, and won an overwhelming majority of votes in the Russian presidential election of 1990. Although widely distrusted by many Western observers, who dismissed him as a rabble-rouser, he gave strong moral support to the Baltic states in their move for independence and called for the liberalization of the Soviet state and establishment of a decentralized and market economy. During the abortive coup against Gorbachev of August 1991, he evaded capture and took refuge in the Russian parliament building, where he and his allies, such as SHEVARADNADZE and YEVTUSHENKO, publicly defied the organizers of the coup. In the aftermath of the failed coup, Yeltsin emerged as the most powerful figure within the disintegrating Soviet Union.

Yevtushenko, Yevgenii Aleksandrovich (1933-) Russian poet. Regarded as the most influential post-STALINist poet in Russia, he attracted huge crowds to his public readings in the 1950s and 60s, which often included outspoken denunciations of Stalinism, and was allowed to travel freely in the West. His best-known poem is *Babi Yar* (1962), a denunciation not only of the Nazi crimes against the Jews, but also of Russian anti-semitism (SHOSTAKOVICH set this and other Yevtushenko poems to music). He also gave public support to SOLZHENITSYN. *See also* YELTSIN.

Yukawa, Hideki (1907-81) Japanese physicist. He became the first Japanese to be awarded the Nobel prize for physics, in 1949, for his prediction (in 1935) of the meson within the atomic nucleus.

Z

Zanuck, Darryl F[rancis] (1902-79) American film producer. He began his Hollywood career as a scriptwriter, becoming a producer in 1927, and was one of the founders of 20th-Century Fox (1935). The many films he produced include *The Jazz Singer* (1927), *Little Caesar* (1930) and *The Grapes of Wrath* (1940).

Zapata, Emiliano (1879-1919) Mexican revolutionary. An Indian tenant farmer, he led (1910-19) a guerrilla campaign against the Mexican government in the name of land reform. He succeeded in occupying Mexico City three times (1914-15), and was assassinated by a government agent. *See also* VILLA.

Zappa, Frank (1940-) American rock musician and Czech diplomat. Founder of the rock band Mothers of Invention, his songs include "Weasels Ripped My Flesh" and "Hot Rats." Noted for his witty observations on popular entertainment ("rock journalism is people who can't write interviewing people who can't talk for people who can't read"), HAVEL's government appointed him Czechoslovakia's "cultural liaison officer to the West" in 1990.

Zátopek, Emil (1922-) Czech athlete. One of the greatest long-distance runners of all time, he won the 5,000 and 10,000 metres and the marathon in the 1952 Olympics.

Zeffirelli, Franco (1923-) Italian stage and film director and designer. His films include *Romeo and Juliet* (1968), *Brother Sun, Sister Moon* (1973), in which St Francis and St Clare are portrayed as proto-hippies, and the TV film *Jesus of Nazareth* (1973), a highly reverential work once described as "Christ Among the Guest Stars."

Zhivkov, Todor (1911-) Bulgarian Communist statesman. He became prime minister (1962-71) and president (1971-89). Under his rule, Bulgaria became the most servile of the satellites of the Soviet Union, at whose disposal Zhivkov placed his notoriously ruthless secret service. Zhivkov was deposed in 1989, following the collapse of Soviet hegemony.

Zhou En Lai *see* **Chou En-Lai.**

Zhukov, Georgi Konstantinovich (1895-1974) Russian soldier. Appointed army chief of staff by STALIN in 1941 following the German invasion, Zhukov's forces repulsed the Germans from the suburbs of Moscow in December, successfully defended Leningrad and captured the German 6th Army at Stalingrad. He took Warsaw in September 1944, delaying his assault while the Germans eviscerated the Polish resistance, and took Berlin in May 1945.

Zia ul-Haq, Mohammed (1924-88) Pakistani general. He led the military coup against BHUTTO in 1977 and became president (1978-88). His refusal to commute Bhutto's death sentence was condemned worldwide. He opposed the Soviet invasion of Afghanistan (1979) and pursued a domestic policy designed to make Pakistan a totally Islamic culture. His death in a plane crash is generally assumed to have been due to sabotage.

Ziegfeld, Florenz (1869-1932) American theatre manager. His spectacular revues, the "Ziegfeld Follies," which were produced annually (1907-31), were designed as an American equivalent of the *Folies Bergères* in Paris. The revues featured music by composers such as BERLIN and KERN, and were important stages in the careers of many entertainers, e.g. W. C. FIELDS and Fred ASTAIRE.

Zinoviev, Grigori Yevseevich (1883-1936) Russian politician. He became chairman of the Comintern (1919-26) and Politburo member (1921-26). He allied himself with STALIN against TROTSKY following LENIN's death, and was subsequently himself purged by Stalin in 1927 and executed in 1936 after a show trial. The so-called "Zinoviev letter" allegedly written by him to the British Communist Party contributed to the electoral defeat of Ramsay MACDONALD's Labour government in 1924.

Zuckerman, Solly, Baron (1904-83) South African-born British zoologist. He was chief scientific adviser to the British government (1964-71) and served on many government committees. He was also noted for his work on primates. His books include *The Social Life of Monkeys and Apes* (1932), the essay collection *Man and Aggression* (1968), and *Nuclear Reality and Illusion* (1982). His autobiography is *From Apes to Warlords* (1978).

Zweig, Stefan (1881-1942) Austrian biographer, dramatist, essayist, poet and novelist (British citizen from 1938). Highly regarded as a translator and for his psychoanalytic biographies, e.g. of Dickens and Balzac, he also wrote the libretto for Richard STRAUSS's opera *The Silent Woman* (1935). He was Jewish and a pacifist, and died by his own hand.